**W9-AVE-680**

The richness of more than 3,000 years of Egyptian civilization comes alive in the pages of this book. From the geology of the land, the first cities, social structure, religion, mummification and burial practices, languages, temple and house architecture, and art, *Egypt and the Egyptians* is a comprehensive treatment of ancient Egypt. The illustrations, many appearing for the first time, and extensive quotes from ancient Egypt letters, hymns, funerary texts, and law codes, enliven the text. The result is a rare combination of up-to-date Egyptological and anthropological research, giving the reader the most current and expansive examination of Egypt. It is written for students and for general readers interested in this ancient land and its people. The extensive bibliography, suggestions for further reading, and glossary, make this book an excellent resource for exploring any aspect of ancient Egypt.

DOUGLAS J. BREWER is Professor of Anthropology at the University of Illinois, Urbana, and Director of the Spurlock Museum. He has written three books and numerous articles on Egypt, and has spent eighteen years involved in field projects in Egypt, including research on the natural history of the Eastern Desert, the Palaeolithic/Neolithic transition in the Fayum, and excavations concerned with the Predynastic and Dynastic culture of the Nile Valley.

EMILY TEETER is Associate Curator at the Oriental Institute Museum, University of Chicago. She is the author of a wide variety of books and scholarly articles about Egyptian religion and history, and has participated in expeditions in Giza, Luxor, and Alexandria.

# EGYPT
## AND THE
# EGYPTIANS

DOUGLAS J. BREWER and
EMILY TEETER

CAMBRIDGE
UNIVERSITY PRESS

PUBLISHED BY THE PRESS SYNDICATE OF THE UNIVERSITY OF CAMBRIDGE
The Pitt Building, Trumpington Street, Cambridge, United Kingdom

CAMBRIDGE UNIVERSITY PRESS
The Edinburgh Building, Cambridge, CB2 2RU, UK   http://www.cup.cam.ac.uk
40 West 20th Street, New York, NY 10011-4211, USA   http://www.cup.org
10 Stamford Road, Oakleigh, Melbourne 3166, Australia

© Douglas J. Brewer and Emily Teeter 1999

First published 1999

Printed in the United Kingdom at the University Press, Cambridge

Typeset in Monotype Apollo 11½/13½ [SE]

*A catalogue record for this book is available from the British Library*

*Library of Congress cataloguing in publication data*

Brewer, Douglas J.
Egypt and the Egyptians / Douglas J. Brewer, Emily Teeter.
p.     cm.
Includes bibliographical references (p.     ) and index,
ISBN 0 521 44518 3 (hbk.) – ISBN 0 521 44984 7 (pbk.)
1. Egypt–Civilization–To 332 B.C.   I. Teeter, Emily.
II. Title.
DT61.B68   1999   932–dc21   98-33986   CIP

ISBN 0 521 44518 3 hardback
ISBN 0 521 44984 7 paperback

# CONTENTS

*List of illustrations*   vi

*List of tables*   xi

*Outline chronology of Egypt and major rulers*   xii

*Preface*   xvii

1   *An Egyptian revival*   1

2   *The river, valley, and desert*   16

3   *A chronology and history of Egypt*   27

4   *Cities, towns, and villages*   52

5   *The government and the governed*   69

6   *Religion and religious practices*   84

7   *Society and its expectations*   95

8   *Language and writing*   110

9   *Homes for the people, the pharaoh, and the gods*   125

10   *The quest for eternity*   147

11   *Egyptian art: craftsmen, techniques, and conventions*   169

12   *Cultural death or transformation of a civilization?*   188

*Bibliography*   191

*Glossary*   202

*Index*   209

# ILLUSTRATIONS

1.1    Sequence dating chart (after Petrie *et al.* 1901).                          *page* 13
1.2    Predynastic and Early Dynastic vessels (courtesy of the Carnegie
       Museum).                                                                     14
2.1    Map of Egypt and the Nile Valley.                                            18
2.2    Cross-section of the Nile flood plain (after Butzer 1976).                    19
3.1    Naqada II vessel painted with a representation of boats (*ca.* 3200 BC)
       (courtesy of the Brooklyn Museum of Art).                                    31
3.2    The Narmer Palette, Egyptian Museum, Cairo (Dynasty 0–1) (photo
       courtesy of the Petrie Museum, University College London).                   32
3.3    Map of the Middle East, *ca.* 1500 BC                                        44
4.1    Plan of the town of Tell el Amarna (Dynasty 18) (Pendelbury 1951).           55
4.2    Plan of the Central Quarter at Tell el Amarna (Dynasty 18)
       (Pendelbury 1951).                                                           56
4.3    Plan of the workmen's village at Deir el Medina at Thebes (New
       Kingdom).                                                                    59
4.4    Plan of the Middle Kingdom fort at Buhen (after Emery, Smith *et al.*
       1979).                                                                       61
4.5    Plan of the Middle Kingdom fort at Semna (after Emery, Smith *et al.*
       1979).                                                                       62
6.1    King Ramesses III offers incense and libation to Ptah (Dynasty 20)
       (courtesy of the Oriental Institute of the University of Chicago).           87
6.2    The sacred boat carried in procession by priests (Dynasty 20)
       (courtesy of the Oriental Institute of the University of Chicago).           88
6.3a   The god Osiris (after Hobson 1987).                                          89
6.3b   The god Horus (after Hobson 1987).                                           89
6.4    Ramesses III runs the ritual circuit of the jubilee festival (Dynasty 20)
       (courtesy of the Oriental Institute of the University of Chicago).           90
6.5    Stela incised with a representation of the ears of the god (Dynasties
       21–24) (courtesy of the Oriental Institute of the University of Chicago,
       OIM 16718). Drawing by J. Brett McClain.                                     92
7.1    Woman's sheath dress typical of the Old Kingdom (after Erman 1971).          100

7.2    Man's typical wrap-around kilt (Dynasty 6) (courtesy of Douglas J.
       Brewer).                                                                101
7.3    Man's kilt showing inverted box pleat (Dynasty 5) (after Erman
       1971).                                                                  102
7.4    New Kingdom clothing with elaborate pleating (Dynasty 19) (after
       Erman 1971).                                                            103
7.5    Senet game (Dynasty 18) (courtesy of the Metropolitan Museum of
       Art).                                                                   104
7.6    A woman who over-indulged (Dynasty 19) (after Erman 1971).             106
7.7    Musicians entertain at a banquet (Dynasty 18) (courtesy of the Oriental
       Institute of the University of Chicago).                                107
8.1    The Rosetta Stone (copyright the British Museum).                       112
8.2a   The name Ptolemaios on the Rosetta Stone.                              113
8.2b   The name Cleopatra on the Rosetta Stone.                               114
8.3    A brief hieroglyphic text written (top) from left to right; (bottom) from
       right to left.                                                          116
8.4    Hieratic script with hieroglyphic equivalent.                          117
8.5    Chart with alphabetic hieroglyphic signs, their phonetic values and the
       hieratic, demotic, and Coptic equivalents.                             118
8.6    Hieroglyphic signs arranged symmetrically around a doorway.
       (Dynasty 20) (courtesy of the Oriental Institute of the University of
       Chicago).                                                               120
8.7    "Mutilated" hieroglyphs (Dynasty 18) (courtesy of the Oriental
       Institute of the University of Chicago).                                122
9.1    Architectural features: torus molding; *khekeru* frieze; cavetto cornice.
       Drawing by J. Brett McClain.                                            126
9.2    Brick-making, tomb of Rekhmire at Thebes (Dynasty 18) (after
       Norman de Garis Davis 1944).                                           127
9.3    Niched "palace façade" wall treatment on the enclosure wall of the
       Stepped Pyramid complex at Saqqara (Dynasty 3).                        127
9.4    Hememieh hut circle (courtesy of the Petrie Museum, University
       College, London).                                                      129
9.5    Egyptian soul houses and offering trays showing types of domestic
       architecture: (a) simple hut enclosure; (b) house with roof terrace;
       (c) multiple-storied home with stairs and portico (Dynasty 11–12).
       (a)  Courtesy of the Museum of Fine Arts, Boston, MFA 07.1026.         130
       (b)  Copyright the British Museum.                                     130
       (c)  Courtesy of the Ashmolean Museum, A 141.                          131
9.6    Plan of residential quarter at Kahun (Dynasty 12) (after Kemp 1991).   132

9.7    Floor plan of a house at Tell el Amarna (Dynasty 18) (after Fairman
       1949).                                                                 134
9.8    Plan of a house at Deir el Medina, Thebes (Dynasty 19) (after Bierbriar
       1982).                                                                 135
9.9    A townhouse as shown in the tomb of Dheutynef at Thebes
       (Dynasty 18) (after Museum of Fine Arts, Boston 1982).                 136
9.10   Plan of the Malkata palace of King Amunhotep III (Dynasty 18)
       (after Smith 1958).                                                    138
9.11   Plan of the North Palace at Tell el Amarna (Dynasty 18) (after Smith
       1958).                                                                 139
9.12   Plan of the palace of Merneptah at Memphis (Dynasty 19) (after
       Fischer 1917).                                                         140
9.13   Artist's reconstruction of the throne room in the palace of Merneptah
       at Memphis (Dynasty 19) (University of Pennsylvania Museum,
       Philadelphia, neg. S4-141816).                                         141
9.14   Detail of a shrine with arched roof line symbolizing Upper Egypt in
       the jubilee courtyard of the Stepped Pyramid complex at Saqqara
       (Dynasty 3) (courtesy of Emily Teeter).                                143
9.15   Reconstruction of the Karnak temple complex in eastern Thebes
       (courtesy of Editions Errance, Paris).                                 144
10.1   The soul (*ba*) in the form of a bird with human head, sitting in a garden.
       Tomb of Usherhat (Dynasty 19) (courtesy of the Oriental Institute of
       the University of Chicago).                                            148
10.2   Predynastic burial (*ca.* 3500 BC) (courtesy of the Oriental Institute
       of the University of Chicago, OIM 11488).                              149
10.3   Canopic jars (Dynasty 25) (courtesy of the Oriental Institute of the
       University of Chicago, OIM 14672–5).                                   150
10.4   Scene from the "Book of the Dead" (Dynasty 19) (copyright the
       British Museum).                                                       151
10.5   Section of mastaba tomb.                                               153
10.6   View of the interior of the mastaba of Mereruka (Dynasty 6) (courtesy
       of the Oriental Institute of the University of Chicago).               154
10.7   Tomb of King Qa'a (Dynasty 1) at Abydos (after Petrie 1900).           156
10.8   The Stepped Pyramid of Djoser at Saqqara (Dynasty 3) (photo
       courtesy of Douglas J. Brewer).                                        157
10.9   Elevation of the Stepped Pyramid (after Fakhry 1961).                  158
10.10a Plan of the Stepped Pyramid enclosure at Saqqara (Dynasty 3).          159
10.10b Reconstruction of the Stepped Pyramid enclosure at Saqqara
       (Dynasty 3) (courtesy of the Oriental Institute of the University of
       Chicago).                                                              159

10.11  The jubilee (*Sed*) festival court of the Stepped Pyramid complex at
       Saqqara (Dynasty 3) (courtesy of Emily Teeter).                        160
10.12  The pyramids at Giza (Dynasty 4) (courtesy of Douglas J. Brewer).      161
10.13  Architectural components of the Giza pyramid complex (Dynasty 4).      162
10.14  Tomb of Amunhotep II (Dynasty 18) (courtesy of the Oriental Institute
       of the University of Chicago).                                         165
10.15  Plan of the tomb of Seti I (Dynasty 19).                               166
10.16  Artist's reconstruction of the eastern façade of the mortuary (royal)
       temple of Ramesses III (Dynasty 20) (courtesy of the Oriental Institute
       of the University of Chicago).                                         166
10.17  Royal tombs at Tanis (Dynasty 21) (courtesy of Emily Teeter).          167
11.1   Artisans finishing granite statues of the king and a limestone sphinx
       and offering table with rubbing stones (Dynasty 18) (courtesy of the
       Oriental Institute of the University of Chicago).                      172
11.2   Baked clay figurine of a king (Dynasties 21–24) (courtesy of the
       Oriental Institute of the University of Chicago, OIM 15556).           173
11.3   Stone and glass pectoral from the reign of Senwosert II (Dynasty 12)
       (courtesy of the Metropolitan Museum of Art, MMA 16.1.3, Rogers
       Fund, 1916).                                                           174
11.4   Procession of offering bearers from the tomb of Rekhmire at Thebes
       (Dynasty 18) (after Norman de Garis Davies 1944).                      175
11.5   Drawing of a box employing western perspective (after Robins 1986).    176
11.6   Scene of a garden and pond (Dynasty 18) (after Robins 1986).           177
11.7   Boats on the Nile (Dynasty 18) (after Nina de Garis Davies 1926).      178
11.8   Male figure superimposed over proportional eighteen-square grid (after
       Robins 1986).                                                          179
11.9   Female figure superimposed over proportional eighteen-square grid
       (after Robins 1986).                                                   180
11.10  Figure from Ptolemaic relief (third century BC) superimposed over
       twenty-one square grid.                                                181
11.11  Standard representation of the human figure (Dynasty 3–4) (courtesy
       of the Brooklyn Museum of Art, Charles Edwin Wilbour Fund
       57.178).                                                               182
11.12a Woman with v-neck dress shown in relief.                              183
11.12b Statue of a woman wearing a v-neck dress similar to that depicted in
       figure 11.12a (Dynasty 5) (courtesy of the Oriental Institute of the
       University of Chicago, OIM 10618).                                     184
11.13  Classic representation of the human figure showing an arch in both
       feet and identical hands (Dynasty 6) (courtesy of the Oriental Institute
       of the University of Chicago).                                         185

11.14   Differing representations of Nefertiti (Dynasty 18) emphasizing the
        symbolic nature of Egyptian art:
            (a)  The idealized form. Replica of Berlin 21300 (courtesy of the
                 Oriental Institute of the University of Chicago).                      186
            (b)  The radical style (courtesy of the Ashmolean Museum,
                 1893.1–41[71]).                                                        187

# TABLES

2.1   Nile evolution and geologic time.                          *page* 21
3.1   Predynastic chronology of ancient Egypt.                          29
4.1   Textual evidence for Nile Valley settlement hierarchy.            67

# OUTLINE CHRONOLOGY OF EGYPT AND MAJOR RULERS

All dates are approximate. Chronology based on Murnane, 1983.

## ARCHAIC PERIOD: DYNASTIES 0–2 (3150–2686 BC)

### DYNASTY 0 (3150–3050 BC)
Scorpion
Narmer

### DYNASTY I (3050–2890 BC)
Aha
Djer
Djet
Den

### DYNASTY 2 (2890–2686 BC)
Hetepsekhemwy
Perisbsen
Khasekhemwy

## OLD KINGDOM: DYNASTIES 3–6 (2686–2181 BC)

### DYNASTY 3 (2686–2613 BC)
Djoser
Sekhemkhet
Khaba
Huni

### DYNASTY 4 (2613–2498 BC)
Snefru
Khufu
Djedefre
Khafre
Menkaure
Shepseskaf

### DYNASTY 5 (2498–2345 BC)
Userkaf
Sahure

Neferirare-Kakai
Niuserre
Unis

DYNASTY 6 (2345–2181 BC)
Teti
Pepi I
Mernere
Pepi II
Nitocris (?)

---

FIRST INTERMEDIATE PERIOD: DYNASTIES 7–11 (2181–2040 BC)

DYNASTIES 7–10 (2181–2160 BC)

DYNASTY 11 (2133–2160 BC)
Wahankh Antef II
Mentuhotep I-III

---

MIDDLE KINGDOM: DYNASTIES 12 and early 13 (2040–1782 BC)

DYNASTY 12 (2060–1991 BC)
Amunemhet I
Senwosret I
Amunemhet II
Senwosret II
Senwosret III
Amunemhet III
Queen Sobeknofru

DYNASTY 13 (1782–1650 BC)
Khendjer

---

SECOND INTERMEDIATE PERIOD: DYNASTIES 14–17 (1782–1570 BC)

DYNASTY 14 (1650 BC)

DYNASTY 15–16 (1663–1555 BC)
Hyksos kings

DYNASTY 17 (1663–1570 BC)
Sekhenenre Tao II
Kamose

## THE NEW KINGDOM: DYNASTIES 18–20 (1570–1069 BC)

### DYNASTY 18 (1570–1293 BC)
Ahmose
Amunhotep I
Thutmose I
Thutmose II
Thutmose III
Hatshepsut
Amunhotep II
Thutmose IV
Amunhotep III
Amunhotep IV/Akhenaten
Smenkhkare
Tutankhamun
Ay
Horemheb

### DYNASTY 19 (1293–1185 BC)
Ramesses I
Seti I
Ramesses II
Merneptah
Amenmesse
Seti II
Siptah
Twosret

### DYNASTY 20 (1185–1070 BC)
Sethnakht
Ramesses III
Ramesses IV-Ramesses XI
Herihor

## THIRD INTERMEDIATE PERIOD: DYNASTIES 21–25 (1069–656 BC)

### DYNASTY 21 (1069–945 BC)
Smendes
Psusennes I
Pinedjem I (Thebes)
Amenemope

### DYNASTY 22 (945–712 BC)
Shoshenq I
Osorkon I

DYNASTIES 23–24 (818–712 BC)
"Libyan" Kings

DYNASTY 25: KUSHITE PERIOD (772–656 BC)
Piankhy (Piye)
Shabaka
Taharqa

LATE PERIOD: DYNASTIES 26–31 (656–332 BC)

DYNASTY 26: SAITE PERIOD (656–525 BC)
Psammethicus I
Necho
Psammethicus II
Apries
Ahmose III
Psammethicus III

DYNASTY 27 (525–404 BC)
(First Persian Domination)
Cambyses
Darius I
Xerxes

DYNASTY 28 (404–399 BC)

DYNASTY 29 (399–380 BC)

DYNASTY 30 (380–362 BC)
Nectanebo I
Nectanebo II

DYNASTY 31 (342–332 BC)
(Second Persian Domination)

PTOLEMAIC PERIOD (332–30 BC)
Ptolemy I–XII
Cleopatra VII

ROMAN PEROD (30 BC–AD 323)
Augustus Caesar

BYZANTINE PERIOD (AD 323–642)

ARAB CONQUEST (AD 642)

# PREFACE

In 1960 UNESCO, on behalf of Egypt and the Sudan, issued an appeal requesting international action be taken to preserve the treasures of Nubia from the large reservoir that would be created when the High Aswan Dam went into operation. When full, the reservoir would extend 560 kilometers from the first cataract in Egypt south over the Sudan–Egyptian border to the third cataract, covering all of what is known as Lower Nubia, and all archaeological evidence in the region would be lost.

Through the efforts of the United Nations and government officials of several member nations, many archaeologists from Europe and North America agreed to become involved in what is now regarded as a marvelous example of international cooperation in order to save as much of Egypt's historic and prehistoric record as possible. It was at this time (1961 to 1966) that the different disciplines conducting research in Egypt began fully to perceive the benefits of a multi-disciplinary approach to understanding Egypt's ancient past. Geologists, botanists, paleontologists, prehistorians, and Egyptologists, among others, began to work together to achieve their goals. Today Egyptologists, archaeologists, anthropologists, zooarchaeologists and paleobotanists are frequently included on the same expedition team; each specialist provides information on a piece of the ancient puzzle and each works to fulfill complementary goals. It is in the spirit of this cooperative effort that this introductory text has been written. The authors come from different academic backgrounds (anthropological archaeology and Egyptology), have different specialties and work in different periods of Egyptian history (and prehistory).

We would be pleased if our professional colleagues working in Egypt learn something – no matter how minor – from reading this volume, but the truth is that this was not written for them. Rather, it was written for those who know little or nothing about ancient Egypt but want some grounding in the basic history and culture of this civilization. To assist our readers, terms particular to Egyptian history and archaeology are printed in italics and defined in the glossary.

Some readers, particularly those with a background in anthropological archaeology, might question the lack of complicated hypotheses and models related to Egyptian cultural evolution. Unfortunately, despite the copious archaeological research conducted in Egypt and the variety of questions posed, the preponderance of work to date has been directed at mortuary and religious complexes and thus has provided little information on issues relating to the socio-political or economic evolution of Egypt. Such biases and the relative paucity of data collected from controlled systematic excavations of secular sites make it difficult to analyze Egyptian cultural evolution within any modern anthropological/archaeological paradigm. In fact, it has been argued that so little relevant archaeological evidence exists that it is impractical at this time even to test complicated hypotheses and models related to much of Egyptian cultural evolution. Any such analysis must, therefore, focus first on the general contexts in which this society evolved. It is partly for this reason that summary accounts of Egypt's history such as this one are still needed.

Although it is standard practice in academic works to provide citations of other works in the text itself, we have not done this here because we do not want to interrupt the text with lengthy lists of the works on which we have depended so heavily. Instead, each chapter contains a suggestion for further reading with a complete bibliography provided at the end of the book. Keeping our intended audience in mind, we have attempted to provide a balance of primary and secondary sources in the list of readings for each chapter. The reader is encouraged first to review the secondary sources, which are often historical or topical reviews in themselves, before attempting to digest the primary sources.

Many people and institutions contributed to this volume. We are especially grateful to David Grove, Mindy James, Donald Redford, and Norm Whitten for reading and commenting on earlier drafts, and Steve Holland who donated his time and artistic skills to produce most of the figures presented here. Ann Hutflies Brewer deserves special thanks for her continued support and editorial comments. The Oriental Institute of the University of Chicago, the Metropolitan Museum of Art, the Museum of Fine Arts, Boston, the British Museum, the Brooklyn Museum of Art, the Egypt Exploration Society (London), the University Museum, University of Pennsylvania, the Ashmolean Museum, the Petrie Museum, University College London, and the Carnegie Museum provided illustrations for this volume. Special thanks are extended to John Sanders and John A. Larson of the Oriental Institute for their assistance in processing images. Finally, Jessica Kuper of Cambridge University Press deserves special thanks for her advice and patience throughout the research and writing process.

## Chapter 1

## AN EGYPTIAN REVIVAL

Ancient Egyptian monuments have been admired through the ages by many peoples, including later Egyptians. One graffito, written by an Egyptian of Dynasty 18 (1570–1293 BC), recounts how a day was spent admiring the great Step Pyramid complex of Djoser, by that time already more than 1,200 years old. But the Egyptians not only appreciated their monuments, they also took active steps to preserve them. One of the earliest documented examples of monument excavation, a task undertaken by Prince Thutmose around 1440 BC, is recorded on a stela uncovered by T. B. Caviglia in 1811. According to the text on the stela, the young prince was hunting near the pyramid complex of Giza. He became tired and chose to nap under the head of the Sphinx, whose body was buried under the desert sands. In a dream, the Sphinx asked Thutmose to clear the sand away so that he (the Sphinx) could breath more freely; if Thutmose accomplished the task, the Sphinx would reward him by making him king of Egypt. The young prince removed the sand and, as promised, was later crowned King Thutmose IV.

A number of other less apocryphal records document Egyptian efforts to conserve their heritage. Prince Khaemwese, fourth son of Ramesses II, is credited with relabeling some of the tombs in the Saqqara complex after the original inscriptions bearing the names of the owners had worn away. Later, during the Saite Period (664–525 BC), the artistic styles of the Old Kingdom were copied so faithfully that it can be difficult to differentiate the original art from that created 2,000 years later.

The earliest foreign interest in Egypt's monuments was exhibited by ancient Greek and Roman travelers. Although a number of Greeks are known to have sojourned in Egypt, the earliest records were probably produced by Hekataios of Miletos in the sixth century BC. His actual writings have never been recovered, but references to his travels are found in works by other authors, especially Herodotus. Thales, the father of Greek geometry, also visited Egypt in the sixth century BC and made some computations on the Great Pyramid. In fact, it became fashionable for Greek intellectuals to travel to Egypt to study with priests: Solon, Pythagoras, and Plato are all reported to have done so.

About 450 BC the Greek historian Herodotus (490?–425 BC) traveled to the Nile Valley. Famous for his interest in the early history and ethnography of different cultures, he compiled the information he gathered from his travels into a multi-volume treatise called *The Histories*. In Book II he described Egypt, then under Persian control during the waning years of the pharaonic period. Portions of his account are the only record of many aspects of Egyptian culture. His discussion of mummification, for example, is the only complete description that survives to the present day. Unfortunately, many of his accounts were not based on first-hand knowledge but were told to him by local guides and other informants through an interpreter. By the time of his travels, Egypt had been visited by so many conquerors and curiosity-seekers that much of the information relayed to Herodotus was intentionally exaggerated or false. In addition, Herodotus embellished certain stories to emphasize what he believed were significant differences between Greece and Egypt. The following passage shows that Herodotus found Egyptian culture and people very different from his own:

> The Egyptians appear to have reversed the ordinary practices of mankind. Women attend markets and are employed in trade, while men stay at home and do the weaving! Men in Egypt carry loads on their head, women on their shoulder. Women pass water standing up, men sitting down. To ease themselves they go indoors, but eat outside on the streets, on the theory that what is unseemly, but necessary, should be done in private, and what is not unseemly should be done openly.
>
> (Herodotus II: 33–37)

A century after Herodotus, Alexander the Great marched into Persian-controlled Egypt (332 BC) and was hailed as a liberator. After he visited the great oracle at the Temple of Amun in Siwa Oasis he claimed to be of divine descent. Thereafter, Alexander spent relatively little time in the Nile Valley, but was so impressed with Egypt that he wished to be buried at Siwa. In June of 323 BC Alexander died of a fever in Babylon. His body was embalmed and placed within an elaborate funerary shrine, which, according to Diodorus, was dragged to Egypt by sixty-four mules. Alexander's successor in Egypt, General Ptolemy, met the funeral party and ordered the body be taken to Memphis. It remained there for several years until a tomb could be constructed in Ptolemy's capital, Alexandria, rather than in Siwa.

Ptolemy's successor, Ptolemy II Philadelphus, appointed Manetho, an Egyptian priest and Scribe of the Sacred Shrines of Egypt, to write (in Greek) a history of Egypt. This work, now known only from excerpts quoted by other authors, was the first comprehensive history of Egypt.

## EARLY TOURISTS

Egypt's ancient and splendid culture began its final decline in 30 BC when the armies of Octavian Caesar marched into Egypt, and Cleopatra VII, under threat of public humiliation by the conquering Romans, committed suicide. Rome reduced Egypt to a vassal state and exploited it for its agricultural potential. The Roman administration also moved against the native Egyptian temples, curtailing their tax-exempt status and carefully controlling the priesthood. Five years after the Roman conquest, the Greek geographer Strabo noted that many sites were already in disrepair from lack of use, and some were partially buried by encroaching desert sands. However, Rome did improve lines of communication within Egypt by establishing a road system and maintaining a police force to ensure safe travel throughout the country. News of the wonders of Egypt, as well as the increased security, prompted many tourists to visit the Nile Valley. To meet this new demand, small inns sprang up for weary travelers, and enterprising contractors hired out boats, pack animals, and tour guides to visitors wishing to see the ruins. In actuality, many elements of today's tourist trade are little changed from Roman times.

Many tourists began their travels at the port of Alexandria, which had an international reputation for scholarship, medicine, and entertainment of all types. Once satisfied by Alexandria's varied offerings, the tourists' next stop was the Giza pyramids, which at that time were still adorned with white limestone casing. Travelers often inscribed comments or names on the casing stones, and by the time of the Arab conquest the graffiti were so numerous that it was said it could fill a book of ten thousand pages.

Other tourist attractions included the Temple of Apis at Memphis and the famous "Labyrinth" in the Fayum, a vast funerary installation of Amunemhet III (1850–1800 BC). While in the Fayum, visitors were also invited to see and feed the sacred crocodiles. From the Labyrinth, the tourists traveled upriver to Thebes to visit the temples at Luxor and Karnak, as well as royal and private tombs that by that time had already been heavily plundered. The highlight of many trips was a visit to the Colossi of Memnon. Partially destroyed by an earthquake, one of the two statues emitted mysterious sounds in the early morning. Tourists flocked to hear and speculate about the origins and meaning of the sound. When Emperor Septimius Severus visited the statue in AD 202, the statue was not obliging, and in an attempt to persuade the god to speak, Severus restored the head and torso, unintentionally silencing the statue forever. Today it is believed the moaning sound was caused by a combination of wind, evaporating dew, and the expansion of the stones in the early morning heat.

The Romans were greatly impressed with the culture of Egypt, and it was fashionable to own and display a few Egyptian artifacts. Obelisks were highly prized, and they were exported throughout the Mediterranean world where they were erected in gardens and public squares. Pyramid-shaped tombs were built even in Rome. The emperors themselves indulged in Egyptianizing fantasies, adopting Egyptian customs or trappings. Hadrian (AD 117–138) adorned his Villa Adriana at Tivoli with an imitation Egyptian landscape complete with canals and temples and Roman-manufactured copies of Egyptian statues. Perhaps for the sake of true antiquity, authentic statuary was also imported from Egypt.

The earliest account of a non-Greek or Roman European to visit the ancient sites of

Egypt was that of Lady Etheria of Gaul. In AD 380 this intrepid nun ventured to the Holy Land in an attempt to identify sites mentioned in the Bible. In Egypt she visited Alexandria, Tell el Maskuta, possibly ancient Pithom (the city of the Israelites' labor in the Book of Exodus), and several other sites.

The rise of Christianity in Egypt marked the end of the ancient way of life. Unlike the Roman tourists who had been curious about Egyptian religious beliefs, native Christians were determined to erase all traces of ancient "heretical" ways. The edict of Theodosius (AD 392), ordering the closure of pagan temples throughout the Roman empire, officially sanctioned Christian efforts. In AD 397 the fanatical patriarch Cyril and his army of monks destroyed the Serapeum at Memphis and other Egyptian temples. The official persecution of the pagan religion was continued by Emperor Justinian, who in AD 580 ordered the arrest of the last priests of the Temple of Isis on the Island of Philae and the silencing of the oracle at Siwa. The ancient Egyptian religion was decreed illegal, and its symbols were regarded as evil and sinful.

The native Egyptian literary tradition also disappeared. During the Graeco-Roman Period, Egypt was multi-cultural, and the ruling elite spoke and wrote Greek. With the official closure of the temples, the only guardians of the old hieroglyphic literary tradition – the priests – were eliminated. Yet the ancient script continued to intrigue Europeans, and for the next millennium there was much speculation about the nature and content of the ancient texts.

## THE ARAB CONQUEST

The Arab conquest of North Africa in AD 640 instigated another wave of interest in the culture of ancient Egypt. While the rest of Europe was in the Dark Ages, the Arabs, who had a passion for literature, astronomy, mathematics, and geography, were the most enlightened people of their day. The Arabs, like all visitors to the Nile Valley, marveled at the temples and pyramids and speculated about their purpose. To broaden their knowledge, they translated Greek texts into Arabic. Unfortunately, their appetite for knowledge often led them to destructive investigations of the monuments in search of new texts. Most famous of the Arab explorers was Caliph Harun Al-Rashid (AD 786–809, whose feats were celebrated in the *Arabian Nights*), who paid translators gold based on the weight of each translated manuscript. For centuries the Arabs pursued treasure hunting with an intensity rivaled only by that of nineteenth-century European collectors. It was so widely practiced that, by the fifteenth century, treasure hunting was classified as a taxable industry, and writing guidebooks was a lucrative business. Even more devastating than treasure hunting was the large-scale dismantling of the pharaonic monuments near Cairo; the stones were then used to build aqueducts, mosques, and fortification walls for the growing Arab city.

One of the most reliable records of the condition of Egyptian monuments during

Arab rule was written by a medical and philosophy instructor in Cairo, Abdel Latif (*ca.* AD 1200). He reported that it took half a day to cross the ruins at Memphis and that the sights were so marvelous, they confounded the mind. Additionally, Abdel Latif described the head of the Sphinx in detail (the body was then covered by sand): the face was brownish red and the nose and beard were still intact. As reported by Makrizi, another Arab historian, the nose of the Sphinx was wantonly shot off in 1378 by Mohammed Sa'im al-Dahr, who, in retribution for the damage, was lynched by the local inhabitants.

More information about the wonders of the Holy Land and Egypt was relayed to Europeans by the Crusaders as they returned to Europe in the twelfth and thirteenth centuries. After the Turkish conquest of Egypt in 1517, traders and explorers from outside the Islamic world regularly entered Egypt and reported their findings. About 1624 Pietro delle Valle returned to Europe with a large quantity of papyrus and parts of mummies. The papyri stirred a great deal of excitement among European scholars and stimulated Athanasius Kircher, a German Jesuit and professor of Oriental languages, to publish the first treatise on hieroglyphs in 1643.

Things Egyptian caught the public's attention and fantasy. "Mummy" became a household word. In the seventeenth century, eating the dried flesh of a mummified corpse was considered a medical cure-all. It is ironic that the zeal for mummy may have been a case of mistaken identity. Bitumen (in Arabic, *mummiya*) is a mineral pitch that is reputed to have some medicinal value. The flesh and wrappings of Egyptian mummies were covered with a dark resinous substance, likened to bitumen, and were therefore referred to as mummy. This confusion, linked with the assumed esoteric knowledge of the ancient Egyptians, may well have contributed to the misplaced notion that consuming the dried flesh of a mummified corpse served a medicinal purpose.

As with any lucrative business, fraud soon entered into the mummy trade. Modern corpses were covered with bitumen, wrapped, dried in the sun and sold as mummy to Europeans. Eventually the Turkish governor of Egypt, probably seeking to profit from the mummy trade himself, imprisoned all traders and levied such harsh taxes on mummy that trade soon dwindled. Yet the threat of government regulation did not entirely prevent fraud or the export of mummy, which persisted until the early nineteenth century.

## THE DAWN OF SCIENTIFIC INQUIRY

Scientific efforts to study and document Egyptian monuments began in 1639 when the astronomer John Greaves of Oxford arrived in Egypt and initiated the first extensive survey of the Giza plateau. As a mathematician and student of ancient Greek, Arabic, and Persian, he was well qualified for the undertaking. His 1646 publication,

*Pyramidographia*, provided the most accurate survey of the structures available at that time. Furthermore, he presented a critical assessment of the accounts of ancient authors and correctly identified Khufu as builder of the first pyramid, Khafra the second, and Menkaure the third. He also described the Arab accounts of the pyramids, including the opening of the Great Pyramid by el-Mamoun in AD 820.

European scientific inquiry into Egypt's past was strongly linked to the political conditions of the late eighteenth century, which centered on nationalistic expansion in the Middle East and the control of sea routes that served lucrative colonies. England, France, Italy, and other European powers installed resident consuls, government-appointed men of widely varying abilities and experience, to oversee national trade interests and protect the "special rights" of their citizens in Egypt. The consuls often behaved as if they were a law unto themselves, with only moderate respect for the Mamluks who then ruled the Nile Valley. The foreign officials extended legal protection to their citizens who traveled in Egypt to collect information and antiquities, and the consuls themselves became major forces in the widespread and aggressive acquisition of antiquities, often at the behest of the European national museums, which were bitter rivals attempting to amass great collections.

### NAPOLEON'S INVASION AND ITS AFTERMATH

In April 1798 Napoleon was authorized by the French government to mount an expedition to seize Malta and Egypt and build a canal at the Isthmus of Suez to ensure the isolation of Britain from her Indian colonies. By July of the same year, Napoleon entered Cairo victorious.

Napoleon's campaign in Egypt ushered in a new era of Egyptian studies. In addition to 40,000 soldiers, Napoleon brought a special scientific commission of approximately 150 specialists in the disciplines of geography, geology, history, botany, zoology, medicine, and linguistics. These specialists were equipped not only with the appropriate instruments for their respective scientific inquiries but also with a library holding virtually all the then-published works on Egypt and a printing press (the first in Egypt). To ensure the coordination and dissemination of the research, Napoleon founded the Institut d'Égypte in Cairo.

In August 1798 the British navy under Admiral Nelson trapped and destroyed the French fleet east of Alexandria at Abukir Bay. The French, who were still battling the Mamluks, were stranded in Egypt. As the French forces moved south in pursuit of the Mamluk armies, the scholars continued their documentation of the land, its fauna, flora, customs, and ancient monuments. They marched an average of 40 to 50 kilometers a day, sometimes stopping only long enough to do a quick sketch and at times working with the drifting smoke of gunpowder around them. During their journey they were harassed by armed locals and plagued by hunger and disease. The military escort, in spite of the overwhelming difficulties, was quite aware of the importance of the scientific mission and on several occasions offered their musket shot to be melted down for pencil lead. On 27 January 1799 the expedition arrived at Luxor; they were so impressed with the magnificence of the temples that they broke into applause and spontaneously formed ranks and presented arms.

By 1801 the French were readying themselves for another British attack. The French scholars, exhausted and demoralized, fled to Alexandria with their scientific samples, notes, and antiquities in hope of leaving the country. With them was one of their most important finds, a large granite (previously identified as basalt) slab engraved in hieroglyphic, demotic, and Greek scripts that had been discovered reused in the fort at the port of el Rashid (known to Europeans as Rosetta) in July 1799. The importance of the multi-lingual inscription was immediately apparent to the French scholars, and the stela had been placed on exhibit in the Institut d'Egypte shortly after its discovery. When the French scholars fled to Alexandria, they were not about to leave the Rosetta Stone, as it had come to be called, behind. Their plan to leave the country with the monument was not to be, however, for the French were defeated by the British military at Alexandria, and, as part of the capitulation, were forced to cede the antiquities held by the scientific mission to Britain. After the war the French scientists returned home with their remaining collections and notes, as well as several casts of the Rosetta Stone.

The most lasting legacy of the French campaign in Egypt was the publication of *La Description de l'Egypte*, a massive, twenty-four-volume work that documented the geography, architecture, natural history, and ancient monuments of Egypt. Engravings of the ancient monuments were done by Dominique Vivant Denon (1747–1825), who traveled throughout Egypt with the Napoleonic mission. Denon was an accomplished artist, author, diplomat, and confident of both Louis XV and Napoleon. In spite of not being able to read the hieroglyphs that covered the monuments, Denon's engravings are so accurate that they are still used by scholars today.

The publication of *La Description* lured many scholars and artists to Egypt. One of the most accomplished was David Roberts (1796–1864), whose renderings of the ancient monuments of Egypt and the Holy Land are so accurate that they, too, are used by modern scholars to determine the condition of the monuments in the nineteenth century.

Engravings and illustrations by Denon, Roberts, and others were widely circulated in Europe where they made a tremendous impact. Not only were accurate images of Egyptian temples available to scholars, but also the interest of the general public was sparked, and clothing, furniture, and decorative arts were embellished with Egyptian motifs.

The cessation of war in Egypt, the installation of foreign consuls, and the "Egyptomania" sweeping across Europe resulted in a dramatic increase in European visitors to Egypt. One of the most colorful and enterprising was the Italian Giovanni

Belzoni (1778–1823). Belzoni and his young wife initially travelled to Egypt in 1812 to interest Mohammed Ali Pasha in a new invention, an ox-driven water pump. Unfortunately, Belzoni found the Pasha less than exuberant about the new water-wheel, but while he was in Egypt he was introduced to Henry Salt, the influential British consul-general. Utilizing his engineering skills, Belzoni helped the British agent move a colossal head known as the "Young Memnon" from the temple of Ramesses II in Luxor. The success of that project (the statue is now in the British Museum) led to more commissions, notably the removal of the sarcophagus of Ramesses III. Belzoni explored much of the west bank at Luxor, discovering six tombs in the Valley of the Kings and many private sepulchres. His techniques were often crude, as reflected in the following passage from his memoirs recounting the discovery of a cache of mummies:

> I sought a resting place, found one, and contrived to sit; but when my weight bore on the body of an Egyptian, it crushed it like a band-box . . . I sunk altogether among the broken mummies, with a crash of bones, rags and wooden cases . . . and every step I took crushed a mummy in some part or other.
>
> (Belzoni in Vercoutter 1992: 182)

Belzoni performed many other salvage projects for Salt during his career in Egypt, including clearing the entrance of the temple of Ramesses II at Abu Simbel. There he employed techniques more sensitive than those he used in Luxor, and he managed to document the reliefs and inscriptions within its chambers. He also spent several days at Giza, where, on 28 February 1818, he found the entrance to the pyramid of Khafra. He immortalized this achievement by writing his name and the date on the wall of the burial chamber. Approximately 6 meters in length, this defacement remains one of the largest examples of graffiti in the world.

In 1821 Belzoni returned to England and held a great exhibition of his artifacts in Piccadilly, including facsimiles of two chambers of the tomb of Seti I. His treasures eventually found their way to the British Museum and form the basis of its collection. Belzoni never returned to Egypt but died of dysentery on his way to Timbuktu.

Britain was not alone in the aggressive exploitation of Egyptian antiquities. Her principal rival was France, represented by the French consul-general, an Italian named Bernardino Drovetti (1776–1852). During the execution of his diplomatic duties, Drovetti and his agents collected myriad antiquities that were sold to the great museums in Paris, Berlin, and Turin.

By 1820 the rivalry between Salt and Drovetti became so acute that they entered into an astounding gentleman's agreement: all antiquities on the west bank of the Nile were fair game for Salt while those on the east bank were reserved for Drovetti. With the help of a spyglass, the French consul trained a watchful eye on his domain from his house perched atop the first pylon of the Karnak Temple.

In 1858 the viceroy of Egypt, Said Pasha, took steps to control excavation and to reg-
ularize the removal of artifacts by forming the Egyptian Antiquities Service under the
direction of a Frenchman, Auguste Mariette (1821–1881). This development marked
the beginning of a new age in the exploration of Egypt.

### THE ACADEMICS

Although the tales of treasure hunters such as Belzoni are entertaining, there are many
academic heroes in ancient Egyptian studies dating to this same period. The work of
Auguste Mariette, Sir John Gardner Wilkinson, Karl Lepsius, and Sir William Flinders
Petrie laid the foundation for modern study, and many of their conclusions remain
unchallenged. Employing evidence provided by artifacts and inscriptions on statues
and stelas, these scholars began to reconstruct the history and culture of ancient
Egypt.

As mentioned above, in 1858 the viceroy of Egypt appointed Mariette to head the
Egyptian Antiquities Service. A noted archaeologist, his discoveries include the Valley
Temple of Khafra and the Serapeum. He is also credited with assisting Verdi in the
libretto of the opera *Aida*, which was written for the opening of the Suez Canal in 1869.

Mariette attempted to impose government control over all excavations in Egypt.
Under his supervision, dozens of mastabas at Meidum and Saqqara, part of Karnak, the
Serapeum, and the temples at Dendera, Luxor, and Edfu were excavated, making them
accessible to scholars and tourists. He was fair in personal dealings, pleasant, likeable,
and a diligent worker, qualities that were instrumental in building good relations with
the foreign excavators who were now dependent upon his permission to work.
Although his excavation techniques, strained by the great number of sites and
workmen, were somewhat crude even for his day, he was widely respected.

Unfortunately, few detailed records were made of most of his discoveries, and little
attempt was made to conserve what had been exposed during excavations. Although
his techniques were not significantly different from those of the robbers he wished to
curtail, his finds were deposited in government storehouses rather than on the antiquities market; and, although he could not entirely prevent tomb robbers from continuing their work, he did curtail the dealers by enforcing a ban on the export of
antiquities from Egypt.

One of Mariette's greatest achievements was the establishment of the Egyptian
Museum in 1863, the first national museum in the Near East. This was no small feat,
for although scholars appreciated the need for safeguarding Egypt's past and the establishment of a national collection, this goal interfered with the growth of the collections
throughout Europe. In addition, the very government that established the Antiquities
Service often undermined it. In 1855 the best of the Egyptian national collection was
presented to Archduke Maximillian of Austria by Khedive Sa'id for diplomatic

purposes. When Princess Eugenie requested a similar gift in 1867, Mariette refused, damaging his standing with the Egyptian viceroy.

Mariette's flexibility and fairness allowed him to maintain generally good relations with his foreign colleagues. He promoted men of other nationalities (especially British) to positions of "Inspector." He allowed duplicate pieces to be awarded to the excavators, and he sometimes sold off surplus antiquities in his effort to refine the museum collection. Mariette was so successful and influential that, even during the later years of British dominance, the Antiquities Department was always headed by a Frenchman until Egypt's independence in 1952.

Another early scholar to work in Egypt was Sir John Gardner Wilkinson (1797–1875), who is credited with being the founder of Egyptology in Britain. His scholarly career began, however, on a far from auspicious note. After leaving Oxford without a degree, Wilkinson planned to join the army but was persuaded by his parents to travel. During his travels he met Sir William Gell, who had a passion for archaeology and who persuaded Wilkinson to sail for Egypt in 1821. There Wilkinson learned to speak Arabic and to read and write Coptic, which many at that time believed to be the key to deciphering hieroglyphs. Wilkinson traveled throughout Egypt recording the temple and tomb scenes. As he worked, he gradually began to see patterns in the hieroglyphs. Availing himself of the work of Thomas Young and Jean François Champollion (see chapter 8), Wilkinson became particularly proficient at determining the phonetic values of royal names and geographic terms. Unlike Young or Champollion, however, he had the great advantage of working in Egypt where he had an inexhaustible supply of comparative materials.

Wilkinson eventually consolidated his work into a three-volume treatise, *The Manners and Customs of the Ancient Egyptians* (1837). The images of daily life and religious rituals in this work provided a virtual encyclopedia of life in ancient Egypt. For this landmark publication, Wilkinson was awarded a knighthood.

Although the scholarly rivalry between Britain and France was the most famous, other European nations were interested in ancient Egypt. Inspired by *La Description*, Count Humboldt of Prussia persuaded Kaiser Wilhelm IV to sponsor an expedition under the leadership of a young prodigy, Karl Lepsius (1810–1884). Although only in his twenties, Lepsius was considered one of the finest philologists of his day. Unlike the French expedition under Napoleon, the Prussian survey was purely academic, and its schedule was fully devoted to recording the ancient monuments and the scenes that decorated their walls. Between 1842 and 1845 the Prussian team visited nearly every major site in Egypt and Nubia. On the Giza and Saqqara plateau alone the scholars explored, mapped, and drew scenes and plans of over 130 mastaba tombs. Everywhere they went, the Germans collected artifacts and made papier-mâché casts of the inscriptions and scenes they encountered. Upon the expedition's return to Prussia, Lepsius supervised the production of one the finest works on Egypt ever printed: the twelve-volume *Denkmäler aus Ägypten und Äthiopien*, which is still a basic research tool. The 15,000 antiquities brought back to Germany by the scholars formed the basis of the Berlin Museum's collection.

Although the first pioneers in the decipherment of the hieroglyphic language were French (Champollion) and British (Young) (see chapter 8), the Germans were leaders in the publication of journals and basic reference works. The earliest journal devoted solely to ancient Egypt, *Zeitschrift für Ägyptische Sprache*, was established in Berlin in 1863. The monumental, and still unsurpassed, dictionary of the Egyptian language, the *Wörterbuch der Ägyptischen Sprache*, appeared between 1926 and 1931.

Through the work of Mariette, Wilkinson, and Lepsius, Egyptian archaeology was born, but it was through the efforts of Sir William Flinders Petrie (1853–1942) that it came of age. Petrie was inquisitive by nature and enjoyed problem solving. He taught himself geometry by age fifteen and learned to use a sextant and map sites by age eighteen. His first published work, *Inductive Metrology, or the Recovery of Ancient Measurements from Monuments* (1877), dealt with measurements of Stonehenge and introduced to archaeology the importance of documenting the precise location of artifacts when attempting to reconstruct the past. Petrie was greatly influenced by Charles Piazzi Smyth (1819–1900), a Scottish astronomer whose 1864 work *Our Inheritance in the Great Pyramid* suggested that the pyramids held all mathematical and astronomical knowledge and that the ancient Egyptians had based their pyramid measurements on the value of $\pi$. Although Piazzi Smyth's ideas were heavily criticized, Petrie went to Egypt to vindicate his theories. To his dismay he found that Piazzi Smyth's measurements were inaccurate. Petrie published his work *Pyramids and Temples* in 1883 and so impressed the director of the British-sponsored Egypt Exploration Fund that he was appointed the chief archaeologist for the organization.

Petrie's contributions to Egyptian archaeology were many, but perhaps the most important was his insistence that even pieces of broken pottery, bones, bricks, beads, worked flint, and other unimpressive objects were significant and should not be ignored. He also was a proponent of the excavation of less glamorous sites such as towns and houses, which, although they may not yield fine art and reliefs for museum collections, do much to elucidate the culture of ancient Egypt.

Petrie's insistence on noting all artifacts as well as their provenance took on further significance in his later work: the development of sequence dating. Petrie believed that cultural change was reflected in stylistic change and that relative chronologies could be established in the absence of stratigraphy by examining how artifacts stylistically change through time. Although this concept may seem relatively simple, in practice it is an extremely complex idea to test because it requires very large sample sizes. Petrie, however, was undeterred. Studying an immense number of graves and artifacts recovered from the Upper Egyptian Predynastic cemeteries at Abydos, Naqada, Ballas, Abadiyeh, and Hu, he divided broad classes of artifacts such as ceramics, slate palettes, flint tools, and figurines into several types. In the case of ceramics, nine types were devised (fig. 1.1). He recorded the contents of each tomb and noted not only the artifacts present, but which of his defined artifact types co-occurred. He then grouped them to establish a plausible progression of stylistic change – that is, how one pattern developed into another over time (fig. 1.2). Petrie did not initially attempt to assign absolute dates but rather established a relative "sequence" of changing artifacts from oldest to more recent, hence the term "sequence date." By assigning sequential numbers from 30 to 80 to each object on the basis of its stylistic complexity, he worked out a system of relative dates. Objects with designations in the 70s were latest; those in the 30s, earliest. Other archaeologists were now able to compare their finds with Petrie's and place them in his relative chronology. Through this process Petrie was able to cross-date Aegean, Mycenaean, and Cretan artifacts with those of ancient Egypt, establishing for the first time a temporal framework from which cross-cultural comparisons could be made.

Petrie's ingenious technique of sequence dating is similar to modern methods of computer-enhanced seriation analysis. Although today the analysis of ceramic vessels has become far more sophisticated since Petrie's original discoveries (especially since the advent of thermoluminescence dating that gives a range of absolute dates), chronologies based on stylistic change are still created.

Petrie excavated almost every major site in Egypt, and he is still admired for the speed with which his publications appeared. He was and still is considered to be a "character." He insisted on rigorous discipline in the field and maintained his staff on a spartan diet of canned food, which often had to be shared cold. Tourists often witnessed him neck-deep in filthy canals or surveying on the Giza plateau in his long underwear. As an archaeologist, Petrie set the standard for scientific research. His meticulous excavation, thorough analysis, and careful and immediate publication were unequaled. He further contributed to Egyptian archaeology by training Egyptian field assistants known as Kuftis (from the town of Kuft) and students, who later went on to conduct their own research. Many of the next generation of archaeologists were trained by Petrie and were highly influenced by his methods.

A new generation of scholars entered Egypt in the 1960s, when the rising waters of the newly built High Dam at Aswan began to threaten the Nubian monuments in southern Egypt and northern Sudan. In addition to Egyptologists, archaeologists versed in European and North American archaeology came to Egypt to help with the preservation efforts. After the Nubian campaign was completed, many of these archaeologists continued to work in the Nile Valley and began addressing new questions about Egypt's past, ushering in a new era of multi-disciplinary research.

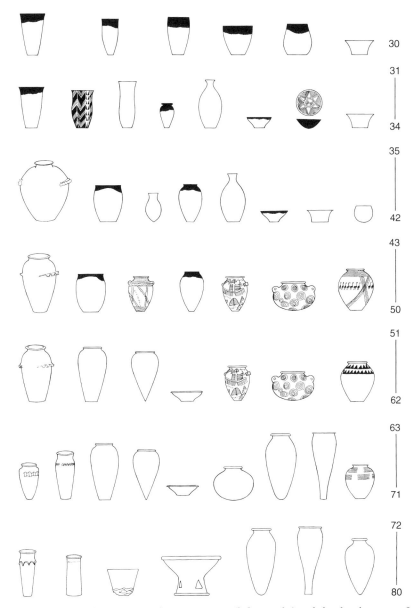

1.1 Sequence dating chart showing Petrie's pottery types (left to right) and the development of pottery styles (top to bottom) in the Predynastic and Early Dynastic periods. This developmental sequence was used as a means of establishing a relative chronology for the era before written records.

1.2 Predynastic and Early Dynastic vessels illustrating the evolution of wavy handle decoration into a raised band of decoration, and finally into a thin line encircling the vessel.

## SUMMARY

The rich culture and great monuments of Egypt have always had a special allure. Greeks and Romans who conquered the country imitated aspects of Egyptian culture. Arab scholars sought the knowledge implicit in the ancient monumental architecture. European expansion in the seventeenth through nineteenth centuries led to military campaigns and political domination, and scientific surveys brought the study of ancient Egypt to a new level. Early European exploration in Egypt was largely an expression of western national pride as government officials collected antiquities for their state museums. With Egypt's mid-nineteenth century reawakening to the richness of her own past and alarm over the exportation of her cultural legacy, strictures were placed upon unauthorized excavation. By the end of the century, most excavations were more scholarly and methodical in nature, and the excavators were expected to share their results through publication. With Sir William Flinders Petrie, archaeology was further refined with emphasis shifting from the excavation of great statues and temples to the investigation of towns, houses, and an understanding of the importance of every shred of evidence. During the 1960s international efforts organized to save the Nubian monuments from the rising waters of the High Dam's reservoir ushered in the modern era of ancient Egyptian research, characterized by cooperative efforts across disciplines and national boundaries.

## FURTHER READING

Andrews, Carol, *The Rosetta Stone*. London: The British Museum, 1981.

Ceram, C. W., *Gods, Graves and Scholars*. New York: Alfred Knopf, 1951.

Curl, James S., *Egyptomania: The Egyptian Revival: A Recurring Theme in the History of Taste*. Manchester: Manchester University Press, 1994.

Deuel, Leo, *The Treasures of Time*. New York: World Publishing Co., 1961.

Drower, Margaret S., *Flinders Petrie: A Life in Archaeology*. London: Gollancz, 1985.

Fagan, Brian, *The Rape of the Nile*. New York: Charles Scribner's Sons, 1977.

Greener, Leslie, *The Discovery of Egypt*. New York: Dorset Press, 1966.

James, T. G. H. (ed.), *Excavating in Egypt*. Chicago: University of Chicago Press, 1982.

Moorehead, Alan, *The Blue Nile*. New York: Harper and Row, 1961.

Thompson, Jason, *Sir Gardner Wilkinson and his Circle*. Austin, Tex.: University of Texas Press, 1992.

Vercoutter, Jean, *The Search for Ancient Egypt*. New York: Harry Abrams, 1992.

*Chapter 2*

# THE RIVER, VALLEY, AND DESERT

Egypt is a land of sharp contrasts. Located on the boundary between the cooler temperate and hotter tropical belts, Egypt is part of the great African desert zone where the earth's surface is subjected to intense heat, aridity, and wind. These harsh conditions denude the landscape and fracture even the hardest stones. Egypt was and is characterized by a hot, almost rainless, climate. The average annual rainfall for the entire country is only about 10 millimeters; even along Egypt's Mediterranean coast, where most of the precipitation occurs, annual rainfall is less than 200 millimeters. Through this vast wilderness the Nile River flows.

As the Greek historian Herodotus remarked, Egypt was the gift of the Nile. Indeed, the river and the ecosystem of the Nile Valley defined Egyptian culture. Daily life was so intertwined with the environment that much of ancient Egyptian culture and history is barely intelligible without reference to the ancient ecology within which the culture developed and flourished. The natural rhythms of nature – the cycle of the sun, the rise and fall of the Nile, the seasonal agricultural cycles – became a primary theme in theology. The local fauna and flora were incorporated as signs in hieroglyphic writing. The floral columns and capitals, the great pylon gateways, and the rock-cut tombs were all echoes of the surrounding environment.

The idea that environment and culture are closely related is not a new concept. In the 1950s V. Gordon Childe, in his now famous "oasis hypothesis," related the rise of civilization to a deteriorating environment; later concepts, such as Carneiro's "environmental conscription," proposed to explain the rise of complex societies, postulate a similar relationship between culture and environment. More recent studies, such as those by Hassan, Brewer, Butzer, and Wenke, differ from the earlier, more simplistic models by acknowledging the interplay of a variety of factors that contribute to the co-evolution of humans, culture, and the environment, as well as the need to be cognizant of the researcher's own culturally based biases.

Few scholars will contest that the Nile River was the most dominant geographic feature influencing the daily life of the ancient Egyptians. The river flows from the mountains in the south to the Mediterranean in the north. This directional flow served as a natural compass for the ancient Egyptians, who thought of travel in terms of movement on the Nile. When Egyptians traveled to other lands, they noticed that the rivers ran the "wrong" way, that is, north to south: A text of Thutmose I at Tombos in Nubia describes the Euphrates as "the inverted water that goes downstream in going

16

upstream." The Nile's northward flow also serves as a basis for modern geographic terminology: southern Egypt, because it is upstream, is referred to as Upper Egypt, and the Delta, or northern Egypt, is known as Lower Egypt. During ancient times, Egypt was divided into four main geographic areas formed by the imaginary intersection of the river and the east-west passage of the sun. That is, the river flowed from the valley to the Delta, and the sun rose over the Eastern Desert and set behind the Western Desert. Each of these geographic regions possessed unique physical and ecological characteristics and each influenced the local inhabitants in different ways.

## THE DELTA

The Delta, representing 63 percent of the inhabited area of Egypt, extends approximately 200 kilometers from south to north and roughly 400 kilometers from east to west (fig. 2.1). It probably reached these modern dimensions by about 4000 BC. The Delta is a flat and almost featureless plain, dropping only 12 meters from its apex near Cairo to the sea.

The overall shape and topography of the Delta can be compared to the back of a triangular leaf: the raised veins represent the river levees and mark the higher ground, and the basins and lowlands between the major channels are represented by the rest of the leaf. Today the Nile flows through the Delta via two principal branches, the Damietta and the Rosetta. In antiquity there were three principal channels, known in pharaonic times as the "water of Pre," "the water of Ptah," and "the water of Amun" and in classical times as the Pelusiac, the Sebennytic, and the Canopic branches. The other branches mentioned by classical writers such as Herodotus were not principal channels, but were subsidiary branches from the Sebennytic (e.g., the Mendesian and Saitic) or artificially cut channels (e.g., the Bolbitine and Bucolic). Throughout history the course of minor canals has been highly variable, and many extinct branches have been recognized. The Mediterranean coast of the Delta is an extensive marshy area, the Bareri, interspersed with a series of lagoons and lakes, some of which are connected to the sea. The major lakes of the Delta, from east to west, are Lake Manzala, Lake Buruillus, and Lake Edku. The northern shores of these lakes are separated from the sea by strips of sand forming straight, regular borders, but the southern shores are irregular and often grade into marshes and swamps, which are frequently misused to characterize the Delta as a whole.

The most dominant topographic features in the Delta are the sand *geziras*, or turtlebacks, that rise above the cultivated fields. These *geziras* are deposits of sand, sandy clay, and sandy silt that appear as islands rising 1 to 12 meters above the surrounding area. The origin of the *geziras* is debated; they may represent relics of old buried branches of the Nile or be windblown, sand-dune-like deposits. The *geziras* follow a pattern roughly associated with a geological fault that crosses the Delta in a

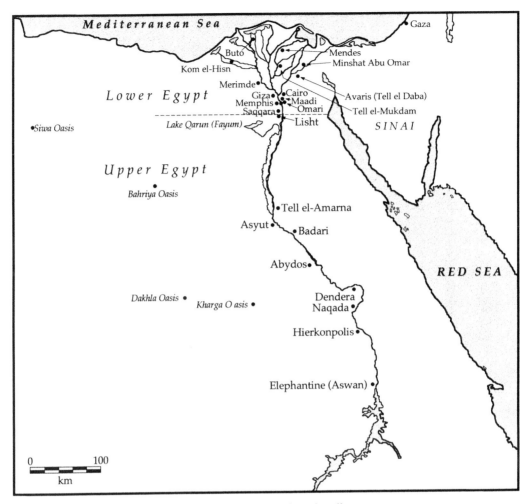

2.1  Map of Egypt and the Nile Valley

northeast–southwest direction and divides the Delta into two parts: southeast of the
fault line *gezira*s are present, but northwest of the line they are not. This distribution
may have contributed to an ancient Egyptian distinction between the western Delta
adjacent to the Libyan frontier and the eastern Delta adjacent to Sinai, the vital land
bridge to Asia. *Gezira*s are important archaeologically because they were ideal sites for
Predynastic and Early Dynastic settlements. Villages and cemeteries built on the sterile
*gezira*s were safe from normal floods, and the surrounding fertile land was ideal for
agriculture. The location of the earliest habitation sites in the Delta on these *gezira*s is
echoed in the ancient belief that all life began on a mound of earth that emerged from
the primordial waters of Nun.

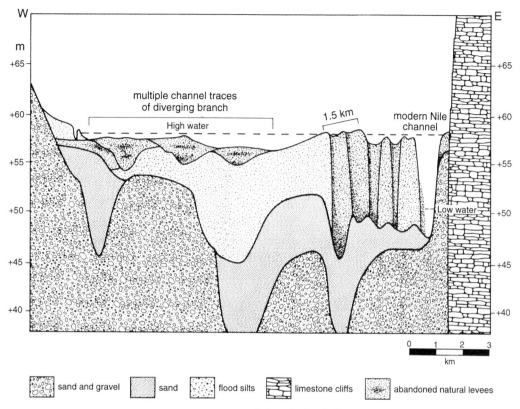

2.2 Cross-section of the Nile flood plain.

## THE VALLEY

Along most of its course through Egypt the Nile has scoured a deep, wide gorge in the desert plateau and deposited a thick layer of rich, dark silt on the valley floor. It is this deep carpet of silt that gives the valley its astonishing fertility. The annual flood waters also added nutrients to the land and helped to curtail the build-up of salts. For 965 km between Aswan and Cairo, the Nile follows a generally south–north course and drops only 71 meters, from 83 meters above sea level near Aswan to 12 meters near Cairo (fig. 2.1).

At Aswan the Nile passes through a formation of hard igneous rock, which is more resistant to erosion than the softer sand and limestone found downstream, and this has resulted in rapids or "cataracts," which formed a natural boundary to the south. Before the inauguration of the Aswan High Dam in 1971, the cataract at Aswan stretched for about 10 kilometers, and along this stretch the river was divided into several smaller streams by rock islands. Today this stretch is an exceptionally wide channel ranging from 1.5 to 4.7 kilometers. On both sides of the Nile steep igneous scarps rise directly from the water's edge. Sheets of sand cover most of the face of the western scarp and sand dunes fill the *wadis* cut into the scarp.

North of the first cataract at Aswan the Nile is deeper and the surface water smoother. Igneous rocks are still obstacles, however, and form sand- and silt-covered islands. Cliffs border both sides of the valley, but those on the west bank rapidly lose height to the north. The scarp east of the Nile runs contiguous to the river, and the water reaches the base of the cliff during most of its course except for a few areas, such as the Kom Ombo plain. The average width of the Nile between Aswan and Luxor is 2.8 kilometers, the maximum is 7.5 kilometers at Edfu, and the minimum is 350 meters at Silwa Gorge.

Downstream from Aswan the Nile flows in a northerly direction for about 200 kilometers to Armant before taking an acute bend, known as the Qena Bend. Running from Armant to Hu, it extends for approximately 180 kilometers and marks off the relatively narrow southern valley from the wider valley to the north. From Luxor to Cairo the Nile flows sinuously, and the flood plain is nearly 20 kilometers wide in some places.

North of Asyut the west bank becomes broader, the western cliffs fade into a low escarpment, and a winding parallel offshoot of the Nile, the Bahr Yusef, flows to the west of the river. Because of its distinctive character, the term "Middle Egypt" is often used when referring to the area between Asyut and Cairo.

In antiquity, the Nile Valley was called Kemet, the "Black Land," in reference to the rich agricultural plain. It was conceived of as being composed of Two Lands: *Ta-mehu*, the north (from the Fayum to the Mediterranean), and *Ta Shemaw*, the south (from Aswan to perhaps the Fayum). Although the Egyptians were aware of the desert oases, these peripheral areas did not enter into the traditional sense of duality formed by the Nile Valley.

OASES AND DESERTS

The deserts stood in stark contrast to the Nile Valley. The arid east and west were collectively referred to as *Djseret*, the Red Land, in contrast to *Kemet*, the Black Land of the Nile Valley proper.

The major oases of the Western desert – Fayum, Kharga, Dakhla, Bahriya, and Siwa (fig. 2.1) – were considered to be part of Egypt in ancient times, although they were always regarded more as frontier outposts than as integral parts of the country. The oases served as military garrisons and as stopping points along the caravan routes that connected Egypt with the deserts and with sub-Saharan Africa. One of these caravan routes, still in use today, is the Darb el-Arbayin, the "road of 40 (days)," that runs from Darfur in Sudan to Asyut. The western steppes were favored hunting grounds for gazelle, antelope, and other mammals. Herds of wild animals still existed as late as

Table 2.1 *Nile evolution and geologic time*

| Geologic time period | Nile phases | Date (BC). |
| --- | --- | --- |
| Holocene | Nile | 18,000 |
| Upper Pleistocene | Neonile | 30,000 |
| Upper Pleistocene | Prenile | 500,000–150,000 |
| Middle Pleistocene | Protonile | 600,000 |
| Pliocene | Paleonile | 3,000,000 |
| Miocene | Eonile | 5,000,000(+) |

Dynasty 18, as indicated by King Amunhotep III's claimed to have bagged 96 wild bulls in the region of Shetep, near the Wadi Natrun.

The most important oasis is the Fayum, a depression whose waters were connected to the Nile via the Bahr Yusef canal. It was always a popular hunting and fishing center, and during the Middle Kingdom the capital (Itchtowy) was situated here. The Fayum was exploited for its agricultural potential and later became one of the most agriculturally productive areas of Egypt. By the New Kingdom, population densities were already higher in the Fayum than in the Nile Valley proper. Ambitious land reclamation projects under the Ptolemies increased the extent of arable land to perhaps 1,300 square kilometers. Census records of the Byzantine Period indicate there were at least 198 towns in the Fayum, housing more than 300,000 people. The pattern of growth continues today, for the area's rich vineyards and plantations of flowers and fruit trees make it one of the most agriculturally productive areas in Egypt.

### GEOLOGIC AND CLIMATIC HISTORY OF THE NILE VALLEY

Over the past 5 million years the Nile has undergone five main episodes (table 2.1). Each of these episodes is characterized by a river that drew a large part of its waters from outside Egypt. Toward the end of each of the first four episodes, the river appears to have dramatically declined in size or ceased to flow into Egypt entirely.

The earliest known episode of the Nile is called the Eonile, which flowed through Egypt approximately 5 to 6 million years ago during the Miocene Epoch. The Eonile valley probably looked much like the North American Grand Canyon, with some stretches more than 3 kilometers deep. The Mediterranean Sea also looked quite different than today. It is thought that the ancient sea was significantly smaller than its modern counterpart, and some scholars even believe that sea levels may have been so low that the Mediterranean did not even exist. Modern remnants of deep canyons cut into the Mediterranean basin by rivers such as the Nile are seen as supporting evidence for such a claim. During the Lower Pliocene, the sea level began to rise and fill the huge Nile Valley. The Mediterranean rose to heights so great that marine deposits dating to this period can be found as far south as Aswan. The rising of the sea marks the end of the Eonile.

A second river, the Paleonile, cut into Egypt during the Lower Pliocene approximately 3 million years ago. The source of this river, like the preceding Eonile, is not known, but it was not the same as the modern river. During the timespan of these two prehistoric rivers, it is believed that rainfall was more extensive and these two rivers may have originated in equatorial Africa with water entering the Nile system through a series of large wadis. Over time the area drained by the Paleonile became more arid. The Late Pliocene was also a time of great seismic activity. The combination of increased aridity, accompanied by scouring winds, and seismic activity created the great basins of the Western Desert (e.g., the Fayum Depression, which is 44 meters below sea level) and eventually caused the Paleonile to disappear.

During the Pleistocene Epoch, three ancient rivers can be identified. The Protonile (Middle Pleistocene, *ca.* 600,000 BC) was a braided river with many interwoven channels and a more westerly course than the present river. The Prenile (*ca.* 500,000–150,000 BC) is thought to be the largest river ever to flow through Egypt, carving and shaping much of today's landscape and possessing a Delta twice the size of the current one. The most recent of the ancient rivers is the Neonile (*ca.* 30,000 BC), which is essentially the same river as the modern Nile: when the Neonile cut its bed down to the modern level, it became the Nile (*ca.* 8,000 BC).

The different flow regimes of the ancient rivers cut a series of eight terraces in the rocky cliffs of the eastern and western shores. The sixth terrace from the top, about 25 meters above the present valley floor, is Prenile and has yielded assemblages of crude axes in the style known as *Acheulean*. Although Egypt has produced no human remains associated with these artifacts, finds elsewhere in Africa suggest this tool industry was used by *Homo erectus*. Paleolithic tools of modern *Homo sapiens sapiens* are found with Neonile sediments.

From its source in Lake Tanganyika to its mouth in the Mediterranean Sea, today's Nile runs more than 6,625 kilometers and is the longest river in the world. The river flows virtually due north: its source and its mouth lie within one degree of the same meridian of longitude (31° E). Most of the modern Nile's water flows from two distinct sources. 83 percent of its volume comes from Lake Tanganyika, high in the Ethiopian plateau. Once a year, during the summer, monsoons fill the lake and send water and silt down the Blue Nile. It is this yearly rainfall that causes the annual inundation of Egypt, which deposits the rich agricultural silts. The source of the White Nile, the second main contributor of water to the Egyptian Nile, is in Uganda. It provides a much smaller amount of water than the Blue Nile (approximately 16 percent), but the source is steady. Without the water from the White Nile, the Egyptian Nile would probably run dry in May or June. The Blue and White Nile meet at the modern city of Khartoum, in the Sudan. The River Atbara is a third water source and provides a yearly average of less than 1 percent of the Egyptian Nile's water.

Like the river, Egypt's climate has fluctuated through time, resulting in changes in vegetation in the Nile Valley and desert. These changes, however, seem to be more quantitative than qualitative. During Prenile times, Egypt received more precipitation than today, and many areas of the desert probably resembled modern African savannahs. This precipitation continued and may actually have increased until 50,000 BC, but by Neonile times conditions had become increasingly arid, perhaps as arid as today. A brief pluvial period around 8,000 BC marked the beginning of the modern Nile and brought back savanna-like conditions throughout many parts of the Western Desert. During this time, evidence from rock art shows that giraffes, gazelle, and ostriches roamed what is now the desert. From this time on, although minor fluctuations in precipitation occurred, Egypt became increasingly arid until the modern period of hyperaridity became established some time in the Early Dynastic Period (*ca.* 3100–2700 BC).

Many introductory texts about Egypt describe the prehistoric environment of the Nile Valley as thoroughly inhospitable to humans. The Upper Egyptian valley is described as a tangled jungle and the Delta as an uninhabitable swamp. Modern geological research has disproved both of these characterizations. For example, the Delta, although marshy in places, had numerous elevated *gezira*s, and the central and southern Delta possessed considerable dry land suitable for habitation from very early times. Upper Egypt was always a well-drained flood plain able to support hunters and fishers in the Paleolithic Period and agriculturalists in the Neolithic and Dynastic Periods.

## THE NILE IN CULTURAL CONTEXT

The special character of the Nile, which made it so central to Egyptian culture, was its annual inundation. (If today's floods were not controlled by a series of dams, the inundation would be approximately the same as it was in dynastic times.) During the month of June, the Nile began to rise between Cairo and Aswan, and a quantity of green water appeared. The cause of the color is said to have resulted from the brief efflorescence of myriad minute organisms. During August the river rose rapidly and its waters assumed a muddy red color because of the presence of the rich red earth brought into the Nile by the Blue Nile and the Atbara. The river continued to rise until mid-September, then remained at that level for two or three weeks. In October, the river rose again slightly and then began to fall gradually until May, when the river reached its lowest level.

The Nile has created a convex flood plain. Unlike most rivers, in which sediments (silts and clays) are deposited as a response to channel shifts and erosion, convex flood plains accumulate sediment deposits through flooding. A convex flood plain is marked by natural levees, constituting the low-water channel banks, immediately adjacent to the river. These levees rise a few meters above the seasonally inundated lowlands situated at the margins of the valley; thus, viewed in cross-section, the valley has a slightly convex shape. When the Nile floods, the water passes through channels in the levees and covers most of the low-lying land up to the edge of the desert. When the floods subside, the waters are trapped behind the levees in natural basins (fig. 2.2). The benefit of such topography is obvious: the water can be used where it stands or channeled to other areas as dictated by agricultural needs.

Ancient records, those preserved in texts and the visible evidence on ancient *Nilometers*, indicate that a flood of 6 meters was perilously low and that one of 9 meters was high enough to cause damage to crops and villages. A flood of 7–8 meters, in which low-lying areas and basins throughout the whole valley would be flooded up to the edge of the rising ground of the desert but towns, villages, and dykes that served as paths and water barriers remained above the water level, was ideal.

The ancient Egyptians fully understood the extent to which their lives and prosperity depended on the unfailing regularity of the inundation. The occasional low flood and consequent shortage of food were enough to cause much anxiety among the populace at the beginning of each flood season. Ancient Egyptians, therefore, never regarded the river and its gifts with complacency, even though the annual inundation that brought a layer of fresh rich silt and waters for irrigation made agriculture in the Nile Valley relatively easy. The generally predictable crops and resulting surplus freed a significant segment of the population from agricultural labor, allowing for the development of non-farming occupations, such as full-time craftsmen, bureaucrats, and priests.

The importance of the Nile to Egyptian civilization is reflected in the role that it played in religion and the myths that revolved around the river. The Nile was known in antiquity by the name Iteru. The personification of the inundation was a god named Hapy, who was associated with fertility and regeneration. The ancient Egyptians had various conceptions of the origin of the inundation. Some texts relate that it began in a cavern at Philae, near the first cataract, while others credit Gebel Silsila (about 100 kilometers to the north) as the source. It was believed that veneration of the gods associated with the Aswan area (Khnum, Anukis, and Satis) could ensure a sufficient inundation. The "Famine Stela," a text carved on rocks at Sehêl near the first cataract, records a famine that was averted by making donations of land and goods to the Temple of Khnum at Aswan. This text was originally thought to date from the reign of Djoser, but in reality it dates to the Ptolemaic Period some 2,500 years later.

The Nile River was the principal highway of the land. Because most villages were situated near the Nile, and even the temples on the desert edge were connected to the Nile by canals, there was little incentive to develop land-based transport. Travel on the Nile was easy, facilitated by the direction of the prevailing wind which blows from the north. Therefore, a boat traveling south against the current could use sails; one traveling north could easily paddle with the current. Travel by means of the river was so common in ancient Egypt that the words for "go north" and "go south" were determined in hieroglyphic script by boats with sail unfurled (for "go south," or upstream) and boats with no sail (for "go north," or downstream).

The river offered both an obvious means of mass transit and an easy way to move goods. During the annual inundation, when most of the cultivated area was covered by water, barges could convey heavy cargo such as building stones and monumental sculptures directly from the quarries situated in the cliffs bordering the flooded valley to their destinations, the temples and cemeteries located just beyond the limits of the floodwaters. Even after the introduction of wheeled vehicles during the Second Intermediate Period, boats remained the dominant means of transportation for people and goods.

## SUMMARY

In Egypt, as elsewhere, the physical environment provided the opportunities and challenges from which civilization developed, and civilization in turn shaped and altered the environment. Not merely the stage for history, geography became part of history as land was opened to agriculture, marshes were drained, irrigation canals were built, and a complex ecosystem evolved. Thus, Egyptian history consists of the interaction of humans and nature, each leaving a deep impression on the other. Yet the basic pattern of the land has remained the same.

Egypt's most dominant geographic feature is the Nile River, which divides the land into identifiable regions: a fertile valley and delta bounded by stark desert to the east and west. Keen observers of their environment, the ancient Egyptian people reflected these geographical divisions in their culture. The solar cycle, the annual flood, the local fauna and flora, and the contrasts between the Desert, Delta, and Valley were incorporated into Egyptian mythology and religious beliefs.

The Nile has progressed through five stages, which are closely associated with changes in the environment. These changes, in turn, affected the fauna and flora of Egypt and, ultimately, the people who inhabited the area. Because the Nile created a convex floodplain, it offered Egypt's inhabitants topographical features well suited to irrigation and water control.

## FURTHER READING

Butzer, Karl W., *Early Hydraulic Civilization in Egypt: A Study in Cultural Ecology*. Chicago: University of Chicago Press, 1976.
Carneiro, Robert, "A Theory of the Origin of the State," *Science* 169 (1970), 733–738.
Hemdan, Gamal, "Evolution of Irrigation Agriculture in Egypt," *Arid Zone Research* 17 (1961), 119–142.

Issawi, Bahay, "An Introduction to the Physiography of the Nile Valley," in *Prehistory of the Nile Valley* (F. Wendorf and R. Schild, eds.), pp. 3–22. New York: Academic Press, 1976.

James, T. G. H., *Ancient Egypt: The Land and its Legacy* Austin, Tex.: University of Texas Press, 1988.
    *An Introduction to Ancient Egypt*. London: The British Museum, 1979.

Said, Rushdi, *The Geology of Egypt*. Amsterdam: Elsevier, 1962.

Wendorf, Fred and Schild Romuald (eds.), *Prehistory of the Nile Valley*. New York: Academic Press, 1976

*Chapter 3*

# A CHRONOLOGY AND HISTORY OF EGYPT

Although much is known about the political and social history of ancient Egypt, there are many areas that are still subject to question. The Egyptians did not leave any comprehensive histories, so the historical framework of ancient Egypt must be reconstructed from annals of individual reigns, autobiographical texts, historical sources from outside Egypt, and archaeological materials. Of special importance among these sources are king lists from Turin, Karnak, Abydos, and Saqqara. These unannotated lists of the names of rulers are useful for establishing the sequence of kings and their reigns; they present special problems, however, as their accuracy is impinged upon by political biases of the times in which they were written and by the conflation of legendary and actual historical events.

One of the earliest attempts to compile a comprehensive history of Egypt was undertaken by Manetho, an Egyptian priest of the third century BC. Although this work has been lost in its entirety, excerpts from it are preserved in quotations by later historians. Modern scholars, following Manetho's work, have divided Egyptian history into a series of thirty-one dynasties ranging from the first ruler, Menes, to the conquest of Alexander the Great.

Neither Manetho's work nor the other king lists can be considered real histories of Egypt with comprehensive chronologies, and the days, months, and years of events were marked within individual reigns in only a few of the lists (the Turin king list and Palermo Stone). These notations are valuable for determining the length of a specific reign. One cannot, however, simply add the reigns of all the kings together to determine an absolute duration for the ancient Egyptian civilization. (If one does, the beginning of Dynasty 1 falls around 5500 BC, a figure known by other methods of dating to be off by almost 2,400 years.) This is because some kings reigned simultaneously (co-regencies) and, during periods of social unrest, some dynasties were, likewise, concurrent. Nevertheless, specific dates can be established for a few textual references because celestial events, such as the sightings of the helical rising of the star Sothis (Sirius), were noted by the ancient Egyptians and can be precisely dated by modern astronomers. These "fixed dates," which occurred during the reigns of Senwosert III, Amunhotep I, Thutmose III, and Ramesses II, are used as absolute chronological dates for Egyptian and ancient Near Eastern history.

To measure the passing days, ancient Egyptians employed two calendars, the civil and the religious. Evidence for both exists from the early Old Kingdom, and both

divided the year into twelve thirty-day months. These twelve months of the year were
grouped into three four-month agricultural seasons: the inundation (*akhet*), the
growing period (*prt*), and the harvest period (*shemu*). Each month was divided into
three ten-day weeks. The year began on day one, month of *akhet,* the start of the inundation. One shortcoming of these calendars was that both were only 360 days long, a
figure considerably shorter than the actual solar year (the 365.25 days that the earth
takes to circle the sun). Thus, fixed seasonal events or solar events, such as the start of
the inundation or the sighting of certain stars, gradually moved forward in the calendar, away from the month with which those events were associated. The Egyptians
solved this shortcoming by adding intervals to the end of each calendar (an idea similar
to our modern "leap year"). The civil calendar was followed by five days, while a thirteenth month was inserted into the religious calendar every two to three years to com-
pensate for the gradual disassociation of the actual seasons from their calendar
designations.

### THE PREDYNASTIC PERIOD (CA. 4650–3150 BC)

One of the most impressive yet puzzling aspects of ancient Egypt is the rapid cultural
transformation that occurred in the fifth and fourth millennia BC. We know little about
the transition from hunter-gatherer to agricultural village, nor about the migration patterns that may have brought the earliest domestic plants and animals into the Nile
Valley from other areas of the continent or from western Asia. During the past few
decades, however, modern researchers have begun to focus on this crucial early period
of Egyptian (pre)history. Questions regarding early foreign contact, trade, and the rise
of early state-level society, etc., are all actively being studied by modern scholars.
Because written records do not appear until the late Predynastic Period, sources for the
study of the Predynastic Period include pottery, stoneware, faunal and floral remains,
habitation sites, and *glyptic* evidence. In addition, as is true of so much of Egyptian
history, the form, location, and content of human burials are a major source of information.

   Although the Turin king list and the Palermo Stone record cultural and historical
events that predate Dynasty 1, it was not until the late nineteenth century that corroborating archaeological evidence was produced. This information initially came from
sites in Upper Egypt (Abydos, Hierakonpolis, and Naqada). In 1896, Jacques de
Morgan, excavating the cemeteries of Abydos, recovered slate palettes, beautiful
flaked flint tools, jewelry and figurines made of bone and ivory, and pottery of a
different style than that typical of the Dynastic Period. De Morgan asserted that these
graves and those from other nearby sites predated Dynasty 1 and reflected a society
quickly changing from an egalitarian and agriculturally dominated lifestyle toward a
class-stratified society centered around a living god personified by the king. De

Table 3.1 *Predynastic chronology of ancient Egypt (after Hassan 1985)*

| Date (BC) | Upper Egypt | Lower Egypt |
|---|---|---|
| 3100 | Protodynastic | Protodynastic |
| 3300 | Nagada III | Nagada III |
| 3400 | Late Gerzean (Nagada II) | Late Gerzean (Maadian) |
| 3650 | Early Gerzean (Nagada II) | Omari B (?) |
| 3750 | Amratian (Nagada I) | Omari A (?) |
| 4400 | Badarian | |
| 4800 | | Merimden |
| 5200 | | Fayum A |

Morgan's declaration was particularly profound because he correctly identified the materials as predating Dynasty 1 without referring to the stratigraphic laws of super-position. That is, no one had yet excavated a site in Egypt where it was clearly demonstrated that these early materials were part of a sedimentary unit underlying Dynasty 1 cultural materials.

Although de Morgan correctly identified the Abydos material as Predynastic, it took William Flinders Petrie's organizational skills and six years of study to prove it using his ingenious technique of sequence dating (see chapter 1). De Morgan's discovery in 1896 of the tomb of Queen Neithhotep at Naqada clearly showed the viability of Petrie's system. In the tomb were ceramic vessels corresponding to Petrie's sequence date 80 in association with ivory labels that bore the name of Aha, a king of Dynasty 1.

By comparing artifacts with Petrie's standard types from Upper Egypt, other archaeologists placed their finds into one of three major periods, called Badarian, Amratian (Naqada I), or Gerzean (Naqada II) after the sites where Predynastic cemeteries were unearthed. As other sites were discovered in Upper and Lower Egypt, a more detailed Predynastic sequence began to develop, as well as an understanding that the northern and southern sections of the country underwent a series of different stages of cultural development. Scholars have divided the cultural sequence for Upper and Lower Egypt into four major periods. The sequence for Upper Egypt begins with Badarian and continues through Naqada I, II, and III. The sequence for Lower Egypt begins with the Fayum/Merimden Neolithic and continues through Omari, Maadian, and like Upper Egypt, ends with the Naqada III period (table 3.1). Traditionally, the stages of the Upper and Lower Egyptian Predynastic development are treated as separate events characteristic of their geographic settings. However, it is as yet unclear whether the Lower Egyptian sequences are actually localized cultures, or if they are indeed typical of an entire chronological period. So too, the traditional distinction of northern and southern traditions may be exaggerated by the assumption, now questioned, that there were two separate kingdoms.

The Badarian and the Fayum/Merimden cultures were characterized by a mixed hunting, fishing, and agricultural economy. Dwellings were oval-shaped huts made of light materials suggesting seasonal or short-term occupations. The brevity of occupation of Badarian sites is substantiated at many such sites by only a thin layer of occupational debris. Merimde, however, had a very long history of occupation extending throughout the Predynastic sequence. Other differences between Merimde and the south are evident in recovered material goods. Badarian pottery is best exemplified by a rippled then burnished surface, while Merimden and Lower Egyptian pottery lacks the characteristic rippled treatment and appears to have been locally produced. In the Fayum, local ceramics are easily identified by their thick, straw-tempered walls and low temperature of firing.

Early Badarian burials consisted of simple depressions in the soil, and the body covered with a hide and accompanied by a few artifacts of ornamentation. This pattern evolved by later Badarian times into more elaborate graves with twig or basket coffins more richly endowed with goods. Excavated Fayum and Merimden burials are not numerous, but there appears to have been no strong tradition of burying the dead with surplus wealth in the Delta.

During the subsequent Naqada I/Omari period, a stronger reliance on domestic plants and animals is evident by both the physical remains of sheep, goats, and cattle, and the increasing prevalence of tools associated with agriculture coupled with a decline in projectile points and other hunting implements. Ceramics, many decorated with distinctive geometric and crosslined patterns, take on a unique and identifiable style throughout many parts of Upper Egypt, while the Delta appears to adhere to its own stylistic traditions: pottery production in the Delta apparently remained a local industry with no evidence of widespread decorative trends.

Shelters during the Naqada I/Omari period also take on a more permanent form than the earlier Badari or Fayum structures and are often accompanied by small outbuildings that, based on the presence of thick deposits of animal dung, were used for sheltering some members of the herd. During the Naqada I–II period, house structures shifted from oval thatch to more traditional rectangular shapes made of mud-brick.

By late Naqada II Egypt had moved rapidly toward a complex and socially stratified society. Upper Egyptian ceramics are often decorated with pictures of boats (fig. 3.1) and other scenes that are also found on tomb walls dating to late Naqada II/III (e.g., Hierakonpolis). Cemeteries yield evidence of a growing social elite, and evidence of defensive fortifications both in artistic depictions and around settlements suggest conflict. In addition, by Naqada II/Maadian times, Predynastic Egyptians had clearly entered into a large trading sphere that extended throughout the Mediterranean.

Recent excavations at Buto, in the northern Delta, for example, have revealed clay

3.1 Naqada II vessel painted with representation of a boat equipped with many oars represented as lines descending from the ship's deck. Men and a dancing (?) woman stand on the two cabins. A standard, topped with three triangular forms rises from the right-hand cabin. *ca*. 3200 BC. The Brooklyn Museum of Art, 09.889.400.

cones similar to those used to decorate temples in the Uruk state of Mesopotamia (*ca*. 3200 BC). Buto's location near the mouth of the Rosetta branch of the Nile and its proximity to the sea (then much closer to the site than today) would have placed it on a maritime route over which vast quantities of timber, oil, wine, minerals, pottery, and other commodities were imported and exported.

By Naqada III, Egyptian centers of political power (e.g., Hierakonpolis, Naqada, Maadi, and Buto) had developed in both Upper and Lower Egypt, and it is at this time that local traditions began to merge more fully into a definable national character. Recent work at Abydos and Minshat Abu Omar has revealed that by late Naqada II, the culture characteristic of Upper Egypt was present in the eastern Delta. Excavations at Abydos have demonstrated the existence of Dynasty 0 (Naqada IIIa), a period of cultural unification of Upper and Lower Egypt that culminated with the, possibly legendary, unification of the Egypt at the end of the Predynastic Period (*ca*. 3050 BC). By Dynasty 0, both the northern and southern sections of the country exhibited much the same culture, attesting to the gradual cultural domination of the north by the south.

At the end of the Predynastic Period, many of the features of the Dynastic Period

3.2  The Narmer Palette, Egyptian Museum, Cairo. Dynasty 0–1, *ca.* 3100 BC.

are evident. Tombs at Abydos and the deposits at Hierakonpolis indicate that these areas were ruled by local chieftain-kings who differentiated themselves from their subjects with symbols later assumed by the kings of Dynasty 1. Houses at Naqada were arranged along winding streets, indicating a city plan. Ivory tags with proto-hieroglyphs recovered from Cemetery U at Abydos suggest that by the end of the Predynastic Period writing was already established as a means of conveying rank, title, and ownership.

### THE ARCHAIC PERIOD (FIRST–SECOND DYNASTIES, *CA.* 3150–2686 BC)

According to traditional histories, kingdoms in Upper and Lower Egypt were unified about the year 3050 BC by a chieftain-king from Upper Egypt named Menes or Narmer. Unfortunately, sources for reconstructing the political history of the Archaic Period are minimal, including only the briefest of texts found on such objects as cylinder seals, ivory tags, and king lists of later periods that refer to Dynasty 1 rulers. The traditional view of conquest and subjugation of the Delta by a southern king is based primarily upon the decoration of the Narmer Palette (fig. 3.2) from Hierakonpolis, which shows on the obverse side a king wearing the crown of Upper Egypt subjugating northern peoples, and on the reverse side the same king is shown wearing the red crown of Lower Egypt.

Unfortunately, there are serious difficulties with the historical content of the Narmer Palette and even the identification of the king pictured. Some scholars, on the basis of seals incised with several royal names, have suggested that Narmer is an alternate ritual name for King Horus Aha/Menes, who is credited (in later king lists) with being the first king of Egypt. More fundamentally, there is no evidence that Egypt was composed of two kingdoms that were forcefully united. Rather the picture that is emerging suggests that Upper Egypt was composed of several city-states, each ruled by chieftain-kings, the most important being Naqada, Hierakonpolis, and Abydos. The traditional date of a unification of Egypt at about 3050 BC has also been brought into question by ivory labels recovered from the tombs in Cemetery U at Abydos that attest to kings of a united Egypt who predate Menes/Narmer.

One possible alternative scenario is that the earliest strong kings were at the city-states of Naqada and Hierakonpolis. They gradually extended their power northward, allying themselves with, or being defeated by, the chiefs at Abydos, a site whose special significance in the growth of the early state is indicated by its association with kingship throughout Egyptian history. The mechanics of the final "unification" of the country are not yet known, but until there is additional evidence, hopefully from Lower Egypt, the idea of a battle between two fully formed states should perhaps be regarded as a reference to the sense of duality, or balanced or opposed pairs, that so heavily marks Egyptian thought.

The precise role of outside influences in the formation of the early state is also unknown; however, there are many signs of contact with Mesopotamia and Western Asia. The pear-shaped mace heads, cylinder seals, niche-façade architecture, *glyptic* of animals and heroes, and cone-studded architecture of Buto all have strong associations with the East. Furthermore, some scholars have suggested that the underlying rebus principle of hieroglyphic writing was inspired by the Sumerian writing system.

During Dynasty 1, the Nile Valley from Aswan to the Mediterranean was ruled by a line of hereditary kings who were surrounded by an elaborate ritual that celebrated their office and person. The basic, enduring features of kingship were established at this time. By the reign of Den (fourth king, Dynasty I), two enduring symbols of the unity of the Two Lands had appeared: the double crown and the title *nsw bity*, "King of Upper and Lower Egypt," as well as the *heb sed* (also called the jubilee) a potent ritual for the symbolic renewal of the king. Associated with the gods Horus and Seth, dressed in distinctive garb, referred to by circumlocutions such as "his majesty," the king was, even at this early date, sharply differentiated from his subjects.

By the end of Dynasty 2, the basic fabric of Egyptian culture that was to endure for the next 3,000 years was established. The king controlled a strongly centralized state ruled from the capital at Memphis. He was assisted by a highly articulated bureaucracy headed by two *viziers* (prime ministers), one for the north another for the south. The country was divided into a series of *nomes* (districts), overseen by a *nomarch* (governor) who was directly responsible to the vizier. Although the royal family filled many administrative positions, the deliberate moving of officials from one post to another appears to have been an effort to forestall true hereditary passage of offices. Throughout its history, the Egyptian state apparatus balanced meritocracy with birth, and a recurring theme in literature was the ability of the humble to equal the powerful through skill and eloquence.

### THE OLD KINGDOM (THIRD–SIXTH DYNASTIES, CA. 2686–2181 BC)

More complete and numerous sources from the Old Kingdom allow a better view of the character of the Egyptian state. Society was heavily stratified and ruled by an absolute semi-divine king who was, in theory, omnipotent and omnipresent (see chapter 5). Of course it was impossible for the king to administer all facets of government directly, so he was assisted by a multi-tiered administration dominated by members of the royal family. The provinces were administered by appointed nomarchs who, until the later Old Kingdom, were obliged to make periodic visits to the capital. These mandatory visits served to strengthen the king's control over the provinces.

No better evidence of the tremendous power of the king and the centralization of the state can be cited than the royal tombs. The sheer size of each monument and its location are important indicators of the power and organization of the state. The apogee of royal power was reached in Dynasty 4, the so-called Pyramid Age (although pyramids were certainly built before and after this dynasty). Most of the kings of Dynasty 4 constructed, or began construction of, at least one pyramid tomb. The state had the ability to conscript and mobilize massive numbers of men and materials and to coordinate the myriad aspects of pyramid building, from the cutting and transport of the stone to feeding the workers. The number of workers on the Great Pyramid of Khufu has recently been estimated at 10,000 men, but for each worker there were support crews who hauled water, made pottery vessels, harvested the grain to make the bread that fed the workers, and picked and transported vegetables and other supplies. These mammoth building projects were supported by state funds derived from the annual tax upon agricultural yield. The workers, who were free citizens, were divided into "gangs" who worked in seasonal shifts. Work on the pyramid continued throughout the year, one gang relieving another, toiling on behalf of the glory of the king. The pyramid sites were, in essence, micro-states of their own, and the success of each pyramid was a reflection of the power, prestige, and administrative ability of the early state.

Obviously, these projects required a massive surplus of grain to feed and reward the workers. As was true throughout Egypt's history, the economy was based upon agriculture, and perhaps 75 percent of the population were farmers who grew emmer wheat, barley, and vegetables on their own land or share-cropped fields. In theory, all the land of Egypt belonged to the king, but great parcels were distributed to individuals as a reward for state service. Plots were then handed down by inheritance. Each year, state officials surveyed fields and, on the basis of the estimated level of the Nile flood, assessed the proportion of the yield of grain that was to be deposited in the local state-controlled granaries. These stocks were used to "pay" state employees: commodities could then be obtained by trading extra grain.

A significant proportion of farm land was owned by temples. The harvests from these lands, most of which were removed from the state tax rolls, supported the great numbers of priests and employees of the cult establishments. The tradition of exempting temple lands from state tax rolls was to prove to be a major factor in later economic decline.

The vitality and power of the early Egyptian state is further expressed through its aggressive foreign policy. As indicated by the autobiography of Weni (Dynasty 6), troops of "many tens of thousands," including Nubians, were raised through conscription. Campaigns were directed against Nubians to the south and the "Asiatic Sand Dwellers" to the east. There was little interest in the outright occupation of Nubia; instead, the Egyptian armies were levied to maintain domination over Nubia's economic resources (primarily the gold mines of the Wadi Allaqi) and to ensure the flow of luxury items (feathers, ostrich eggs, and ebony). This foreign policy based on trade also applied to the forested eastern Mediterranean (modern Lebanon), from whence the cedar timbers that were employed for ships originated.

The decline of the Old Kingdom in Dynasty 6 is most evident in the rise of provincial power at the expense of the central authority. Nomarchs were no longer required to visit the capital and were buried in large tombs in their home towns, rather than in the capital near their patron. Their posts became hereditary, further freeing them from government control. The royal tombs became progressively smaller and more shoddily built, reflecting the restricted influence and economic power of the state.

Though the rise of the nomarchs certainly played a role in the breakdown of the Old Kingdom state, climatic change – a factor beyond the control of the state – was also involved. Reliefs from the causeway of Unis (Dynasty 5) show scenes of starving men, which may have been the result of poor inundation levels. Rainfall decreased throughout much of Egypt after about 2900 BC, and some scholars postulate that this would have reduced agricultural resources and eliminated much of the seasonal pasturage adjacent to the Nile Valley.

## THE FIRST INTERMEDIATE PERIOD (DYNASTIES 7–11, CA. 2181–2040 BC)

The First Intermediate Period, an interval of approximately 140 years, was a time of state decentralization as the nomarchs of Herakleopolis (Dynasties 9–10) vied for control of the country with the remnants of the Old Kingdom rulers at Memphis (Dynasties 7–8), who were supported by "kings" at Coptos. The contrast of this era to the Old Kingdom was recognized by the ancient Egyptians themselves who, in later times, referred to it as a time of distress. The "Lamentations of Ipuwer", a text which has been dated to the First Intermediate Period, relates: "The land is full of gangs and a man goes to plow with his shield. . . . All is in ruin, a man smites his brother, plague is throughout the land, blood is everywhere. . . . The land is diminished, its rulers are multiplied . . ." (Lichtheim 1973: 150–151).

The main sources for modern scholars are literary texts like that quoted above, brief autobiographical inscriptions, the Ramesside king lists, and Manetho, the latter two sources being far removed from the time of the actual events.

Although the reasons for this breakdown of central authority and social order are not completely understood, the decentralization of the country was due to the rising independence of the nomarchs, especially those at Beni Hasan, Coptos, and Herakleopolis. The Akhtoy, or Khety, lineage of Herakleopolis was recognized by Manetho as Dynasties 9–10. In spite of the political fragmentation, there was little interest in changing the social or ritual makeup of the country, for the ephemeral kings of Herakleopolis sought legitimacy by being buried near the tombs of the kings of Dynasty 6 at Saqqara.

By about 2100 BC the Akhtoys of Dynasty 10 controlled the northern part of Egypt while the south was held by the Inyotef and Mentuhotep families of Thebes (Dynasty 11), who were aided by a system of shifting alliances with other nomarchs. Although there were areas of peace and stability (e.g., Hatnub and Sheik Said), fierce battles raged between the Thebans and the Herakleopolitans throughout much of Egypt, as reported in the "Teachings of Merikare":

Troops will fight troops;
As the ancestors foretold;
Egypt fought in the graveyard,
Destroying tombs in vengeful destruction . . .
I attacked This [a city north of Thebes] to its southern border . . .
I engulfed it like a flood . . .
I breached their strongholds,
I made Lower Egypt attack them [the Thebans],
I captured their inhabitants,
I seized their cattle . . . (Lichtheim 1973: 102, 104)

Battles raged through Middle Egypt, while autonomous nomarchs like Ankhtyfy of Moalla bragged of capturing Edfu behind the lines of the Thebans. The destruction of the necropolis at Abydos by the troops of Akhtoy III was an evil act that was believed to have brought the retribution of the gods against the Herakleopolitians. By the accession of the Theban Mentuhotep II, the battles were won, and he installed his own officials in Herakleopolis, thereby reunifying the land and ushering in the Middle Kingdom Period.

### THE MIDDLE KINGDOM (DYNASTIES 11–13, *CA.* 2040–1782 BC)

The Middle Kingdom was a time of prosperity, general peace, and long-reigning kings, but also a time in which the role and status of the king was diminished, and in which the Egyptians were forced to become more cognizant of their neighbors.

Amunemhet, the first king of Dynasty 12, attempted to consolidate the state and reduce the power of the provinces. He sent troops against disloyal or independent nomarchs and redistricted the nomes. The capital was moved to Itchtowy ("Seizer of the Two Lands") (Lisht, a city in the Fayum), and royal tombs were built near the new capital at Lahun (Kahun), Dashur, and Hawara. Signs of disorder, however, are evident. As related in the text known as the "Instructions of Amunemhet", King Amunemhet I was assassinated by palace guards. The diminished status of the king is further reflected in the "Loyalist Instructions" that implored men to "fight on behalf of his [the king's] name . . . the one whom the king loves shall be provided for – for there is no tomb for anyone who rebels against his majesty; his corpse shall be cast into the waters" (Simpson 1972: 200). This reminder that the citizen must be obedient to the king is in marked contrast to the implicit loyalty shown to the semi-divine king of the Old Kingdom. The message carried by the "Loyalist Instructions" was implemented not by the restoration of the status of the king, but by political means when Senwosert III further reduced the power of the nomarchs. As part of this reform, the existing nomes were divided among three administrative districts (*warets*) overseen by a "reporter" who answered directly to the king.

The kings of the Middle Kingdom maintained an aggressive policy toward Nubia. Under Amunemhet, Egyptians occupied Nubia to the second cataract. Under Senwosert III, the cataract at Semna was again cleared to facilitate the passage of Egyptian trade and troops. Great brick forts raised at Buhen, Mirgissa, Uronarti, and elsewhere – the defensive capabilities of which were not surpassed until the time of the Crusades – indicate the Egyptians' desire to control trade and immigration. Ironically, a contemporary text, "Prophecy of Neferty," states that Amunemhet I was from the south.

Immigration and aggression from the east was to be controlled by "The Walls of the Ruler," a defensive barrier in the eastern Delta built by Amunemhet I. However, by this era, it is clear that Egyptians were becoming more cosmopolitan. Records from the town of Kahun list many inhabitants with foreign names. Nubians were incorporated into Egyptian society and many served in the police and desert corps (*Medjay*).

The pyramid tombs of the kings of the Middle Kingdom at Lisht, Dashur, Lahun, and Hawara present a mixed view of the society and economy. The tombs are smaller

and built of smaller stones or bricks cased in stone. These tombs were more economi-
cal to build and did not test the state with the conscription of the great masses of men
employed by even the relatively short-reigning kings of Dynasties 5 and 6. Elaborate
systems of portcullises and false passages were employed (most elaborately in the tomb
of Amunemhet III at Hawara) to foil robbers whose activities, even toward the bodies
of the kings, were now anticipated. In contrast to the indifferent construction of the
superstructures of the tombs were the remains of the contents recovered from tombs
of princesses at Lahun and Dashur. The gold jewelry, much of which is inlaid with
colored stone, exhibits a refinement of design and technique that was never surpassed.

Although the end of the Middle Kingdom has been placed at the end of Dynasty 12,
it is evident that the kings of Dynasty 13, ruling from the capital at Itchtowy, were
acknowledged in Upper Egypt. However, growing instability and the threat of political fragmentation was evident in the number of ephemeral rulers known only from
Manetho's history.

By the end of the Middle Kingdom, the Egyptian state was fully formed. Major
cities, governed by appointed mayors who were assisted by lesser administrators and
corps of scribes, dotted the Nile Valley. Egypt controlled Nubia to at least the second
cataract, and provisions had been made for defense of the eastern frontier. Although
the Middle Kingdom traditionally ends with Dynasty 12, it is evident that the kings
of Dynasty 13, ruling from Itchtowy, were acknowledged in Upper Egypt. However,
the number of ephemeral rulers known mainly from Manetho's history indicate
growing instability and the threat of political fragmentation. Indeed, the Second
Intermediate Period saw the fragmentation of the state due to new external forces, primarily from the east.

THE SECOND INTERMEDIATE PERIOD (DYNASTIES 14–17, *CA.* 1782–1570 BC)

The major distinguishing feature of the Second Intermediate Period is the occupation
of the northern part of the Nile Valley by Asiatic peoples known as the Hyksos (from
the Egyptian word for "rulers of foreign lands"). Linguistic evidence (basically a few
known Hyksos names) suggests that the Hyksos were western Semitic speakers.
Although they never occupied or even controlled the entire country, artifacts of
Hyksos manufacture have been recovered all along the Nile Valley as far south as
Thebes (Luxor) and the Sudan.

The Hyksos rule was the first outright occupation of Egyptian soil by a foreign
power. The turmoil of this period is reflected in the Turin king list that devotes six of
its eleven columns to the 175 rulers of this brief era. The idea that this period witnessed the complete destruction of order has been re-evaluated, for not only did
Dynasty 13 continue much in the same manner as Dynasty 12, but the relatively small
number of viziers known suggests that, though the turnover of kings was rapid, the

administration maintained some stability and, as in preceding periods, the social fabric of Egypt showed great continuity.

The historical sources for this period are scanty: scarabs, inscribed statues, king lists, Manetho, autobiographical texts, and recent excavations at their capital at Tell el Daba in the eastern Delta. The tenor and nature of the period is best reconstructed from the Kamose Stele that has come down to us in several versions and from the autobiographical text from the tomb of Ahmose, son of Ibana, at El Kab.

There is little information about the nature of the Hyksos occupation, but it does seem not to have resulted from a single invasion, rather from a coalescing of the foreigners who immigrated into Egypt from Old Kingdom times onward. A Middle Kingdom papyrus (Brooklyn Museum 35.1446) and records from Kahun indicate that there were significant numbers of foreigners working in Egypt. Mentuhotep III boasted of turning back groups of foreigners who attempted to settle in Egypt and, as previously mentioned, the gradual movement of people or, less likely, the threat of sudden invasion was the motivation for Amunemhet I to build fortifications in the eastern Delta. This pattern of gradual immigration rather than invasion was repeated in the Libyan Period (Dynasties 22–23) of the Third Intermediate Period.

The Hyksos king resided in the eastern Delta at Avaris (Tell el Daba). The sense that the Hyksos came as immigrants who wished to adapt to Egypt is suggested by the Hyksos kings' adoption of Egyptian-style names and parts of the traditional royal titulary. The early years of the Hyksos domination were not times of strife, for texts indicate that Upper Egyptian herds were allowed to graze in the Delta areas controlled by the Asiatics. However, one major difficulty for the Egyptians was the Hyksos alliance with the Nubians, for the Thebans were sandwiched between their traditional rival to the south and new opponents to the north. The Kamose Stela relates, "One prince is in Avaris, the other is in Nubia . . . Each man has his slice of Egypt, dividing up the land with me!" (after Pritchard 1969: 232). Hyksos domination was apparently economic, as indicated by the taxes that they levied upon the Thebans. By the reign of Inyotef VII of Thebes, there were signs of growing resistance to the foreign occupation, for inscriptions from Coptos refer to the Hyksos as enemies. The Kamose Stela and the autobiography of Ahmose, son of Ibana, relate the subsequent battles, the interception of spies, and the siege of Avaris, which ultimately resulted in the expulsion of the Hyksos. The horrific wounds to the skull of the mummy of Sekhenenre Tao II of Thebes are usually attributed to the battle to liberate Egypt from the Hyksos.

The work of Kamose was completed by his brother Ahmose, the first king of the New Kingdom. His expulsion of the Hyksos was solidified by his three-year siege of the Palestinian town of Sharuhen (Tell el Ajjul), another Hyksos stronghold, to secure the eastern frontier. Afterward, Ahmose turned his attention to Nubia, initiating a series of campaigns that were continued by nearly every king of the New Kingdom. A glimpse of the influence and power of the Egyptian queens at this time is afforded by a stela of Ahmose that credits his mother, Ahhotep, "the one who looked after the soldiers of Egypt" and the "one who pacified Egypt," with capturing deserters. The furnishings of her tomb at Thebes included a "gold fly of valor" (a military award for bravery in battle) and a golden battle ax, the blade of which was decorated with a scene of her husband smiting enemies.

In spite of their attempt to assimilate themselves into Egyptian culture, the Hyksos were viewed with hatred by the Egyptians, and this era was forever a matter of shame. No longer were the Egyptians able to feel secure within the confines of the Nile Valley. Ironically, the Hyksos introduced the horse-drawn chariot and the more powerful compound bow into Egypt, both military innovations that enabled the Egyptians to compete more successfully in battle with their neighbors.

By the early New Kingdom, the political face of the ancient Middle East had changed. The Egyptians were now forced to protect their boundaries from aggression and undertake constant foreign campaigns for economic and diplomatic means. They also created buffer states against the Mitannians and the growing power of the Hittite and Assyrian empires.

## THE NEW KINGDOM (DYNASTIES 18–20, CA. 1570–1069 BC)

The New Kingdom was a period of extraordinary Egyptian expansion abroad and of the centralization of bureaucratic power. During this period Egypt maintained control over extensive foreign territory, including Nubia and vassal states in the Levant. Diplomatic and commercial contacts were developed with countries throughout the Near East and in Crete.

This period is the best documented of any period of Egypt's long history, and the wide variety of textual, iconographic, and archaeological sources from Egypt are augmented by sources from Western Asia and Nubia. During the New Kingdom, Egypt's history became an integrated part of the history of the Near East, and must be viewed in regard to the political and cultural events of the ancient Near East as a whole.

The New Kingdom's Dynasty 18 is often referred to as "The Golden Age" of Egypt. It was a time of political stability, great prosperity, and achievement in architecture, the arts, and literature. By the New Kingdom, Egypt may have had a population of as many as 3 million people. The land was ruled by a highly articulated bureaucracy that functioned at local and national levels. From the lowly farmer whose fields were surveyed by the government for taxation purposes to high officials, all Egyptians were, at some point, touched by the tremendous bureaucracy of the New Kingdom state.

The head of the highly stratified society was the king, an absolute ruler who served as the head of the military, as chief priest, and as chief judge. Part of the stability of Dynasty 18 stemmed from the continuity of kingship; through Tutankhamun's reign, near the end of the Dynasty, the kings were all members of the Ahmose and

Thutmoside lines. Below the king were one or two viziers who reported directly to the king. They were supported by an immense bureaucracy composed of a multi-tiered system of administrators and overseers aided by corps of scribes that served the provinces and the capital. Autobiographical inscriptions claim that a single administrator often served several kings, a continuity that was an important factor in the stability of New Kingdom Egypt. Nobles, all of whom held some level of administrative or clerical function, came from a number of favored families, some of whom were permitted to pass their offices to their offspring. Unlike the Old Kingdom, being a member of a recognized noble clan or even of the royal family was not a prerequisite for membership in the elite. Indeed, many of the nobles, who boasted about themselves in autobiographical inscriptions, advanced by meritorious civil or military service.

The capital was relocated from Itchtowy back to Memphis. Thebes emerged as a major metropolitan and theocratic center, dominated by the administration of the domains of the god Amun. This god, whose name means "The Hidden One" – perhaps a reference to his multi-faceted attributes and associations – rose to supreme importance among the pantheon of New Kingdom gods. The cult of Amun was closely associated with the king himself, and veneration of the god had implications for the status of the king. Not only did nearly all of the kings of the New Kingdom embellish and expand the temple of Amun at Karnak, but new religious cults and festivals were introduced to stress the symbiotic nature of king and god, and thereby enhance royal prestige. This is most apparent during the reign of Hatshepsut with the introduction of the Opet festival, an annual procession of the sacred images of Amun, his consort Mut, their child Khonsu, and the king from the Karnak Temple to Luxor Temple. Opet, which marked a new mythologizing of the king, ensured the renewal not only of the god but also of the pharaoh.

The wealth of the Egyptian state and the degree of veneration of the god Amun is evident in the frenzy of building and in the economic endowments to the temples, especially to the domain of the god Amun at Karnak. The temples, which had their own administrative bureaucracies parallel to the state, were major factors in the economy of the New Kingdom. The construction of the temples, their upkeep and maintenance, the tremendous amount of food and goods that were offered to the god each day, and the "salaries" of the many temple workers were derived from the lands that were deeded to the temple by the king and by individuals. One document (Ostracon Gardiner 86) from Dynasty 20 refers to the holdings of Amun in the northern part of the country alone numbering more than 35,000 men engaged in raising cattle, goats, and fowl, and another 8,700 raising crops. These lands, scattered throughout Egypt, were generally removed from the government tax rolls. Although all kings of the New Kingdom embellished temples, Hatshepsut seemed specially intent on enhancing the cult of Amun at Karnak. She was responsible for a new sanctuary (the Chapelle Rouge) that served as the holiest part of the temple, rebuilt or re-embellished other areas (e.g.,

Pylon 6) with obelisks and cult chambers, and created a new north–south axis of the temple. Her favoring of the cult of Amun is especially evident in linking the adminis-tration of the domain of Amun with that of the state through joint appointments held by her steward Senenmut.

The expansion of the religious cults and their economic prerogatives are a major theme of the New Kingdom. Temples of mud-brick or stone were renovated, expanded, and founded throughout Egypt, northern Nubia, and the Sinai. The mortuary cult of the ruler himself was celebrated in a royal temple (also referred to as a mortuary temple) on the west bank at Thebes. These huge structures had their own staff of priests. Some of the structures were oriented to the cult temple of Amun on the oppo-site bank, and again were intended to convey the association between king and god. These temples were only a part of the elaborate architectural provisions for the king's afterlife. From the time of Thutmose I, the kings were buried in rock-cut tombs located in the Valley of the Kings and the adjacent West Valley. These tombs are markedly different than the tombs of the Old Kingdom kings. Not only are they rock cut – some more than 250 meters into the limestone hillsides – and capable of being obscured or at least easily guarded, but they also reflect significant changes in theology and the country's economy. The Dynasty 18 tombs have a bent axis, theoretically dividing the tomb into spheres of the light and day, evocative of death and rebirth. Their walls, unlike Dynasty 4 pyramids, are covered with religious texts such as the "Book of Gates," the Amduat, and the "Book of the Heavenly Cow" that further associate the king with the sun god, thereby ensuring his eternal rebirth with the solar cycle. In contrast to the pyramids, these tombs were built by a small group of usually no more than sixty elite work men who labored for the state. They, along with their families and support staff, were permanently settled in a walled "company town" called Deir el Medina, located over the cliffs from the Valley of the Kings. This town had its own administration and judicial system, and the "chief of the gang" reported directly to the vizier of the south rather than to the mayor of Thebes.

Dynasty 18 also saw a new prominence of women, especially those of the royal family. Ahmose Nofertari, the wife of Ahmose, was the first to bear the title "God's Wife of Amun/divine adoratress" indicating a special status and association with the god Amun. This title was held by most of the royal ladies of the New Kingdom. Women of non-royal but elite families were inaugurated into part-time priesthoods of Amun and other gods, serving as a prestigious divine chorus that entertained and amused the deity.

The foreign policy of Dynasty 18 was aggressive, offensive, and imperialistic. This change from the largely defensive posture of the previous era was perhaps in response to the occupation of the Hyksos, and certainly a reaction to changes in the greater polit-ical sphere of the Near East. The objective of foreign policy was no longer to protect the actual borders of Egypt but rather to establish buffer zones and vassal states in Palestine, in order to insulate Egypt from the growing powers of the Near East.

During the second millennium BC, Egypt was surrounded by potentially powerful enemies. To the south lay the first great Sudanese kingdom in history, Kush; the Mediterranean coast west of Egypt was inhabited by hostile Libyans; and to the northeast in western Asia (fig. 3.3), a complete realignment of kingdoms had taken place. Palestine was composed of city-states that paid allegiance to whatever power most threatened their security. The "superpowers" were the Hittites of Anatolia, the Mitannians of north Syria, the Kassites (who occupied Babylon), and the early Assyrians. During the New Kingdom a gradual realignment of these Asian powers occurred, and each shift created a new balance of power with which the Egyptians had to contend. The Mitannians were the dominant power in north Syria, and all the Thutmoside rulers through Thutmose IV undertook campaigns in Palestine and north Syria to thwart them. After that time, the Egyptians increasingly turned away from military campaigns to diplomacy, which was, in the case of Amunhotep III, sealed by his marriage to daughters of two successive Mitannian kings. Diplomatic marriages became a staple part of Egyptian foreign policy, with Amunhotep III also marrying the daughter of the Kassite king of Babylon. In contrast, indicative of their traditional xenophobia, Egyptian princesses were never married to foreign rulers.

Prior to the period of peace in the second half of the long reign of Amunhotep III, repeated campaigns in Western Asia suggest an overall lack of success in Egyptian foreign policy. The Egyptians were loath actually to occupy conquered areas, preferring to leave a few key administrators and to receive promises of fealty from the local governors. Even after Thutmose III's successful siege of Megiddo, which was described as "like the capture of 1,000 towns," the chieftains were allowed to return to their villages where they plotted further actions against the Egyptians. Time after time, after Egyptian troops withdrew, conquered areas would switch allegiance to whatever superior power presented the most immediate threat, thereby precipitating a renewed campaign by the Egyptians. Finally Thutmose III instituted the practice of transporting the eldest son of foreign vassals to Egypt to be indoctrinated with Egyptian policy and world-view, in hope of producing a more loyal vassal.

Diplomacy is best recorded from the reign of Amunhotep III to Tutankhamun by a series of more than 350 clay tablets written in cuneiform script, the majority of which were recovered from Tell el Amarna in Middle Egypt. These so-called Amarna Letters provide a clear view of Egypt's dealings with the powers of the Near East (Assyria, the Kassites, and Hittites). Major concerns expressed in the letters are mutual defense pacts and economic matters, especially the exchange of Egyptian gold, ebony, and ivory for horses, textiles, and lapis lazuli. As one letter stated, "gold is like dust in the land of my brother," rejoined by "there are more horses than straw in the land of my [Kassite] brother." These letters attest to the new sense of diplomacy that had, for the time being, replaced the incessant military campaigns.

Kush (southern Egypt and northern Sudan) was another objective of Dynasty 18

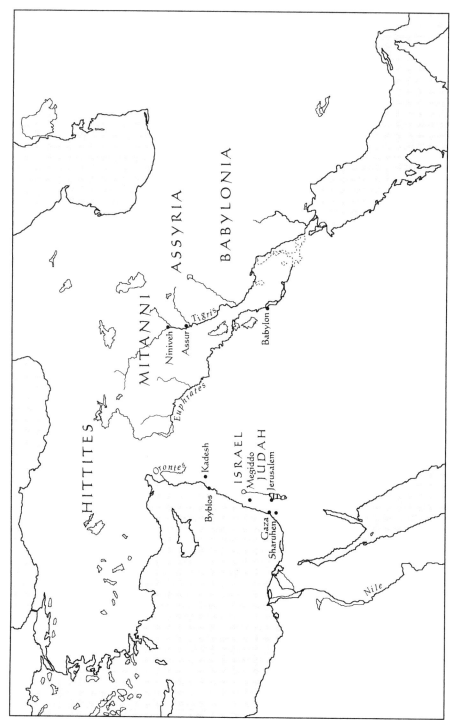

HITTITES

MITANNI

ASSYRIA

BABYLONIA

Nineveh ● ● Assur

*Tigris*

Babylon ●

*Euphrates*

*Orontes*

● Kadesh

ISRAEL

Byblos ●

Megiddo ● JUDAH
Jerusalem ●

Gaza ●
Sharruhen

*Nile*

3.3  Map of the Middle East, *ca.* 1500 BC.

foreign policy. Not only did the Egyptians wish to eliminate any possible threat from the kings of Kush (whose capital was located at Napata between the third and fourth cataracts), but they wished to ensure the steady flow of the natural resources (gold, ebony, ivory, animal skins, and feathers) that fueled the opulence of the New Kingdom elite lifestyle. The south was subjugated and held by continuous military campaigns rather than by diplomatic means. Under Amunhotep I, Kush was annexed into the Egyptian empire. This new province was overseen by an official (initially drawn from the royal family), entitled the "king's son of Kush" who reported directly to the king. Still, subsequent kings needed to send armies south to maintain their control. Thutmose I and Thutmose III may have reached the fifth cataract, while Hatshepsut was forced to mount four separate campaigns to maintain Egypt's hold on the south.

Not all aspects of foreign policy were belligerent. In year 6–7 of Hatshepsut, a trade mission was sent to Punt, probably modern Eritrea on the coast of Africa. As related by the scenes in her temple at Deir el Bahari, the soldiers returned with heaps of precious incense for the cult of the gods, incense trees, and exotic animals, all accompanied by the queen of Punt herself.

The end of Dynasty 18 presents a series of interpretive problems for modern researchers. A discussion of the events must begin in the last years of Amunhotep III, whose thirty-eight years on the throne were an apogée of Egyptian power and influence. Reliefs of Amunhotep III suggest new aspects of the cult of the king. After the king's first *jubilee* in year 30, innovative royal iconography showing a markedly youthful king was introduced to stress the rejuvenation of the king through his association with the sun disk in its incarnation of Horus or Re. Although it is not yet clear whether Amunhotep IV shared power with his father for two or nine years, it is clear that the elder king's particular solar theology had a dramatic impact upon his son. The monuments of the early years of the reign of Amunhotep IV, primarily at the temple of Amun at Karnak, were revolutionary. Not only were they built of sandstone blocks of a small uniform scale, but the iconography also showed tremendous innovation, such as stressing the cultic role of the royal wife Nefertiti beyond that of previous queens. Even more curious were the monumental sandstone statues of the king showing a grossly distorted visage with long drooping chin, narrow oval eyes, and heavy belly and hips. Some statues portray the king nude, without genitalia. The worship of the traditional pantheon was abandoned in favor of the worship of the sun and its life-giving light, initially in the form of Re Horakhty and then, by year 3 or 4 of his reign, in an entirely new form: the globe or disk of the sun, whose rays terminated with tiny human hands. The Aten's names were encircled by a cartouche, formerly a prerogative of kings and queens. In the new decorative program, only the king and royal family were centered under the rays of the sun, and they were the primary communicants with the god. At the same time, the king changed his name from

Amunhotep IV ("Amun is Satisfied") to Akhenaten (perhaps "The One who is Beneficial to the Aten"). In year 5, Akhenaten moved the administrative capital to Tell el Amarna, a spot in Middle Egypt which was, according to the boundary stones, "dedicated to no other god." There an entirely new city was built, surrounded by the homes of the administrators and courtiers who were obligated to follow the king. Between years 8 and 12 of the reign, the worship of all other gods was officially forbidden, and in an effort to enforce this new theology, the names of the other gods were hammered from statues and the temple walls. Scaffolds were even erected around 30-meter-tall obelisks to expunge the name of Amun and other deities. The art of the period took on a dramatically different look: heads were exaggerated to resemble eggs, and bodies – traditionally portrayed as lithe and youthful – became heavy, drooping, and androgynous.

The meaning of these changes has long been debated. Once considered to be the first era of "monotheism," the Amarna interlude is now viewed as a period of henotheism, in which the Aten was elevated above other deities. The continued veneration of the gods Maat, Shu, and Tefnut also contradict the idea of monotheism. The close association of the king, the queen, and the Aten seems to suggest a program designed to bolster the status of the king through his communication with the god. In addition, recent work has suggested that the Aten may be the incarnation of the deceased and deified King Amunhotep III.

The radical changes of the artistic style within Akhenaten's sixteen-year reign, especially when comparing depictions of a specific individual, suggest that the art was not striving for realism or that the royal family were in any way deformed, but rather that the artistic program expressed, as it always had, aspects of theology. Some scholars now propose that the egg-headed figures and androgynous figures perhaps allude to ideas of rebirth.

The religion of Akhenaten did not penetrate deeply into society other than among the courtiers who were forced to move to Tell el Amarna. The "new" theology had shortcomings that limited its appeal, such as the population having to worship the god through the intermediary of the royal family. Perhaps a more serious drawback was the absence of a defined sense of the afterlife that would take the place of the age-old Osirian beliefs (see chapters 6 and 10) that gave comfort and security to the elite and non-elite alike.

The Amarna period had strong repercussions upon the economy and national psyche. Many of the domains of the temple of Amun were transferred to the new cult of the Aten, and direct taxes were placed upon temples and cities throughout the country for the upkeep of the new cult. The state of the old temples as a result of this neglect is described in the later Restoration Stele of Tutankhamun:

> The temple and the cities of the god and goddesses from Elephantine as far as the
> Delta marshes . . . were fallen into decay and their shrines were fallen into ruin,

having become mere mounds overgrown with grass . . . their sanctuaries were like
something that has not come into being, and their buildings were a footpath. . . .

(Murnane 1995b: 213)

This description may be hyperbole, for such a dramatically miserable state of the
temples is not confirmed by signs of widespread architectural restoration.

The foreign policy of Akhenaten must be viewed within the context of the era of
diplomacy established in the second half of the reign of Amunhotep III. Rather than
viewing Akhenaten as a wistful philosopher who meditated while the empire was
ruined, one should consider that the Amarna Letters reflect that the last half of the
fourteenth century BC was generally a time of peace and that Akhenaten's reign coin-
cided with that period of status quo. The king and the queen were both portrayed in
the traditional pose, smiting the heads of enemies, a depiction hardly compatible with
the reign of a complete pacifist.

Within seven years of the death of Akhenaten, the administrative center of the land
was moved back to Thebes and the economic prerogatives of the old cults were restored
under his second successor, the young Tutankhaten. As a sign of his devotion to the
traditional cults, the new king changed his name to Tutankhamun ("Living Image of
Amun"). Although it is doubtful that a king so young actually participated in military
campaigns, Egyptian troops – probably under the leadership of Horemheb, the
commander of the troops – were dispatched to Kadesh to quell new signs of unrest.

The last two kings of the Dynasty (Aye and Horemheb) had indirect ties with the
royal blood line. The former military commander, Horemheb, undertook sweeping
administrative changes in the land, reorganizing the army and the vizirate. Building
activity at Luxor and Karnak temples indicates that the resources of the temple were
fully re-established. On the death of Horemheb, his vizier, another man of non-royal
family, Ramesses I, ascended the throne.

Though the Ramessides (Dynasties 19–20) were unrelated to the Thutmosides of the
earlier New Kingdom, they adopted the ancient iconography and prerogatives of kingship. The fact that the major king lists were compiled in the Ramesside Period may be
a reflection of the family's desire to be considered legitimate.

The foreign policy of the Ramesside kings was, in contrast to that of the kings of
Dynasty 18, more reactive than proactive. The Hittites were now the major power in the
Near East. City-states in the Levant shifted their allegiance back and forth between
Egypt and the Hittites, thereby forestalling any permanent state of peace in the region.
The battle of Kadesh early in the reign of Ramesses II, one of the best-documented battles
of the ancient world, has been described as a debacle for the Egyptians, in spite of
Egyptian claims of victory and personal bravery of the king. The florid peace treaties that
attempted to partition the Near East into Hittite and Egyptian spheres of interest and the
diplomatic marriage of Ramesses II to a Hittite princess did little to forestall friction ten
years later when Egypt became involved in dynastic disputes of the Hittite royal house.

Another challenge that was to have long-range implications for Egypt was the rise of the Assyrians in northern Mesopotamia and Western Asia. The Assyrians absorbed the buffer states that had separated them from the Hittites, ensuring a future war over the Levant. The prospect of powerful and aggressive Assyrian troops on the Egyptian frontier without the states that served as political/military fodder for the major powers was a matter of great concern in Egypt.

The greatest threat to Egypt during the Ramesside Period was the so-called "People of the Sea," a confederation of peoples from the Aegean or western Anatolia, who attacked northeast Africa and the eastern Mediterranean. From early in the reign of Merneptah, the ships of these people, known more specifically as the Sherdan (perhaps from Ionia and Sardinia), Shekelesh, and Peleset, attacked the western and eastern Mediterranean approaches of Egypt while others attempted to colonize via land routes. Much of the thirty-one-year reign of Ramesses III was devoted to thwarting their attacks, and records of great sea battles are carved on the north side of the king's temple at Medinet Habu. The "People of the Sea" ultimately changed the entire balance of power in the Near East, sweeping away the Hittites and setting the stage for Assyria to step into the void as the new dominant power in the Near East.

The Biblical account of the Exodus, which many scholars have argued occurred during this period, cannot be corroborated by Egyptian texts. Hebrew personal names do attest to Hebrew people in Egypt throughout the New Kingdom, and references to them working on state projects can be found in Papyrus Harris and Papyrus Leiden 348, but attempts to date the Exodus to the reign of Ramesses II or Merneptah are frustrated by a later text from Wadi Hammamet (Ramesses IV) that refers to some 800 people with Hebrew names who worked in the quarries. As perplexing, the Stela of Merneptah states that "Israel is laid waste," in reference to a campaign against Israelites already in Palestine during his reign. It is possible that the movement of Hebrew peoples to Palestine was a gradual series of migrations that were not noted by the Egyptians, but were cannonized as a single movement by the Hebrews themselves.

The domestic policy of the Ramesside pharaohs was closely related to their foreign policy. The transferal of the administrative center of the county to the new city Pi-Ramesses near the old Hyksos city of Avaris (Tell el Daba) in the eastern Delta was, no doubt, a reflection of the desire to be closer to the eastern frontier from which the pharaonic armies were continually dispatched to Western Asia. This, however, did not mean that Thebes and the cult of Amun were neglected or ignored. On the contrary, the Ramesside kings lavished tremendous efforts upon embellishing and expanding the temple of Amun at Thebes as well as throughout Egypt and at sites in Nubia. The royal mortuary temples of Ramesses II (the Ramesseum) and Ramesses III (Medinet Habu) are among the largest in western Thebes. In hindsight, it seems inevitable that the orgy of construction and donations to the temples created a detrimental drain on the economy. One section of the Wilbour Papyrus (dating to Ramesses V) indicates that

a full third of the land of Egypt was held by the temples and that one-fifth of the population worked for the temples, three-quarters of whom worked for the domain of
Amun. Although the cult of Amun supported the cult of the king through the association of the king and the god, the functions of the state were slowly strangled by the
economic requirements of the temple administration. This is vividly illustrated by the
strike of the workmen from Deir el Medina. The first such strike was recorded in year
29 of Ramesses III, when the state was apparently unable to pay the wages of the men
who were building one of the most important projects in the realm – the royal tomb.
Economic difficulties are also reflected in the tremendous inflation of grain prices and
in the desperate robberies of the precious objects from the royal tombs in the Valley of
the Kings. Political instability is reflected in the harem conspiracy mentioned in
Papyrus Harris, in which members of the household of Ramesses III were accused of
plotting against the life of the king, and by the irregular succession at the end of
Dynasty 20, a succession engineered by the high official Bay, who in later records was
referred to as "a king maker." As during previous periods, administrative stability
ensured continuity until the end of the Dynasty, when rival factions (the strongest of
which was led by two successive High Priests of Amun) vied for power with the king,
who was aided not by Egyptian troops but by a Nubian commander. Even after the
rival factions were eliminated, at Karnak the high priest of Amun and commander of
the troops, Herihor, claimed limited use of the titles king of Upper and Lower Egypt.
This active political role of the high priest in Thebes and the fusion of military and
clerical offices was to set the stage for the fragmentation of the land in the Third
Intermediate Period.

THE THIRD INTERMEDIATE PERIOD (DYNASTIES 21–25, CA. 1069–656 BC)

The Third Intermediate Period is one of the least-studied eras of Egyptian history; ironically, it is well documented by records within Egypt and without.

   Like the First Intermediate Period, the Third Intermediate Period was a time of state
decentralization. The administrative center of the country was moved to Tanis in the
eastern Delta, northeast of Pi-Ramesses. The temples of Tanis, now almost destroyed,
were largely built of stone reused from the Ramesside monuments of Pi-Ramesses. The
kings of Dynasties 21 and 22 ruled from Tanis while the high priests of Amun at
Thebes, who were – at least during Dynasties 21 and 22 – nominally confirmed by the
Tanite kings, controlled the southern part of the country and paid varying amounts
of fealty to the northern kings. Continuing construction of the temple of Amun in the
name of the Tanite kings and the intermarriage of high priests with daughters of the
Dynasty 21 kings indicate that the land was not cleanly divided along geographic or
state/clerical lines. By Dynasty 22, the kings of which were of Libyan descent, the fragmentation of the land was more pronounced, with rival contemporary dynasties at

Leontopolis (Dynasty 23) and Sais (Dynasty 24), and the development of a hereditary high priest of Amun at Thebes. Battles between the rival dynasties were ultimately resolved by the intervention of the Nubian king Piye, who invaded the lower Nile Valley on the pretense of protecting the god Amun of Thebes, and eventually reunified the land under the Nubian kings of Dynasty 25. As an indication of the continuing power of the domain of Amun, the kings of Dynasty 25 left the administration of Egypt in the hands of their daughters, who bore the title "God's Wife of Amun." These women, who were supposed to be wed to the god Amun, had long and stable reigns that set the stage for the cultural renaissance of Dynasty 26.

Foreign policy of the Third Intermediate Period focused upon the vulnerable eastern frontier of Egypt. Shoshenq (known as "Shishak" in the Bible; Dynasty 22) undertook ambitious campaigns in Palestine against the states of Israel and Judah. A greater and more persistent problem was the growing power of Assyria which, by Dynasty 22, had absorbed Palestinian states as near as Gaza. Following an ill-conceived strategy, the Egyptian kings attempted to forestall the Assyrian advance into Egypt by the presentation of a tribute of horses and gold. That Egypt was truly weak was evident in the failure to send troops to relieve their ally, Hezekiah of Judah, who was under siege by the Assyrian king Sennacherib. By 674 BC the Assyrians under Esharhaddon stormed Memphis. They were dispelled not by Egyptian military might but by a great rainstorm that soaked the enemy's bow strings. The murder of the Assyrian vassal Necho, appointed by Esharhaddon, incited the Assyrian invasions of Ashurbanipal (667 BC and 663 BC) that resulted in the horrific sack of the city of Thebes. In his annals the Assyrian king boasted, "From Thebes I carried away booty, heavy and beyond counting. I pulled out two obelisks, cast of shining bronze . . . and took them to Assyria. I made Egypt and Kush [Nubia] feel my weapons very bitterly" (Pritchard 1969: 295).

Once the Assyrian troops left Egypt, their Egyptian vassal Psammethicus of Sais threw off their rule, instituting Dynasty 26.

## THE LATE PERIOD (DYNASTIES 26–31, CA. 664–332 BC)

Dynasty 26, also called the Saite Period after Sais, the home of the kings of the era, was a time of tremendous artistic achievement. The temples were restored and embellished. A great outpouring of sculpture and relief, some of the finest from any era of Egypt, dates to this time. Art and architecture reflected a conscious feeling of veneration for the past, evidenced in the archaizing of artistic and literary styles, emulated perhaps in an attempt to evoke Egypt's more genuine glorious past.

Egypt, however, had to adjust herself to a new world. Twice (525–404 BC and 343–332 BC) the land was occupied by Persians who had little affinity or respect for traditional Egyptian culture. Alexander the Great's expulsion of the Persians in 332 BC was welcomed as a method of substituting the Greeks, who respected Egyptian culture, for the Persians. The population of Egypt in this era was heavily mixed, being composed of Libyans, Greek traders, Persians, and others who formed a new multi-cultural society. The lack of shared cultural experience and allegiance to a Greek semi-divine king and, ultimately, the introduction of the new Christian theology, may have been responsible for the decay of Egypt's cultural core and the transformation of the ancient civilization (see chapter 12).

## SUMMARY

Egypt's history was a complex, cumulative pattern of evolutionary changes, but in many ways the basic themes established in the Old Kingdom were repeated throughout the eighteen centuries that followed. Although Egypt paralleled other early civilizations in many fundamental ways, it also had distinctive, almost contradictory, cultural characteristics: Egypt was one of the most centralized early political systems and possessed an extraordinarily complex bureaucracy, yet the majority of the populace lived in small, self-sufficient villages and towns, much like their predecessors in the Predynastic Period. Socio-political change appears to have evolved around the king rather than being instigated by market forces. That is, although its agricultural productivity was clearly related to the Nile and the annual flood, Egypt's cultural evolution was linked to a complex series of personalities, eventually melding with Alexander's empire and the classical period of Western history.

## FURTHER READING

Aldred, Cyril, *Akhenaten, King of Egypt*. New York: Thames and Hudson, 1988.
Baines, John and Jaromir Málek, *Atlas of Ancient Egypt*. New York: Facts on File, 1980.
Emery, Walter B., *Archaic Egypt*. Harmondsworth: Penguin, 1961.
Gardiner, Alan, *Egypt of the Pharaohs*. Oxford: Oxford University Press, 1961.
Grimal, Nicolas, *A History of Ancient Egypt*. Oxford: Blackwell, 1992.
Hoffman, Michael A., *Egypt Before the Pharaohs*. London: Ark Paperbacks, 1984.
Kemp, Barry J., *Ancient Egypt: Anatomy of a Civilization*. London: KPI, 1991.
Lichtheim, Miriam, *Ancient Egyptian Literature: A Book of Readings. Vol. I: The Old and Middle Kingdoms*. Berkeley, Ca.: University of California, 1973.
  *Ancient Egyptian Literature: A Book of Readings. Vol. II: The New Kingdom*. Berkeley, Ca.: University of California, 1976.
  *Ancient Egyptian Literature: A Book of Readings. Vol III: The Late Period*. Berkeley, Ca.: University of California, 1980.
Redford, Donald B., *Egypt, Canaan and Israel in Ancient Times*. Princeton: Princeton University Press, 1992.
  *Pharaonic King-lists, Annals and Day-books*. Mississauga, Ontario: Benben Books, 1986.
Spencer, A. Jeffrey, *Early Egypt*: *The Rise of Civilization in the Nile Valley*. Norman, Okla.: University of Oklahoma Press, 1993.
Trigger, Bruce G., Barry J. Kemp, David O'Connor, and Alan B. Lloyd, *Ancient Egypt: A Social History*. Cambridge: Cambridge University Press, 1983.

*Chapter 4*

# CITIES, TOWNS, AND VILLAGES

Any discussion of Egyptian cities, towns, and villages depends in large part on how these terms are defined. Many definitions exist and all are debated. Although the problem seems a minor one, it is anything but straightforward when dealing with archaeological remains. For example, anthropological models have traditionally been based upon the ancient Mesopotamian form of city, that is, a walled community with continuous long-term habitation. Using this definition of city has led some anthropologists (e.g., Wilson 1960) to characterize Egypt as a civilization without cities. The Mesopotamian model, however, probably should not be applied to the Egyptian settlement pattern, for the topography and society of the Nile Valley differed dramatically from that of ancient Iraq. Setting aside the problematical definition of city, additional difficulties can arise when archaeologists attempt to determine the specific type of settlement that archaeologically preceded a city: was the populated area originally a village that evolved into a town and then into a city, or did a city spring up from some yet to be defined proto-city form? A second major problem revolves around how to distinguish between the various habitation types (city, town, or village), which in reality fall along a continuum of settlement types but are defined as if they represent distinct, identifiable units. With no generally accepted definitions of terms, simple comparison and description remains the most common tool for dealing with these concepts.

The ancient Egyptians had several terms for settlements. Unfortunately, the distinction between them (if there ever was one) is now unclear. The most common term is *niwt*, usually translated as "city" or "village." The round sign, thought to represent a round city with intersecting streets, was used as a generic determinative for any habitation. Archaeological remains support this interpretation – Predynastic towns at Abydos and Hememieh were built on round or oval plans. *Niwt* could also denote a large city, for by the New Kingdom, Thebes, the theocratic center of the country and certainly one of the largest cities in Egypt, was referred to simply as *niwt,* "the city." The term *demy,* commonly translated as "town," may come from the root meaning "to touch," referring to an area of the river bank where ships landed. Other early words for types of settlements were *set,* translated as "seat" or "abode," specifically that of a god; and *hwt,* "domain," in reference to land holdings of a temple.

Clearly Egypt possessed a number of settlement types, and one basic way that archaeologists can establish a settlement type hierarchy is by analyzing the number of functions carried out within a population center. That is, within a given culture, settlement types are differentiated by noting what kinds of activities are conducted within each of the respective settlements. Defined in this manner, a city is a polyfunctional settlement that has a dominant regional position among other settlements that perform fewer functions. In villages only one or two functions, primarily agriculture, might be performed. A town or city, on the other hand, serves a number of different roles, and different activities can be identified, ranging from market exchange to agriculture and government affairs. Towns are differentiated from cities because towns maintain a strong agricultural component by offering attractive conveniences to agriculturally based communities (villages) located within easy traveling distance; cities, although often maintaining an agricultural component, serve a greater variety of regional and national administrative functions than towns.

## CITIES

For almost 2,000 years the most important population centers in Egypt were Memphis and Thebes, dominating the northern and southern parts of Egypt respectively. Archaeological remains and textual evidence suggest that these centers were large enough and functionally diversified enough to be labeled as cities. Later in Egyptian history other towns (e.g., Tanis, Bubastis, Mendes, Sais, Pi-Ramesses, Alexandria, Koptos, and Elephantine) also gained prominence as administrative centers.

Excavations have not provided a reliable picture of how the early provincial, and later Old Kingdom, capital of Memphis was laid out, but it is thought to have been a conglomeration of residential areas located around a planned royal fortress-like palace and the temple of Ptah, which were surrounded by the city's famous "White Walls." According to Herodotus, the city was founded by Menes, Egypt's first pharaoh, who, through the construction of a dike, diverted the Nile and built the city on reclaimed land. Modern excavations suggest that this dimly remembered event may have some basis in fact. Advantageously positioned near the confluence of several Nile branches, the settlement grew quickly, enhanced by the foundation of pyramid towns like that of Pepi I. Through urban sprawl, semi-independent settlements coalesced over the ages to create a large population center with distinct neighborhoods or boroughs. Interspersed among the populated quarters were gardens and fields. The city eventually extended for 30 kilometers north to south with a more densely populated downtown (government) core area of 13 by 6.5 kilometers.

Saqqara and Giza served as necropolises for Memphis. The tombs, known in antiquity as "houses of eternity," were imitations of houses, so the cemeteries may give a clue to the ideal appearance of Memphis in the Old Kingdom. The cemeteries are laid out on a grid pattern with straight unpaved streets. The areas are zoned, with officials of certain ranks being allocated specific areas, just as there were, perhaps, elite and less desirable neighborhoods in the actual city.

Like Memphis, Thebes began its long history as a provincial capital and grew from the Middle Kingdom through the Late Period. It was a loosely linked series of settlements and population centers on the east and west banks of the Nile. In contrast to the urban sprawl of Memphis, Thebes proper has been envisaged as a series of clustered houses or neighborhoods built near various temples. One of the tomb robbery papyri (British Museum Papyrus No. 10068) contains a "town register" of 180 households in an area on the west bank. The mixture of professions, from scribe, district officer, and physician to craftsman, fisherman, potter, sandal-maker, gardener, and farmer who lived in the same area suggests that the neighborhoods were not stratified by profession and status. The notion that New Kingdom Thebes consisted of multi-story townhouses jammed together is probably true, but only for the oldest part of the settlement. Much of the city beyond the central district probably contained domestic architecture typical of other areas in Egypt (see chapter 9).

Another relatively well-preserved city is Tell el Amarna (Akhetaten), the planned capital created for King Akhenaten. The city, built in Middle Egypt on the east bank of the river, had an estimated population of 30,000. The actual layout of the city was formed by three roads which ran north to south and roughly paralleled the river. Around these three main roads the city was divided into several well-defined sectors identified as the Central Quarter, the South or Main Suburbs, and the North Suburb (fig. 4.1).

The Central Quarter was the site of the palace, temple, and government offices. Most of Amarna's residents lived in the North and South Suburbs. In general, the South Suburb was home to the court and government officials, and the North Suburb, about 800 meters north of the Central Quarter, was essentially a middle-class suburb with a strong mercantile component. The North Suburb also contained the Northern Palace, as well as what can best be described as a slum area, where numerous housing units were of the simplest and cheapest construction. Given that many residents of the South and even the North Suburb were bureaucrats who worked in the Central Quarter, there must have been periodic commutes between the suburbs and the government offices in the city. Outside of the royal and government buildings of the Central Quarter planning seems to have been virtually non-existent. The three broad, but far from straight, main streets connecting the suburbs to the center of town were intersected by narrower streets running at right angles to the main roadways. Like large cities of today, these cross streets outlined distinct neighborhoods. Within the large neighborhoods, the overlapping of individual house plots further demarcated distinct local community complexes. Sometimes groups were exclusively of larger or smaller houses, but the two types were often intimately mixed, with rich and poor apparently living side by side. There seems to have been little interest in prime location other than frontage on one of the main north–south thoroughfares.

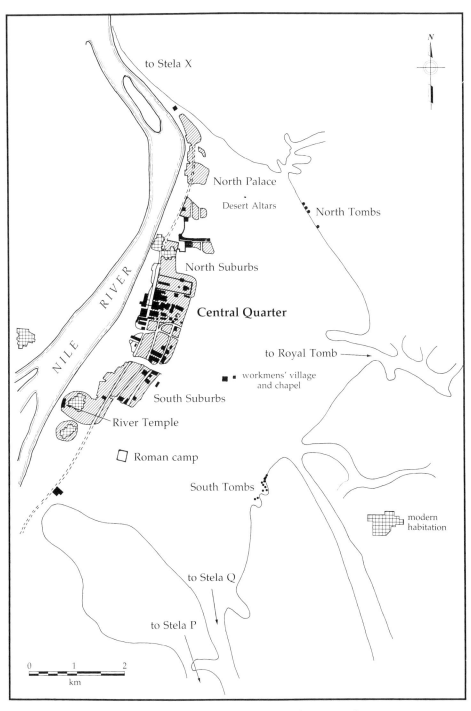

4.1 Plan of the town of Tell el Amarna (Dynasty 18).

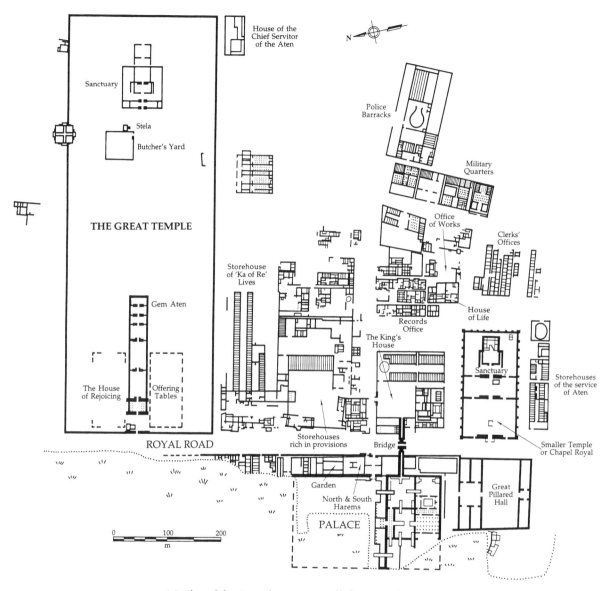

4.2  Plan of the Central Quarter at Tell el Amarna (Dynasty 18).

In contrast to the haphazard planning of the South and North Suburbs, there can be do doubt that the Central Quarter was carefully and deliberately planned as a unit (fig. 4.2). The northern boundary of the area was marked by the Great Temple, set in an enclosure more than 800 meters long and 250 meters wide. The area's western boundary was formed by the immense official palace with frontage on the Royal Road, which at this point was very wide to allow for royal processions. Between the Royal Palace and the Great Temple were two distinct groups of storerooms and kitchens: the south-ern group apparently served the palace, and the northern group was attached to the temple. Government offices lay to the east of these buildings. Most cannot be assigned to specific departments, but some have been identified by inscriptions; for example, the Records or Foreign Office where the famous Amarna Letters, the diplomatic corre-spondence of the time, were found. Behind the Records Office was a building that appears to have been a school and scriptorium. Farther east lay other buildings that may have been devoted to different official departments. To the south of all these struc-tures were long rows of rooms: the offices of clerks and civil servants. Finally, at the desert edge to the east lay the military barracks and police quarters, the latter with long rows of stables ideally situated so that the "Flying Squad" (charioted police) could quickly reach any disturbance.

It is natural to wonder to what extent Amarna was typical of cities of its time. Because it was built specifically and rapidly as the new administrative center of the country, it seems likely that it incorporated some features typical of ordinary cities but did not exhibit the full range of characteristics of ancient cities.

## TOWNS

Towns may have emerged initially as centers of redistribution and, very commonly, as religious centers. Generally, towns had larger populations than villages, were inter-nally more differentiated, served more private and public functions, and offered a greater range of goods and services. Many of the earliest towns were religious cult centers dedicated to a specific deity. Some were once villages located at the terminus of desert routes or adjacent to natural harbors along the river. Included among the array of town types were nome capitals: large towns with mayors where provincial administrative affairs, such as the maintenance of irrigation works, collection of taxes, and mobilization of the rural labor force for local agricultural and building projects, as well as military operations, were conducted.

During Dynastic times it appears that two types of Egyptian towns existed: unplanned and planned. These town types, however, should not be considered mutu-ally exclusive, because even planned settlements experienced unplanned and random building activity. In addition, planned and unplanned towns may be further classified as nuclear (restricted by a wall) or unrestricted.

Unplanned settlements arose over long periods in random fashion according to the immediate needs of the inhabitants. They expanded, often in the course of a single gen-eration, and were rebuilt many times. Archaeological ground-plans of such sites reveal a confusing labyrinth of narrow, oddly twisting alleys, passages, squares, and courts, with little open space. In dense population areas, such as inside town walls, space was at a premium and houses grew upwards to two or possibly three stories. Only temples and palaces, which were surrounded by high walls, presented oases of tranquillity with their regular architectural design and open ground.

Planned towns, on the other hand, tended to be more orderly in general design. One of the best examples of a planned town is Deir el Medina in western Thebes (fig. 4.3). This well-preserved, but atypical, town was built as the residence for the men who built the royal tombs in the Valley of the Kings. The town was surrounded by a 6 meter high wall that served to differentiate it from the rest of western Thebes. As founded during the reign of Thutmose I, Deir el Medina was bisected by a main street. The twenty original one-story houses had common walls and their front doors opened to the main street.

Deir el Medina underscores the difficulties in distinguishing between settlement types. In secondary literature Deir el Medina is referred to as the workmen's "village," yet according to the definitions established here, it clearly is a town. Foremost, it was the seat of the local administration and of the local court, and it was, by virtue of the internal system of trading specialized labor – such as a carpenter exchanging a coffin with a man who would paint the carpenter's tomb chapel – also a center of trade. Yet the trade was largely limited to the inhabitants of the town, and thus the impact of Deir el Medina's economic ties with the surrounding area were very limited. In addition, there was virtually no agricultural component in Deir el Medina, for the food for the workers was supplied through contract with Theban suppliers.

### VILLAGES

From its inception to its ultimate decline, Egypt remained an agricultural country; yet it is very difficult to study early agricultural villages because, built of perishable materials such as reed mats and mud-brick rather than stone, they leave little archaeological record. The earliest Neolithic villages very likely originated in areas where certain environmental conditions allowed agriculturists to sustain herd animals and grow crops within an acceptable margin of risk. In Upper Egypt, the best areas for sustaining Neolithic villages were along the ancient river levees. Levees stood several meters above the surrounding plain and offered the village security from all but the highest floods. A village on a levee allowed the early farmer direct access to adjacent cultivable land and the river, which was important for transportation, communication, and rich fish resources. Such a location also offered proximity to the desert border lands and the wild game that was attracted to those areas.

Though the upper Nile Valley provided optimal areas of the type described here, the Delta offered similar habitats along the main river branches and elevated sand *geziras*. Smaller and less dynamic, given that the forces of the Nile were considerably less in the multi-branched Delta drainage system, such habitats nevertheless provided sites for villages and cemeteries analogous to the Upper Egyptian levees.

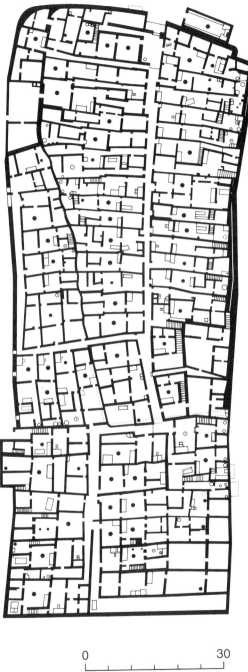

4.3 Plan of the workmen's village at Deir el Medina at Thebes (New Kingdom).

In the Delta, as the prime areas became saturated, secondary and tertiary environmental zones began to be occupied. These areas offered much of what the primary sites offered, but were often farther away from the Nile, or on minor Delta tributaries. Settling in these areas involved compromises: considerable travel might be needed to reach fertile fields or agricultural activity might have to be limited. In contrast, later Upper Egyptian settlements, located, as was usual, near the edge of the flood plain, did not have a particularly disadvantageous situation and merely raised the density of the population in the area.

What did an ancient Egyptian village look like? The earliest Neolithic villages were simple clusters of dwellings with no defensive palisades. As discussed above, the generic determinative used for an inhabited place is a circle bisected by crossroads, suggesting perhaps that the archetypal early village had a generally circular layout. Excavations of an early settlement at Abydos revealed a circular plan about 30 meters in diameter, and Caton-Thompson's work at Hememieh also revealed that a circular or oval village configuration existed there as well. Hememieh was a small community composed of dome-roofed huts with a number of outbuildings of similar construction and shape. This settlement plan, with free-standing domiciles and separate outbuildings, is mimicked in the lower levels of the Predynastic settlements at Merimde, el Omari, and Maadi.

By the time of Naqada II, there seems to have been a shift in house type and community appearance. Mud-brick became the favored building material for houses, walls, and other structures. Work at Merimde shows the evolution from Neolithic and Naqada I dome huts to Naqada II mud-brick rectangular structures. Streets and alleys also appeared at this time, probably as a result of the architectural shift to rectangular or sharply angled structures. In addition, settlements with brick enclosure walls existed. Fragments of a Naqada II model found at Diospolis show two men looking over a low wall; on slate palettes of late Predynastic and Early Dynastic times, settlements are shown as circles or ovals surrounded by stout, often buttressed, brick walls.

### FORTS

During the Predynastic and Old Kingdom periods, the natural boundaries of Egypt served as the main defense against foreign incursions. By the Middle Kingdom, however, these natural boundaries were insufficient, and defensive forts were built along the eastern and western Delta to defend against incursions and to protect Egypt's important trade routes.

Over a period of 130 years, beginning with the reign of Senwosert I and ending with the rule of his grandson, Senwosert III, eleven forts were established along the first and second cataract at points where the Nile was difficult to navigate. The positioning of these forts makes it clear that they were not established to protect Egypt's southern

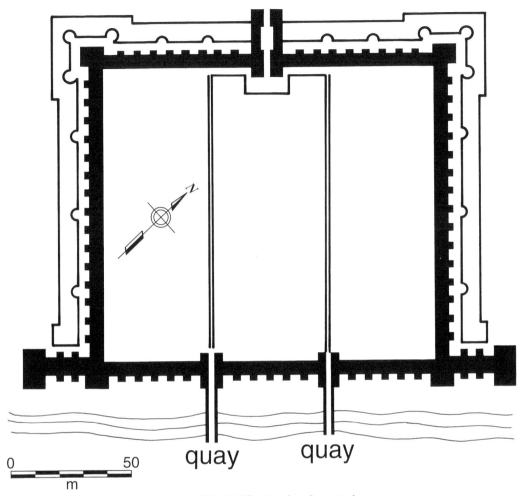

quay          quay

0                    50
                 m

4.4 Plan of the Middle Kingdom fort at Buhen.

border, because they could easily have been outflanked by an army traveling on either side of the river. Rather, it seems more likely that their purpose was to control the flow of traffic and people into and out of Egypt and to enforce the king's monopoly on trade.

Topography and geography played an important role in fort design. Two types of forts can be identified: plains and cataract. Plains forts were constructed in open territory and were the larger of the two. The best example of a plains fort is at Buhen (fig. 4.4), located in Nubia on the Nile's west bank. Probably one of the most elaborate fortresses built in the Nile Valley, it exemplified the use of the natural environment in its positioning. Buhen's defenses included a wall more than 700 meters long, 8 meters high, and 4 meters thick that was strengthened at intervals by 32 semicircular bastions.

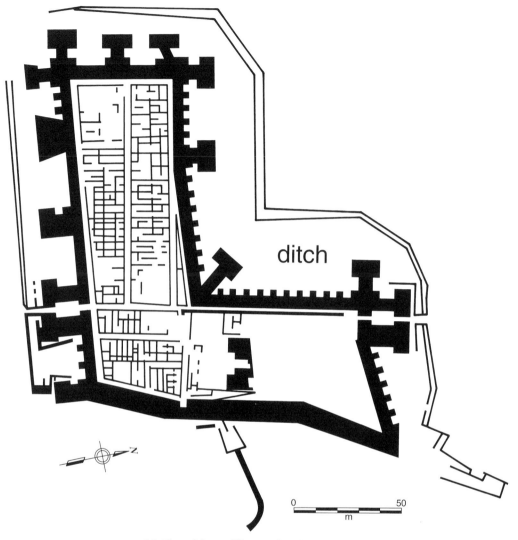

ditch

4.5 Plan of the Middle Kingdom fort at Semna.

Providing additional security was an inner wall 11 meters high and 5 meters thick with bastions every 5 meters from which bowmen could fire down on attackers. Cataract forts departed from the rigid rectangular design of plains forts to take full advantage of the defensive terrain upon which they were built. They were often quadrangular, but use of natural terrain allowed for other shapes as well: Semna West (fig. 4.5) was L-shaped and the fortress of Uronarti was triangular. Modern defense specialists rank the latter among the most efficient of defensive configurations.

All forts had a similar internal plan, consisting of a grid pattern of specialized zones for storerooms, granaries, workshops, barracks, and officers' houses. The various quarters were linked and intersected by a network of well-constructed streets paved with stone. The entire fortress community was usually encircled by a street, running adjacent to the inside of the wall and offering troops speedy access to the battlements. Outside the fortress walls, homes would often spring up; they offered accommodation to families of fort personnel and others doing business with the fort.

## LIFE IN THE SETTLEMENTS

The lifestyle of urbanized Egyptians who resided permanently in cities or towns differed in important ways from the lifestyle of villagers. Every Egyptian, however, was tied to agricultural life; even bureaucrats had to deal with the leasing of land, accounting of harvests, and taxation and redistribution of the proceeds. Town- and city-based governments also intervened in rural society through the leasing of land, tax collection, military and conscripted state labor forces, judiciary endeavors, and regulations that affected daily life. For instance, excerpts from the "Legal Code of Hermopolis West" (*ca.* 300 BC) give us insight into ancient building regulations. Structures were legally described and located, not by a house number, street, or block, but by reference to which buildings or features were located to the north, east, west, and south; this system understandably required strict record-keeping, given that new construction could replace any one of the referenced structures. The code also included the legal rights of home owners from encroachment, such as the inappropriate positioning of a drain under a neighbor's home or the entry way of one home being obstructed by the rubbish heap of another. Encroachment on state-controlled thoroughfares was a violation that could result in the destruction of the offending house, a significant penalty given construction costs. Adherence to the building code seems, however, to have been inconsistent at best. Archaeological evidence suggests that both private lanes and major thoroughfares were encroached upon by builders. In fact, excavations at East Karnak demonstrate that a 2-meter-wide thoroughfare was slowly encroached upon by domestic construction and finally was reduced to a mere 75 centimeters in width.

Excavation plans and modern reconstructions that provide an image of a clean and organized garden or park-like atmosphere for most Egyptian settlements are far from accurate. Ancient Egyptian streets were not surfaced and there was no system of drainage and little proper sanitation (sewage merely drained into the sub-soil). Domestic garbage was piled on rooftops, in alleys, and in just about every available area outside the compounds of the rich. Refuse heaps were particularly large next to public wells and along the smaller winding alleys, thereby reducing access to many homes. As urban areas grew, these rubbish heaps were leveled and even "disinfected" (by burning), and new estates and houses were built on top of them. The North Suburb of

Amarna is particularly instructive in this respect, for it was still being developed when the city was abandoned. Every stage of building can be seen, from leveled and disinfected dumps, to areas where house foundations were planned, to homes nearly completed. Even in planned cities, organization seems to have been fairly superficial.

THE EGYPTIAN SETTLEMENT PATTERN: CITY-STATE OR VILLAGE STATE?

On the basis of available evidence there existed in Egypt, as well as in other ancient state-level societies a continuum of urban types. The working relationships between different types and sizes of settlements have been classified under a number of different headings ranging from city-states to territorial or village states. Egypt and Mesopotamia, for example, traditionally represent the two opposing extremes along a spectrum of possible settlement distributions and types.

Mesopotamian city-state systems were made up of densely populated urban areas that shared common status symbols, language, and economic systems, but whose elites tended to compete with each other, often militarily, to control territory, trade routes, and other resources. Each city-state controlled a relatively small territory, often only a few hundred square kilometers, and had its own a capital city, which in many cases was enclosed by a wall. In addition to its capital, a city-state might govern a number of smaller centers, as well as numerous farming villages and hamlets. Ancient Sumer is a classic example of such a system.

In ancient Mesopotamia, urban centers tended to be relatively large with populations ranging from less than 1,000 to more than 100,000 inhabitants, depending on the ability of a particular city-state to control and exact tribute from its neighbors. Often, a considerable number of farmers lived in these centers to secure greater protection for themselves and their possessions. It is estimated that in southern Mesopotamia (*ca.* 2900–2350 BC) more than 80 percent of the total population lived in cities.

These cities also supported craft production, which sought to satisfy the demands of the urban elite and society as a whole. The development of craft specialization and commercial exchanges between town and countryside as well as between neighboring urban centers encouraged the growth of public markets. Although the evidence for actual marketplaces is less than clear for southern Mesopotamia, the remnants of shop-lined streets indicate vigorous commercial activity involving large numbers of people. This activity in turn promoted competition among city-states to obtain supplies of exotic raw materials. As a result of widespread access to goods produced by full-time specialists and the development of more intensive agriculture close to urban centers, Mesopotamian city-states were able to support numerous non-food producers, possibly as high a proportion as 20 percent of the total population.

In contrast to Mesopotamia, ancient Egypt's population has traditionally been perceived as more evenly dispersed across the landscape, a characteristic of village states.

Topography and the formation of the early state were the major factors contributing to this dispersal. Unlike Mesopotamia, Egypt had relatively secure and defined borders, allowing a single state to dominate the area from the first cataract to the Mediterranean. Additionally, the villages and towns of Egypt, all of which were situated near the Nile on the river's narrow flood plain, had approximately equal access to the river and did not have to compete among themselves for water as their contemporaries in Mesopotamia were forced to do. As the main highway through Egypt, the Nile offered innumerable harbors for shipping and trading, so there was no strong locational advantage to be gained in one area as opposed to another; hence the Egyptian population generally remained dispersed throughout the Valley and Delta in low densities. Trade specialists apparently were evenly spread throughout Egypt, supported by both independent workshops in small towns and royal patronage in the nome capitals. In contrast to the defensive walls of Mesopotamian city-states, the walls of Egyptian towns primarily defined and delineated sections of the town (e.g., a temple precinct from a residential area).

Egypt, however, was not without urban centers. At points where goods entered the Nile Valley via maritime routes (e.g., Buto and Mendes) or overland routes from the Red Sea via *wadis* (e.g., Coptos and Abydos), the right circumstances existed for greater urbanism. Egyptian cities and towns shared certain characteristics with other contemporary societies but also displayed unique traits influenced by the culture and environment of the Nile Valley. Thus, the geopolitical system that evolved in ancient Egypt was different from that of Mesopotamia; Egypt developed a village or territorial state characterized by dispersed settlements of varying size, a form of urbanism that gave Egypt its distinctive identity.

Like other territorial states (e.g., Inca in Peru, Shang in China), Egypt developed a hierarchy of administrative centers at the local, provincial, and national levels, but these urban centers tended to be small with a centralized administrative district and population. Although we have no firm population records, Egypt's capital, Memphis, may have had no more than 50,000 people, a figure no larger than a substantial Mesopotamian city-state. The reason Memphis remained relatively small was that it was inhabited almost exclusively by the ruling class and the administrators, craft specialists, and retainers who served them. Egyptian farmers, on the other hand, took advantage of the security provided by the state and tended to live in dispersed homesteads and villages near their agricultural fields. This settlement pattern is confirmed by the lists of temple domains (lands whose produce supported a specific temple). These domains were scattered throughout Egypt, often far from the temple to which the lands belonged.

Unlike the more fluid economic system of the city-state where the market economy extended to all classes, a clearly demarcated two-tiered economy with distinct rural and urban sectors developed in Egypt. Markets existed but they were small and served the needs of the local population by providing access, through barter and exchange, to raw and finished materials. Elite craftsmen were employed by the state in provincial centers or in the national capital to manufacture luxury goods for the ruling class, often from raw materials imported specifically for that purpose. The only significant economic link between rural and urban centers in territorial states such as Egypt tended to be the payment of rents and taxes and the performance of *corvées* by peasants. The transfer of food surpluses from the countryside to urban centers was principally in the form of assessed taxes and temple domain transfers rather than commercial enterprise.

Archaeologists attempting to assess Egypt's settlement pattern have attempted to classify the hierarchical structure of Egyptian cities, towns, and villages by contrasting them to a number of ideal models that are intended to reflect the settlement pattern of the city or village state: the "primary settlement distribution" model, which is equated with the village state, and the "ranked settlement distribution" model, which more closely resembles the city-state. In the primary settlement distribution, one or two large towns or cities (e.g., provincial capitals) exist among myriad village-size communities. Ranked distributions, on the other hand, possess the full range of settlement sizes, and the settlements fit a statistically predictable distribution.

Unfortunately, cemeteries and *tells* have provided the vast majority of data concerning Egyptian settlement patterns, and few small populations centers have been excavated. This has very likely skewed the perception of Egyptian settlement patterns toward the primary distribution model. More recent archaeological studies are beginning to provide a different perspective. For example, one survey by Dutch archaeologists in the eastern Delta identified ninety-two archaeological settlements in a 35 square kilometer area. The number and size of these settlements do not fit the expected primary distribution, but rather fall well within the predicted relationship of towns to small villages and hamlets that would be expected from a ranked settlement distribution.

The ancient textual record is also a source of information about settlement size and distribution. Using textual sources, Butzer (1976) compiled an inventory of 217 ancient population centers throughout Egypt. He divided the settlements into a four-stage hierarchy: city, large town, small town, and large village. He used the term "city" to refer to large multi-functional settlements, which included the two main administrative centers: Memphis and Thebes; large and small towns served as regional centers of administration and economic exchange; and large villages were settlements that showed some connection to a town through religious and economic exchange networks, but lacked administrative functions. Butzer's list is biased toward larger settlements because most small villages and hamlets were not important to state ideology and were therefore only rarely listed on literary documents, yet the list clearly demonstrates a hierarchical (rank) arrangement of population centers rather than a primary one (table 4.1).

Table 4.1 *Textual evidence for Nile Valley settlement hierachy (after Butzer 1976, table 3)*

|  | City | Large center | Small center | Large village |
|---|---|---|---|---|
| Upper Egypt | 17 | 24 | 29 | 138 |
| Lower Egypt | 1 | 3 | 4 | 1 |
| TOTAL | 18 | 27 | 33 | 139 |

As in other scientific endeavors, representative sampling is the key to understanding the working dynamics of the ancient culture. Like modern opinion polls, a sample representative of the ancient society must be obtained before any results can be considered valid, and a sample can only be considered representative when it has been collected to answer a specific question and when other samples have provided corroborating results. Thus, because work on ancient Egyptian settlement distributions is only now providing researchers with initial results, it is still premature to make concluding statements. However, it is interesting to note that information supplied by both Butzer and the Dutch survey (van der Brink 1988), while using slightly different classificatory definitions for habitation type, both suggest the presence of a rank settlement distribution for pharaonic Egypt. Thus, although it is safe to say that the Egyptian settlement pattern differed from that of Mesopotamia, how it differed and to what extent the hierarchical arrangement of habitation types differed as a functioning system has yet to be fully determined.

### SUMMARY

Egypt was highly urbanized, and there was an array of settlement types ranging from cities and towns to small villages. Each was incorporated into a working bureaucratic network through taxation, corvée labor, and, at local levels, barter and exchange of goods. Distinctions can be made between these settlement types on the basis of the kinds of activities carried out within each type. In typical villages only one or two functions, primarily agriculture, might be performed. Although most towns also maintained a strong agricultural component, they differed from villages by performing more activities, such as controlling market exchange and governmental affairs. Cities, although often still maintaining an agricultural component, played an even greater role in regional and national administration.

The basic form of early Egyptian settlements was a roughly circular, unwalled village. Evidence for planned, unplanned, restricted (walled), and unrestricted towns and cities can be found throughout Egyptian history. The planned capital of Amarna represents an example of the urban sprawl that occurred around larger centers such as

Memphis and probably Thebes. Such sprawl created a number of semi-urban residential districts, both wealthy and poor, where disposal of refuse was always a problem and upkeep of public thoroughfares a continuous endeavor.

Regardless of whether an ancient Egyptian lived in a city, town, or village, he or she was integrated into the overall society. He or she was forced to interact with the central government through bureaucrats who collected taxes and dispensed justice. As shown by archaeological remains and reinforced by documents that relate to zoning and encroachment, the often idealized view of life in ancient Egypt may in fact have been less than pleasant, with areas of crowded housing, a lack of sanitation, and constant economic pressure from the government.

## FURTHER READING

Butzer, Karl W., *Early Hydraulic Civilization in Egypt: A Study in Cultural Ecology*. Chicago: University of Chicago Press, 1976.

David, Rosalie, *The Pyramid Builders of Ancient Egypt: A Modern Investigation of Pharaoh's Workforce*. London/Boston: Routledge and Kegan Paul, 1986.

Fairman, Walter B. "Town Planning in Pharaonic Egypt," *Town Planning Review* 20 (1949), 32–51.

Hassan, Fekri, "Town and Village in Ancient Egypt: Ecology, Society and Urbanization," in *The Archaeology of Africa: Food, Metals and Towns* (Thurstan Shaw, Paul Sinclair, Bassey Andah, and Alex Okpoki, eds.), pp 551–569. London/New York: Routledge, 1993.

Kees, Hermann, *Ancient Egypt: A Geographical History of the Nile*. Chicago: University of Chicago Press, 1961.

Kemp, Barry J., *Ancient Egypt: Anatomy of a Civilization*. London: KPI, 1991.
    "The City of el-Amarna as a Source for the Study of Urban Society in Ancient Egypt," *World Archaeology* 9 (1977), 123–139.
    "The Early Development of Towns in Egypt," *Antiquity* 51 (1977), 185–200.
    "Fortified Towns in Nubia," in Ucko *et al.* (eds.), *Man, Settlement and Urbanism*, below, pp. 651–656.
    "Temple and Town in Ancient Egypt," in Ucko *et al.* (eds.), *Man, Settlement and Urbanism*, below, pp. 657–680.

Lacovara, Peter, *The New Kingdom Royal City*. London/New York: Kegan Paul, 1997.

O'Connor, David, "The Geography of Settlement in Ancient Egypt," in Ucko *et al.* (eds.), *Man, Settlement and Urbanism*, below, pp. 681–698.

Smith, Henry S. and Rosalind Hall (eds.), *Ancient Centres of Egyptian Civilization*. Shooter's Lodge, Windsor Forest, Berkshire: Kensel Press, 1983.

Trigger, Bruce G., "Determinants of Urban growth in pre-industrial societies,' in Ucko *et al.* (eds.), *Man, Settlement and Urbanism*, below, pp. 575–599.
    *Early Civilizations*. Cairo: American University in Cairo Press, 1993.

Ucko, Peter J., R. Tringham and G. W. Dimbleby (eds.), *Man, Settlement and Urbanism: Proceedings of a Meeting at the Research Seminar in Archaeology and Related Subjects at the Institute of Archaeology, London University*. London: Duckworth Press, 1972.

Uphill, Eric P., *Egyptian Towns and Cities*. Aylesbury: Shire Press, 1988.

van den Brink, Edwin C. (ed.), *The Archeology of the Nile Delta: Problems and Priorities*. Amsterdam: Netherlands Foundation for Archeological Research, 1988.

*Chapter 5*

# THE GOVERNMENT AND THE GOVERNED

Any discussion of the government of ancient Egypt is complicated by the fact that the civilization lasted more than 3,000 years and during that time there was significant modification in the forms and systems of administration. Indeed, Egypt's socio-political structure was a dynamic entity evolving in response to the changing local and international events of the Eastern Mediterranean in the second and third millennia BC.

## THE KING AND THE COURT

The institution of kingship was central to the Egyptian state and government. The office can only be traced with certainty to Dynasty 0, but the Egyptians themselves considered the institution to date back to "the time of the gods," a mythical era in which the land was ruled by deities. Mythologically, all kings were considered to be descendants of the early gods. Each king was the incarnation of the god Horus who succeeded his father Osiris on earth in an unbroken chain of direct descent (see chapter 6). Even kings who were acknowledged to be of non-royal blood (e.g., Horemheb and Ramesses I) assumed the mythical mantel of Horus. In practical terms, however, the king was known to be mortal, but he was differentiated from his subjects by his multi-faceted nature, some aspects of which expressed divinity. Although the status of the king changed from era to era, the best expressions of the mortality of the king are the explicit claims of divinity, such as divine birth, and iconography stressing his divine nature – features that would have been unnecessary if he were routinely considered to be divine. More concrete symbolism that was employed to set the king apart from his subjects was his regalia: the *shendty* kilt, the straight false beard, various crowns, and his scepters: the crook and flail.

The multi-faceted character of the king was expressed by his names, titles, and epi-thets. He was most commonly referred to by the polite circumlocution 𓈖, "his majesty," or from the Ramesside Period, by the name of his residence 𓉐 , *pr-aa*, "the great house," from which the Greeks derived the title "pharaoh." The most common element of his titulary, 𓇓𓏏, *nesw bity*, "king of Upper and Lower Egypt," reflected the sense of duality and balance so evident in Egyptian thought (see chapter 2). Another common title, 𓅭𓇳 , *sa Ra*, "son of Re," reflected both his association with the sun god and his distance from true parity with the god. In laudatory texts he was extolled as

69

the "perfect god," the "great god," and "a god by whose nature people live," thereby differentiating him from his subjects.

The complex character of the king was also expressed by his formal five-fold titulary. From Dynasty 5 onward, it included two names, each enclosed in an oval cartouche, the hieroglyph for "eternity," which may have meant that the king ruled all Egypt forever. The first of these cartouche names was the prenomen, the name which the king assumed upon coronation. During at least some periods, this name was composed by lector priests and proclaimed at the coronation. The second cartouche name was the nomen, the king's family name, such as the repeated names Amunhotep, Thutmose, and Ramesses.

Throughout the dynastic period the king (📜, *nesw*), was the apex of the political and religious hierarchy. He was an absolute monarch who ruled for the duration of his lifetime. He served as the chief executive officer of the state, the supreme chief justice, the commander of the troops, and the highest priest, and he was responsible for upholding the cosmic order of the universe embodied in *Maat*. Though at least three female pharaohs are known to have existed (Nitocris of Dynasty 6, Sobekneferu of Dynasty 12, and Hatshepsut of Dynasty 18), the office was normally held by a man.

The pattern of succession was patrilineal, and the eldest son usually succeeded his father. Although royal women were influential, there is no evidence to support the idea that the successor to the throne had to marry a woman of royal blood; indeed, the chief wives of Thutmose III, Amunhotep II, and Amunhotep III were not of the royal family. Succession was occasionally ensured by co-regencies of father and son, or, when a king died leaving a young successor, a member of the royal family might act as regent on his behalf, such as Hatshepsut who was regent for Thutmose III.

In theory, the king led all activities. In reality, a complex hierarchy of thousands of bureaucrats who served as advisors and functionaries were appointed to carry out his duties and wishes. During the Old Kingdom, most of the highest officials were members of the royal family, but by the Middle Kingdom and later there was an increasingly professional corps of civil service workers. Theoretically, any qualified person could enter the civil service, but in actuality it was predominately composed of upperclass males.

The chief advisor and administrator of the king was the *chaty*, 📜 conventionally translated as "vizier" or "prime minister." The earliest evidence for the office of vizier dates to Dynasty 3, but little is known about the responsibilities of the office until the Middle Kingdom. By that time, the authority and the degree of power held by the vizier was second only to the king and, in periods of weak centralized power, perhaps rivaled that of the king. The office was filled at the pleasure of the king, and the fact that a single vizier served a succession of kings attests to the stability of the office. The autobiographical text of Vizier Ankhu of Dynasty 13 refers to other members of his family who served as vizier and indicates that the office, at least during some periods, was passed from father to son. During Dynasty 5, much of Dynasty 6, and from the end of the Second Intermediate Period or the early New Kingdom onward, there were two viziers. The vizier of Lower Egypt resided at Memphis; the vizier of Upper Egypt was posted in several different cities during the Old Kingdom, apparently reflecting governmental priorities and needs, while during the New Kingdom, his seat was Thebes. At least two women held the title of vizier, one during Dynasty 5 and the other during Dynasty 26.

The clearest information that we have about the duties of the vizier come from New Kingdom Theban tombs. The best preserved records are from the tomb of Vizier Rekhmire (Dynasty 18). In these texts Rekhmire refers to himself as "second to the king," "the heart of the Lord," and "the ears and eyes of the sovereign." More specifically, the texts relate that the vizier was responsible for civil order, the assessment and collection of taxes, the maintenance of archives and the organization of their retrieval for consultation, the mobilization of troops, the appointment and supervision of officials, the examination of land claims, the inspection and surveillance of provincial governments, the monitoring of natural phenomena such as the inundation, and the exercise of the law over civil cases. Some viziers also served as mayor of their city, be it Memphis or Thebes. In keeping with the lack of clear division between the secular and clerical realms, Rekhmire also claims to be one "who goes into the sanctuary, from whom the god keeps nothing"; in other words that his post put him on the level of the highest priest. In sum, all internal affairs of the kingdom were the responsibility of the vizier. He was treasurer, chief justice, high priest, chief architect, and the king's closest advisor.

The king and his vizier were aided by many departments of state that are known most clearly by the titles of their chief administrators: overseer of the treasury, overseer of all the works of the king, overseer of the granaries, overseer of the king's documents, and overseer of the armies. The temples, which had their own parallel administration and, at least by the New Kingdom, were semi-autonomous, may be considered to be yet another department, for the king himself was considered to be the chief priest of each cult.

Each of these departments was managed by a hierarchy of officials and a huge civil service of scribes, the latter being the fulcrum which supported the entire government. The actual duties of many of these bureaucrats is difficult to discern because once-meaningful titles, such as *haty-a* ("mayor"), *repat* ("count"), and *rekhet-nesw* ("king's acquaintance") had become purely honorary by late Old Kingdom times. Adding to the confusion is that many of these bureaucrats served several departments and also held priestly rank. The bureaucracy touched all aspects of Egyptian life in its quest to assess taxes, collect the prescribed amount of grain, store it, and distribute it to finance the works of state and temple.

### PROVINCIAL ADMINISTRATION

At the local level, Egypt's government was composed of a series of administrative districts called ⌗, *sepat*, known by the Greek term "nome." Although the earliest record of the existence of nomes appears in Dynasty 3 (reign of Djoser), they may have existed in earlier times. They do not, however, appear to be vestiges of chiefdoms originating in the Predynastic Period, as was once thought. On the basis of topographic lists in the Abu Sir Papyrus of the reign of Niuserre (Dynasty 5), Egypt was divided into forty-two nomes. Upper Egypt achieved its total of twenty-two at an early date, but the Delta, because of slow and progressive land reclamation and settlement, reached the figure of twenty only in the first millennium BC.

The chief of the nome, the head of provincial administration, is referred to as the nomarch after the Greek *nomarchos*. The nomarch, originally a royal appointee or a member of the royal family, could also bear titles such as "judge" and "overseer of priests." By Dynasty 6, it is evident that nomes were grouped administratively into larger units and an "overseer" interacted with the respective nomarchs (e.g., the overseer of governors of the fourth, fifth and sixth nomes of the Delta).

Essentially, the nome was a miniature version of the state, with its own treasury, court of justice, land office, service for the maintenance of dikes and canals, militia, and a host of scribes who compiled records for the provincial archives. The nomarch, as a member of the ruling elite, conducted his life in much the same manner as the royal aristocracy in the capital, but on a smaller scale. He was also very much dependent upon the central administration, primarily through the economic ties of taxation. Officials from the central administration visited the nomes regularly to assess the condition of the fields and, on the basis of the predicted level of the inundation, calculate the grain tax that would be transferred to the royal treasury outposts. Temple administrators also served to tie the provincial nomes to the central authority, for the land holdings of specific temples were spread throughout Egypt. For example, officials of the temple of Ptah in Memphis who derived some of their income from farms in Upper Egypt, were in constant contact with officials of the area in which their domains were located.

Nomarchs were given titles and estates and, as the greatest Old Kingdom reward, some were granted the right to build their own tomb in the royal necropolis. The power of individual nomarchs is most evident during the First Intermediate Period, when the post became hereditary and led to the establishment of semi-autonomous fiefdoms. Middle Kingdom kings competed with the nomarchs for power, and by the reign of Senwosert III (1848–1841 BC) the post of nomarch was abolished, presumably because it presented a threat to national unity. As a part of the Middle Kingdom administrative reforms, the country was divided into three departments, or *waret*, that controlled the north, the south, and the "Head of the South" (the vulnerable area of Elephantine and the Nubian border). Each *waret* was overseen by a "reporter" aided by heralds. After the Middle Kingdom, the *waret* system was replaced by the traditional division of Upper and Lower Egypt, each overseen by a vizier. During the reign of Amunhotep I (Dynasty 18), an additional department for Nubian affairs was added. This department was overseen by the "king's son of Kush," initially a king's actual son but later a man of non-royal birth who reported directly to the king.

The administration of the empire in Western Asia, particularly the taxation of its holdings, was supervised by the "overseer of foreign lands." Often this administrator was a local official from the conquered area left to govern on behalf of the Egyptian king. In fact, it was common policy that sons of conquered rulers were sent to Egypt to be indoctrinated into Egyptian ways, later to be returned to their home country to serve as an advocate for the Egyptian cause.

During all periods, but never more so than in the New Kingdom, the most prominent feature of the bureaucratic system was the archives. Everything – wills, title deeds, census lists, conscription lists, orders, memos, tax lists, letters, journals, inventories, regulations, and transcripts of trials – was recorded. No one of substance, whether vizier, army officer, or priest, eluded identification in government files.

Although the king was theoretically the highest judge in the land and the vizier was technically the second highest, the law was generally administered on a local level, although appeals to successively higher levels of the administration were possible. Few actual law codes have survived (e.g., Edict of Horemheb, the Hermopolis Code), but it is clear that the judicial system was based upon precedent and case law. Texts found in the tomb of the vizier Rekhmire (Dynasty 18) comment that "everything is done according to what is specified by law," and references to the retrieval of written legal documents that recorded previous judgments, as well as thousands of actual documents of trials, inheritance, and transfers of real and personal property, attest to the functioning legal system. Like the government, the courts (*kenbet*) were formed on local and provincial levels. As with so many aspects of the state, religion played a part in the judicial system, for on the local level oracles were often employed to settle minor cases such as petty theft.

Justice in Egypt appears to have been relatively fair and impartial. Texts such as Ptahhotep (13.1), which implores judges to "Hew a straight line . . . do not lean to one side," and the tale of the Eloquent Peasant, which relates how a simple farmer's complaint against a superior was ultimately heard by the king himself, relay at least the ideal. The inscription of a man named Mose (Dynasty 19) indicates that court cases could even be reopened, reassessed, and judgments overturned in light of new evidence. Tomb robbery papyri of Dynasty 20 indicate that some of the accused were acquitted, suggesting that real justice existed even in such delicate matters as the royal tombs. All of these sources suggest that the Egyptians generally did not fear the legal system but considered it a fair forum to air complaints. Justice was available to everyone, and even peasants believed the law was on the side of truth, even if in reality justice did not always favor them.

There is no evidence that Egypt ever had a standing professional army. Although there were probably professional corps of officers and palace guards, the regular troops were apparently drawn through temporary conscription on a local level, for the autobiography of Weni (Dynasty 6) relates that the army that fought the "Asiatic Sand Dwellers" was composed of men from Upper and Lower Egypt and even Nubia. He relates that the army was led by men who did not have military titles and who apparently were the local leaders of the conscriptees:

> My majesty sent me at the head of this army, there being counts, royal seal-bearers, sole companions of the palace, chieftains and mayors of towns of Upper and Lower Egypt and chief district leaders, chief priests of Upper and Lower Egypt . . . at the head of the troops . . . from the villages and towns that they governed and from the Nubians of those foreign lands.

(Lichtheim 1973: 20)

The existence of military titles from later periods indicates that professional ranks of career commanders of troops and military administrators did develop. Although troops continued to be temporarily mustered, the distinctive dress of soldiers and their arrangement into formations, as seen in the Middle Kingdom models from the tomb of Mesheti and in New Kingdom tomb paintings, suggest that conscripted soldiers were well drilled and expected to conform to standard regulations. During the New Kingdom and later, residents of some temple domains were protected from military service by so-called exemption decrees.

The military was composed primarily of infantry. In the battle of Kadesh (Ramesses II, Dynasty 19), the infantry was organized into four divisions named for the gods Amun, Ptah, Re, and Seth. The essential weapons of the army were bows and arrows, slings, spears, battle axes, and maces. The infantry carried round or oval shields covered with hide. By the New Kingdom, infantrymen wore light body armor of padded fabric or bronze scales.

The battle of Megiddo (Thutmose III, Dynasty 18) may mark the appearance of an organized chariotry division. Chariots, which functioned mainly as mobile platforms for archers, were expensive and were limited to use on flat, open ground. Consequently, although they were prestigious, they were never a significant element in the Egyptian military. Cavalry was, until the campaigns of Shoshenq I (Dynasty 22), limited mainly to scouting parties.

For most of its history, Egypt did not have a separate navy. Although sea battles are depicted and described, especially in reliefs of Ramesses III's battles against the Sea People and the annals of Piye (Dynasty 25), sailors – at least for most of Egyptian history – appear to have been regular soldiers who used boats simply as water-born platforms.

Like modern armies, the Egyptian army was organized into a strict hierarchy. It was under the command of the king, who had an advisory council made up of the vizier, "the overseer of the troops," the generals, and the most senior functionaries. Divisions, companies, and platoons had supervisors equivalent to modern officers and NCOs, and, as in every other sphere of the Egyptian bureaucracy, there were scribes who were in charge of unit administration (including enlistment), allocation of weapons and equipment, and registering casualties, booty, and prisoners.

During the Old Kingdom, with the exception of Nubians who were valued archers, the Egyptian army was largely a national one, but foreign units began to form with the gradual subjugation of neighboring peoples. During the New Kingdom, some units were composed of men from various nations of Asia, the Mediterranean, and Libya. From the time of Ramesses II the army included a contingent of *Sherdan* mercenaries, originally from the Mediterranean islands, who fought with swords, spiked helmets, and shields. It was not unusual for foreign mercenaries to reach the senior ranks or even join the king's elite bodyguard. Amenhotep III's guard, for example, was composed of Nubians and Canaanites. Beginning in the Second Intermediate Period, use of the *Medjay* (pastoral people who lived in the Eastern Desert) as police within Egypt and in the deserts was common. By the New Kingdom, the Medjay became virtually synonymous with "police." Like the military, the police were formed in a hierarchical structure, headed by the chief of the Medjay, i.e., "chief of police."

Many New Kingdom pharaohs campaigned in Western Asia on a nearly annual basis. As might be expected from a temporarily mustered force, the troops left Egypt after the harvest was gathered and returned in time for the planting season. There is no evidence for supply trains, and the armies presumably requisitioned necessary food and fodder from their allies or took it more forcibly from others. There is no evidence that the soldiers' families accompanied the troops, perhaps because Egyptian campaigns were of limited duration.

### THE PRIESTHOOD

Religion cannot be separated from the overall fabric of ancient Egyptian civilization. The great temples were economic powers, and their tens of thousands of employees, both priests and support staff, were organized into an administration that paralleled the government's civil service. Many people held both priestly and secular administrative titles. This interdependence of temple and state was possible because religion impacted upon all aspects of culture, because the king was acknowledged to be the highest priest in the land, and because many of the priests served in the temples on a part-time rotating basis, allowing them to have several professions.

Priests, both male and female, were drawn from a broad swath of society. Many followed their fathers or mothers into temple service while others were appointed by the king. Tutankhamun (Dynasty 18) claimed, "I installed lay priests and higher clergy from among the children of their cities, each one being 'the son-of-man' whose name is known," (i.e., from elite families). The selection and confirmation of a high-ranking priest could also be through oracular selection, as in the case of Nebwenenef, whose name Ramesses II presented to Amun for the god's approval.

Priests were organized into hierarchical ranks. Lists of titles indicate that a man or woman could serve in the priesthoods of several deities simultaneously. For instance, Seti, the high priest of Seth, was also responsible for the religious festivals of Banebdjed, and he was in charge of an important ritual at Buto where different gods were worshiped.

The most complete information about the administration of priests comes from the Temple of Amun (New Kingdom and Third Intermediate Period). The domain of Amun was headed by prophets 𓍝 (*hem netcher*), who were arranged in rank from "first" through "fourth prophet" who were assisted by others who were simply called "prophets." According to the texts recording the installation of Nebwenenef as the first prophet of Amun by Ramesses II, Nebwenenef became "superintendent of the treasury, of the granary, the work force and craftsmen in Thebes. All the domains of Amun, all his property and all his staff were assigned to his authority . . ." This was a powerful position, for contemporary texts relate that the domain of Amun alone employed over 81,000 people and that the temple owned vast tracts of land throughout Egypt.

Below the prophets were ranks of other priests: the lector priests (*khery-hebet*) who read liturgical texts; the "god's fathers"; *sem* priests; priests who cared for the fabric, perfumes, and goods that were used in the daily offering service of the god; the *Iwenmutef* priests who officiated at funerary functions; and great numbers of low-level priests simply called *wab* ("pure ones"). Although the upper levels of priests were literate, there is little evidence that the *wab* could read and write. Not only did these different ranks of priests perform different functions within the cult, but they were considered to possess different levels of purity before the god. Inscriptions on the door jambs of temples bear instructions such as "everyone who enters here be four times pure," which would exclude lesser levels of priests. Purity in this context certainly refers to rank, not to physical condition.

Working in the temples did not appreciably change the way a priest lived his or her life. Priests were not cloistered, and male priests and most ranks of female priestesses could marry and raise families. Herodotus (*ca.* 450 BC) states that priests were obliged to shave their entire body for cleanliness, but this was either misinformation or a custom of the later period, for priests of the earlier eras are seen both with and without hair. The *is* priest for example, wore a distinctive tonsure that bared the top of his head but left a fringe of hair around the sides.

Some classes of priests were distinguished by their garb and accoutrements. Nebwenenef states that he was given a gold staff and two gold rings when he was installed as the first prophet of Amun. The high priest of Heliopolis wore a robe covered with stars, while the *Iwenmutef* priest and the *sem* priests wore real or imitation leopard-skin cloaks. Lector priests wore broad sashes across their chests. The lower levels of priests, such as the *wab*, were indistinguishable from the non-clerical person.

Fewer ranks of priesthood were available to women than men. During the Old Kingdom women from elite families served as prophets of Hathor, but by Middle Kingdom times the office was filled exclusively by men. During the New Kingdom, women served primarily as singers in temples, comprising divine choruses for the gods. As with other types of priests, the singers were divided into various ranks distinguished by their headdresses and ritual implements: rattles (*sistra*) and beaded necklaces (*menat*). During the Third Intermediate Period the office of God's Wife of Amun took on much of the power and influence of the first prophet of Amun, and by late Dynasty 25 the holder of the title served as the theocratic ruler of the Thebaid.

### LEARNED INDIVIDUALS AND SCRIBES

The intelligentsia of Egyptian society were literate, and the scribe (𓏞𓏠 *sesh*) was the cornerstone of the bureaucracy. Literacy was highly prized in ancient Egypt because it was a means of advancement between social classes and within the government bureaucracy. Yet in spite of the emphasis placed upon writing and literacy, during most of Egyptian history probably no more than 1 percent of the population was literate, and even during the Ptolemaic Period literacy probably did not exceed 10 percent. Thus, the scribal class was highly esteemed. As stated in the "Satire on the Trades," "It is the greatest of all callings; there's none like it in the land. . . . See, there is no profession without a boss except for the scribe, he is the boss. Hence if you know writing, it will go better for you than [other] professions" (Lichtheim 1973: 184, 198).

Scribes were most often the sons of scribes, but theoretically the profession was open to anyone. There is limited evidence for female literacy, and virtually none for female professional scribes. This is especially ironic, for the goddess Sheshet was associated with writing.

The scribe's position as a civil servant of the king, court, or temple demanded independent thought, decision-making, and management skills. Scribes were well aware of their social position and status. They were mid-level managers who gave orders, checked results, took records, and granted or denied permission. Numerous texts and tomb scenes demonstrate how the managerial and auditing function of the scribes entered into the people's daily life. Everything was noted: size of herds, amount of grain harvested, amounts of seed-grain and materials issued from store, types and quantities of objects manufactured, building supplies, and tools and artisan supplies requested. Records were kept on a wide range of matters, including work attendance, wages paid, kinds and quantities of booty seized, and numbers of hands and phalluses cut from the bodies of fallen enemies. Although listing all that was produced, crafted, and captured throughout Egypt seems pedantic, scribal records provided an account of Egyptian stocks and reserves and made taxation and eventual redistribution of goods possible. The precision with which quantities were reckoned shows that a good scribe had to be adept at mathematics, including practical geometry for reckoning field size.

In dealing with the public the scribe filled many roles. He served the ordinary Egyptian by drawing up wills and marriage contracts and noting financial arrangements such as purchases, loans, sales, and the tally of taxes owed and paid. Letters and other private documents were also handled by the scribe for the illiterate masses.

Scribes learned their skill in informal schools, some of which were connected with temples. According to textual references, boys entered scribal school prior to their adolescence and remained in what amounted to a day school until well into their teens. Their training consisted of rote memorization of groups of signs, initially in cursive hieratic, then progressing to the more complicated hieroglyphs. The students wrote with ink on a gesso-covered board that could be erased or on flakes of inexpensive limestone or pottery. As related in Papyrus Anastasi V, the teachers were demanding: " Scribe do not be idle. . . . Do not give your heart to pleasures, or you shall be a failure. . . . Persevere in action every day, that you may gain mastery. Spend no day of idleness or else you will be beaten – a boy has a back, and he listens to a beating" (Caminos 1954: 231).

The equipment of the scribe was simple and portable. The hieroglyphic for scribe, 𓈒, depicts a rectangular box that contained two round depressions for ink, one for black pigment made from soot and the other for red pigment made from finely ground ochre. The palette was attached to a small bag with powdered pigment and to a slender pen case. Actual palettes were often equipped with a slot to hold the pens. Statues of scribes from the New Kingdom show that their equipment also included a seashell, probably to hold water. For most of Egyptian history the scribe wrote with a reed, the tip of which was chewed to produce a frayed brush, but from Ptolemaic times on a thicker reed cut to a point and split at the end like a quill was used. The material on which the scribe wrote was determined by the type of document to be produced. For instance, if it was a draft of a letter, informal notation, or brief account, he might use an inexpensive chip of limestone or pottery, called an *ostracon*. In contrast, formal documents such as wills, literary works, and funerary texts might be written on *papyrus*, a paper-like substance made by overlapping strips of the papyrus stem. These formal documents were usually written from right to left in horizontal or vertical columns. Once completed, the document might be rolled or, in the case of letters, folded into a packet with an address added to the outside.

## SKILLED LABOR

Craftsmen and women were highly specialized. Like scribes, they generally inherited their trade from their parents or other members of their family. Craftsmen usually learned their trade through apprenticeships as youths. Most craft positions were filled by men, although women were important textile workers and potters. Because most of the commentary that we have about the relative desirability of specific trades was written in order to compare them to the exalted position of scribe, it is unclear whether some crafts were more prestigious than others.

Craftsmen worked for temple and royal workshops making the wide range of objects (e.g., statues, vessels, textiles, perfumes, furniture) required for the daily rituals and for the pharaoh, and they also undertook private commissions. They generally received payment in the form of grain, which they could exchange for other necessary goods. Records from Deir el Medina indicate that craftsmen also relied on the barter system.

Probably the most common skilled professional was the potter, for pottery was nearly ubiquitous throughout society, and all but the smallest villages must have had their own potter. Until the end of the Second Intermediate Period, pottery styles were distinctive to certain regions of the country, suggesting local manufacture. After that time, pottery became less distinctive, and the same general forms were used through-out the country, suggesting that the profession had become more standardized.

On the basis of scenes in tombs and wooden models recovered from Middle Kingdom tombs, some inferences can be drawn as to the inner working of a craft shop. It is evident that collective production was followed, and that many large craft shops worked like an assembly-line factory, with most objects passing through the hands of several individuals, each of whom carried out a particular activity. This method of work is especially clear in the case of decorated tombs, where an entire gang of men, including stone masons, those who specialized in smoothing surfaces, and those who applied the gesso, worked together. Some workers drew preliminary outlines of designs, while others, presumably the master craftsmen, corrected the initial sketches. Still others specialized in the techniques of carving and painting. This teamwork approach may explain why there are so few signed pieces of art from ancient Egypt – a single object was not the product of an individual craftsman.

### THE PEASANT CLASS

Most of the population of Egypt was engaged in the production of food, be it grain, fish, fowl, or meat. Throughout Egyptian history grain (barley and emmer wheat) production was the main agricultural activity, and the average peasant farmer was basically a field-hand who worked the land of others in exchange for part of the harvest. Information from a variety of sources presents a rough outline of how an Egyptian farms operated. First, heredity played an important role in matters concerning the availability of land for cultivation. Not only was title to land passed from one generation to the next, but leasing rights to temple or government-controlled lands may have been based on inheritance as well. The farm itself was thus not a discrete, contiguous expanse of land, but rather a composite of plots – owned, rented, or leased – that were scattered across the countryside and worked by contracted laborers.

Considered among the lowest members of the peasant class were fishermen. Why such an aversion to the fisher-folk of Egypt existed is difficult to surmise. According to the "Satire on the Trades", it might have been simply that fish, and therefore those that caught and prepared fish, smell. Furthermore, the image of a fish was used in the Egyptian word *bwt,* which meant forbidden, religiously impure, or taboo. These sources may be misleading, however, for fish, like grain, was given as wages and constituted one of the main sources of sustenance.

Although members of the peasantry, even under the best of circumstances, were probably destined to live out their lives in the same social station, several means were available to change one's status. One was through literacy, for if one could read and write there were far more opportunities for advancement. As Papyrus Anastasi V relates, "Better is that trade [writing] than any other, it makes men great. He who is skilled in it is found fit to be an official." The texts also stress that eloquence could advance a man. Another means of acquiring status was through recognition of bravery in combat or some other action that resulted in the honor of having a title bestowed by the pharaoh.

Although these avenues were theoretically open to any Egyptian, in practical terms the great bulk of the population – farmers, herdsmen, and laborers – had to be content with their place in life for they had no real opportunity to rise through the ranks. They could at least console themselves with thoughts of the afterlife, for after death all people who had lived their lives according to Maat equally enjoyed the pleasures of eternal life after death (see chapter 6). In the realm of eternity, the lowly peasant could walk among the ranks of the grandees.

### TAXATION

The population was directly tied to the central administration through a system of obligations that could take the form of direct taxes or labor owed to the state. The direct taxes were normally levied on the basis of crops and, prior to the harvest, the grain yield of any given field was estimated for the purposes of taxation. This audit was carried out by a party of government officials, including several scribal assistants. Fields were surveyed by means of a premeasured knotted cord that was stretched over the cultivated area to the boundary stone marking the edge of the deeded land. From several documents, it appears that about one-tenth of the total harvest was assessed for taxes that were apparently paid by the land owner. Another 10 percent of the crop allotted to the landowner was saved for seed.

How a crop was divided between owner and cultivator is not entirely clear, and the arrangements may never have been standardized by region or era. The Hermopolis Code (*ca*. 300 BC) states that one who rented or leased a field and cultivated it would receive one-quarter of the harvest, and that the seed corn was to be provided by the owner of the land. The same code specifies that if it was impossible to irrigate due to a low inundation, then the farmer was not liable for the rent of the fields but that he must return the seed corn to the field's owner. The Hekanakht Letters (First Intermediate Period) relate that the rent on flax fields could be paid in finished lengths of linen fabric.

From Dynasty 5 on there are references to conscripted labor forces (corvée) working on state-owned lands or state projects. Texts in the tomb of the vizier Rekhmire (Dynasty 18) refer to his responsibility to call up men for various duties and to dispatch regional officers to construct dikes throughout the entire land. The Nauri Decree (Dynasty 19) refers to corvée labor being used in the fields, and a Dynasty 19 letter mentions corvée workers being employed to haul stone. One might assume that actual conscription was, like irrigation management, organized and supervised at the local level.

The pervasiveness of the idea of corvée is reflected by the *shabti*, figurines that became a standard part of tomb furnishings from the Dynasty 13 onward. These mummiform figures were considered to be substitute workers who would perform the corvée for the deceased in the afterlife.

In theory, every Egyptian was subject to government corvée as a form of public service, but in actuality some people did evade service by hiring substitutes. Others were protected by immunity decrees, and still others may have been protected by their rank, for one document that enumerates corvée workers does not list any titles or professions for the men and women. Punishment for illegally avoiding conscription was severe. A papyrus dating to the late Middle Kingdom refers to a group of men and women who were accused of fleeing their temporary – but mandatory – work assignments. As punishment they were permanently assigned to the government work project and in some cases they were fined and members of their family were taken hostage to ensure their good behavior.

Another section of the same papyrus indicates that individuals permanently assigned to government work as punishment could be transferred to private hands through unknown means, and, in the status essentially of "slave," be inherited and sold like any material property. Prisoners of war were also numbered among the unfree in ancient Egypt. References to slavery or serfdom are rare, but at least by the late Middle Kingdom, both Egyptians and foreigners could be enslaved. Slavery was never an important part of the economy or society, however, and most of the workers on the great temple and state projects were paid workers.

## SUMMARY

The Egyptian bureaucratic system, although traditionally thought to be static, conservative, and resistant to change, did undergo restructuring throughout the Dynastic era. Though the overall power structure remained relatively stable through time, the degree of influence of important officials such as the vizier did change; as Egypt evolved, so did its bureaucratic system. The addition of a foreign affairs office during the New Kingdom is but one example of the way the government met changing needs, and change in one part of the hierarchical system necessitated adjustments and changes in other parts of the system. Egypt's burgeoning empire brought a large amount of additional wealth into the country, which the king was able to use to much advantage. To him went the credit for military victories and the extra revenues claimed from the conquered lands, which could be distributed as the king directed to ensure the fidelity of the recipients. The New Kingdom government was highly centralized, and it seems the king held more power than ever; this power was secured by the redistribution of the empire's taxed wealth.

Stability in the bureaucratic system was somewhat illusory, but in the lower echelons of society it was more of a reality. The life of peasants changed little from the Protodynastic Period to the end of the Dynastic era. Peasants lived out their lives much as they had always done, their occupations predetermined by a hereditary system. The impact on daily life of fluctuations in the power of the state increased with proximity to the seat of power.

## FURTHER READING

Eyre, Chris J., "Work and the Organization of Work in the Old Kingdom," in *Labor in the Ancient Near East* (M. Powell, ed.), pp. 5–47. New Haven: American Oriental Society, 1987.

Grimal, Nicolas, *A History of Ancient Egypt*. Oxford: Blackwell, 1992.

James, T. G. H., *Pharaoh's People*. Chicago: University of Chicago Press, 1984.

Leprohon, Ronald, "Royal Ideology and State Administration in Pharaonic Egypt," in *Civilizations of the Ancient Near East*, Vol. I (J. M. Sasson, ed.), pp. 273–287. New York: Scribner's, 1995.

Malék, Jaromir, *In the Shadow of the Pyramids: Egypt During the Old Kingdom*. Norman, Okla.: University of Oklahoma Press, 1986.

O'Connor, David and David Silverman (eds.), *Ancient Egyptian Kingship*, Probleme der Ägyptologie IX. Leiden: E. J. Brill, 1995.

Sasson, Jack (ed.), *Civilizations of the Ancient Near East*. 4 vols., New York: Scribner's, 1995.

Sauneron, Serge, *The Priests of Ancient Egypt*. New York: Grove, 1960.

Schulman, Alan R., "Military Organization in Pharaonic Egypt," in *Civilizations of the Ancient Near East*, Vol. I (J. M. Sasson, ed.), pp. 289–301. New York: Scribner's, 1995.

Strouhal, Eugene, *Life of the Ancient Egyptians*. Norman, Okla.: University of Oklahoma Press, 1992.

van den Boorn, Guido P. F., *The Duties of the Vizier: Civil Administration in Early New Kingdom Egypt*. London: KPI, 1988.

Wise, Terrance and Angus McBride, *Ancient Armies of the Middle East*. London: Osprey, 1981.

*Chapter 6*

# RELIGION AND RELIGIOUS PRACTICES

Because the role of religion in Euro-American culture differs so greatly from that in ancient Egypt, it is difficult to fully appreciate its significance in everyday Egyptian life. In Egypt, religion and life were so interwoven that it would have been impossible to be agnostic. Astronomy, medicine, geography, agriculture, art, and civil law – virtually every aspect of Egyptian culture and civilization – were manifestations of religious beliefs.

Most aspects of Egyptian religion can be traced to the people's observation of the environment. Fundamental was the love of sunlight, the solar cycle and the comfort brought by the regular rhythms of nature, and the agricultural cycle surrounding the rise and fall of the Nile. Egyptian theology attempted, above all else, to explain these cosmic phenomena, incomprehensible to humans, by means of a series of understandable metaphors based upon natural cycles and understandable experiences. Hence, the movement of the sun across the sky was represented by images of the sun in his celestial boat crossing the vault of heaven or of the sun flying over the sky in the form of a scarab beetle. Similarly, the concept of death was transformed from the cessation of life into a mirror image of life wherein the deceased had the same material requirements and desires.

## ORIGINS AND NATURE OF THE GODS

It is almost impossible to enumerate the gods of the Egyptians, for individual deities could temporarily merge with each other to form syncretistic gods (Amun-Re, Re-Harakhty, Ptah-Sokar, etc.) who combined elements of the individual gods. A single god might also splinter into a multiplicity of forms (Amun-em-Opet, Amun-Ka-Mutef, Amun of Ipet-swt), each of whom had an independent cult and role. Unlike the gods of the Graeco-Roman world, most Egyptian gods had no definite attributes. For example, Amun, one of the most prominent deities of the New Kingdom and Late Period, is vaguely referred to in secondary literature as the "state god" because his powers were so widespread and encompassing as to be indefinable.

To a great extent, gods were patterned after humans – they were born, some died (and were reborn), and they fought amongst themselves. Yet as much as the gods' behavior resembled human behavior, they were immortal and always superior to humans.

Gods are attested from the earliest time of Egyptian civilization. Standard anthropological models that suggest that gods in early civilizations are derived from a mother goddess or that they are the incarnation of aspects of nature do not fit the Egyptian evidence. Further complicating our understanding of the early gods is the fact that a single deity could be represented in human form, in zoomorphic form, or in a mixed animal–human form. Although the animal forms and therianthropic forms slightly predate anthropoid manifestations, it is unlikely that the gods were derived from totemic animals or that the Egyptians practiced zoolatry. Rather, animal forms were probably used to suggest metaphorically something about the characteristics of the god.

Certain gods were associated strongly with specific localities, although their worship was not limited to those regions. The gods were organized into groupings that expressed male and female elements (Amun/Amunet), family triads (Amun, his wife Mut and their child Khonsu), and other groupings such as the ogdoad of eight gods and the ennead of nine gods.

Many aspects of Egyptian theology are elusive to modern researchers. This results from the fact that there was tremendous development of religious ideas throughout the 3,000 years of Egyptian civilization, yet few concepts were discarded; instead, they were layered upon each other in an ever more complex and seemingly convoluted manner. Although sometimes dismissed as the signs of a primitive culture or of the Egyptians' confusion about their place in the universe, the seemingly contradictory beliefs are better interpreted as extended metaphors used to explain the intangible. For example, there are several different and seemingly contradictory ideas about creation. In some theologies, the god Ptah brought mankind into being by the force of his thoughts while others recount that mankind was created by Khnum on his celestial potter's wheel. In still others, the god Atum performed the first act of creation from his spittle or semen. All of these solutions were an attempt to explain a phenomenon that was beyond human understanding in more comprehensible metaphors.

### CULT OF THE GODS

The deities required food, drink, clothing, and rituals of purification to sustain them as the protectors of mankind against the forces of chaos. These needs were met in the course of rituals perfomed before a cult statue of the god that was thought to provide an abode for the deity's soul. Although no complete example of such a cult statue has been identified, the Restoration Stela of Tutankhamun describes the Amun statue as "his holy image being of electrum, lapis lazuli, turquoise and every precious stone." In theory, the king, as the highest priest of the land, approached the sanctuary where the statue stood three times each day (in actuality, the high priest of the temple, accompanied by choirs of temple singers and ranks of other priests, substituted for the king).

He opened the doors of the shrine that enclosed the statue and performed purification rituals (fig. 6.1). The cult statue was washed, anointed with perfumes, and dressed in clothes and necklaces. Food and drink were laid before the image of the god for divine sustenance. After a suitable interval for the god to consume the offerings, they were removed and reverted to the temple staff.

Processions of the god were an important feature of the cult. During festivals the statue of the god was removed from his or her sanctuary and placed in a portable shrine which was, in turn, placed on a boat (fig. 6.2). These ritual craft could be quite large; indeed, the texts from Tutankhamun claim that it was carried by eleven pairs of priests. The sacred boat processions might circumambulate the temple or make a pilgrimage from one temple to another, accompanied by temple personnel and local residents who sang, danced, and acclaimed the god.

### MAAT, THE KING, AND HIS SUBJECTS

Central to Egyptian religion and thought is the concept of maat, the embodiment of truth and the universal balance of the universe. This sense of order, personified as a goddess named Maat, intertwined all aspects of correct daily behavior and thought with cosmic order and harmony. Individuals were personally responsible for the maintenance of the universal order. If one transgressed against the forces of order, chaos – a state antithetical to everything the Egyptians knew and valued – would ensue and in this frightening realm the sun would not rise, the Nile would not flood, crops would not grow, and children would abandon their elderly parents.

One of the most fundamental duties of the king was to maintain maat through his intercession with the gods and especially through the cult actions performed in the temples each day in his name. Yet each of his subjects, through their correct behavior, shared that responsibility. What constituted proper morality is illustrated by the negative confession that the deceased recited at his or her judgment before the gods. This litany, Spell 125 of the "Book of the Dead," stipulated what was considered sinful such as: "I have not done wrong; I have not slain people; I was not sullen; I have not caused anyone to weep; I have not had intercourse with a married woman." Protestations such as "I have not disputed the king" indicate how closely religion was tied to the state, and that political obedience was an important part of the individual's religious duty.

### THE KING, OSIRIS, AND RITUALS OF REJUVENATION

One of the most significant functions of Egyptian ritual and myth was the reinforcement and protection of the office and body of the king. The most important myth associated the entity of the king with the gods Osiris and Horus (fig. 6.3). According to the myth, Osiris, the first king of Egypt, was murdered by his evil brother Seth. His death

6.1 King Ramesses III offers incense and libation to Ptah while the god stands in his shrine. Medinet Habu (Dynasty 20).

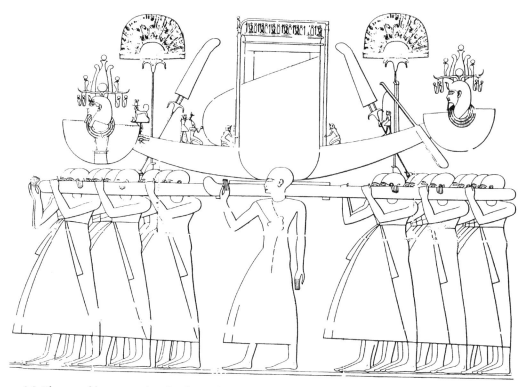

6.2 The sacred boat, carrying the shrine that shelters the divine image, being carried in procession by priests. The shrine is partially covered by a billowing veil. Medinet Habu (Dynasty 20).

was avenged by Horus, the son of Osiris, and mourned by his sister/wife Isis and her sister Nephthys. This basic outline has myriad variations, the most elaborate version of which appears in the second century AD writings of Plutarch, but the focus of the myth was to associate the living king with the god Horus and his deceased predecessor with his mummiform father Osiris. In this way, each king of Egypt was incorporated into a mythological descent from the time of the gods. The myth also stressed filial piety and obligations of a son to his father. Osiris (or, according to various versions of the myth, at least part of the god's body) was thought to have been buried at Abydos, accounting for the sacred nature of the site throughout Egyptian history.

By the late Old Kingdom, posthumous identification with the god Osiris was adopted by the common people. After death, if they had lived their lives according to Maat and could truthfully confess that they had not committed any mortal sin before the divine judges in the Hall of Two Truths, they were admitted into the company of the gods. Coffins and funerary objects of the New Kingdom record that the name of the deceased was compounded with that of the god, and that the face of coffins belonging to men bore the false beard of Osiris.

6.3a  The god Osiris.

6.3b The god Horus.

Many rituals were dedicated to the eternal rejuvenation of the living king. The most important was the *Sed* festival (also known as the "*jubilee*"), which is attested from the Early Dynastic Period and was celebrated up to the Ptolemaic era. Throughout most of Egyptian history, the ritual was celebrated on the thirtieth anniversary of the king's accession to the throne and thereafter at three-year intervals. During the course of the festival, the king alternately donned the red crown of Lower Egypt and the white crown of Upper Egypt and, grasping implements such as a slender vase, a carpenter's square, and an oar, ran a circuit between two B-shaped platforms (fig. 6.4). The king was then symbolically enthroned. Because the central act of the ritual – running the circuit – was physical, the Sed festival may be the vestige of a Predynastic ceremony wherein the king proved his continued virility and physical ability to rule. Although there is great emphasis upon the celebration of the jubilee in annals and autobiographies of courtiers who served kings who celebrated the Sed, little is known about the specific ceremonies.

6.4 Ramesses III, wearing the red crown of Lower Egypt and grasping two ritual vessels, runs the ritual circuit of the jubilee festival. Medinet Habu (Dynasty 20).

By the reign of Hatshepsut (Dynasty 18), another ritual was introduced that, like the Sed, emphasized the power of the king. This festival, called *Opet*, was celebrated annually at Thebes. The ritual took the form of a procession of the sacred barks of the Theban triad (Amun, Mut and Khonsu) accompanied by the bark of the king himself. Once within the sanctuary of the Luxor Temple, the *ka* (spirit) of the king (see chapter 10) was rejuvenated for another year by its temporary fusion with the gods.

## POLYTHEISM, HENOTHEISM, AND MONOTHEISM

Throughout their history the Egyptians worshipped a great number of gods. Tomb and literary texts indicate that an individual did not ally himself with a single god. For example, the opening formula of Late Ramesside letters recounts: "I call upon Amun Re, King of the gods, Mut, Khonsu and all the gods of Thebes to bring you back safe."

The religion of Akhenaten during the Amarna Period (Dynasty 18) has been described as "monotheism," and heralded as a possible indication that the Egyptians were the source of Judeo-Christian thought. Indeed, in the Amarna Period, Akhenaten elevated his god, the Aten, to a supreme place in the pantheon, and later in his reign his agents traveled through Egypt physically expunging the name of other gods from monuments. The interpretation of the religion of the Amarna age as true monotheism, however, cannot be sustained in light of the simultaneous worship of other gods. Maat, both as a concept and in her personification of a goddess, continued to be venerated, and indeed the ritual of the presentation of her image reached new prominence in the Amarna age. So too, in some circumstances, the king and queen were associated with the gods Shu and Tefnut, respectively. Statuettes of Bes and other members of the traditional pantheon have been recovered from houses at Amarna. The greatest objection to the religion of the Amarna age being true monotheism is the elevation of the king and his queen Nefertiti (and perhaps, posthumously, Akhenaten's father, Amunhotep III) to divine status. The vestiges of the old gods, as well as the triad formed by Akhenaten, Nefertiti, and the incarnation of the solar light as the Aten, consisted of yet another conventional grouping of gods, not the formation of a transcendent monotheistic godhead.

The religion expressed in the Amarna age is better termed henotheism, the temporary elevation of one god above others. This trend to henotheism continued in the Ramesside Period, with the elevation of various forms of Amun to the supreme god, but without the intolerance for other gods seen in the late Amarna Period. Some theologians even argue for the presence of a transcendent god into whom all other gods were subsumed during the Ramesside Period.

## POPULAR RELIGION

The great temples of the official state religion do little to elucidate the piety and religious practices of the common folk. Ordinary Egyptians had limited access to the temples, and were normally only allowed into the outer courtyard and the first and second courts of some temples on special festivals. Most manifestations of personal religion were remote from the great temples; instead, they focused on solving the cares of everyday life such as resolving disputes, praying for children, or medical cures. The means of contacting the gods were intensely personal, and by the late New Kingdom

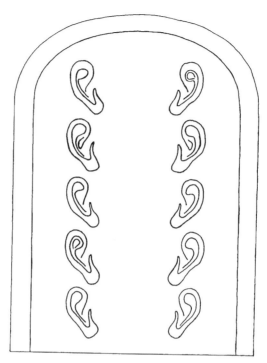

6.5 Stela incised with the representation of the ears of the god. It was thought that prayers said to the stela would be transmitted directly to the deity (Dynasties 21–24 ).

there were ever-increasing numbers of ways in which an individual could communicate with a deity. Specially decorated or shrouded areas on the outer walls of the temple, referred to as "chapels of the hearing ear," were places where a petitioner could whisper his or her prayer into representations of the ear of the god. Small stelae, most of which date to Dynasty 18 and later, were decorated with the ears of gods and presumably served as portable access lines to the deities (fig. 6.5). Statues of famed scribes were believed to intercede on behalf of a petitioner and to relay prayers to the god. A statue of Amunhotep, son of Hapu, the chief architect for Amunhotep III is inscribed with the text: "Oh people from Upper or Lower Egypt . . . who come upstream or downstream to pray to the lord of the gods, come to me and I will relay your words to Amun of Karnak . . . for I am the spokesman appointed by the king to hear your words of supplication" (Wildung 1977a: 87).

Common folk also had access to their gods during the many processions when the cult statues were removed from the interior of the temples and carried throughout the community. When a god rested in wayside shrines, individuals would approach him or her with questions such as "Was it the craftsman Amunwashw who took my fabric?" The movement of the statue of the god indicated a yes or no answer. Because the oracle statues were carried by members of the community, to modern eyes it appears that the oracle proclaimed public consensus about a community problem.

Small shrines and holy places associated with a specific god, such as Hathor, Thoth, or Meretseger, dotted the landscape. Common people could visit these places and leave votive offerings to demonstrate their piety. On a more formal level, the elite followed the same practice, placing statues of themselves in the temple hallways where they were thought not only to attest to their piety but also to pass the sanctity of the priests' prayers and actions to the owner of the statue. The tremendous number of animal mummies (it is estimated that more than 4 million ibis mummies were buried in the catacomb at North Saqqara alone) are related to this practice, for the purchase and dedication of the mummy of an animal associated with a particular god was also thought to accrue merit and favor from the god.

## SUMMARY

The formative principles behind Egyptian religion, cosmologies, and gods were not logical, but symbolic. The metaphors employed to explain the universe and the gods attempted to reduce cosmic, and thus unknowable, phenomena to an earthly scale. One of the fundamental principles of Egyptian theology was Maat, the personification of universal order and truth. The balance represented by Maat against the forces of chaos was maintained by the ritual actions of the king and the everyday actions of his subjects. Among the obligations that kept the forces of chaos at bay was obedience to the king, thereby intertwining the secular and religious spheres.

Another major focus of the religious system was the support of the office of kingship through its association with the cycle of Osiris and his son, Horus, and the ritual maintenance of individual king's power and well-being through the Sed and Opet festivals. The royal and non-royal spheres coalesced in the late Old Kingdom with the Osirian belief that any justified person would, like the king himself, be associated with Osiris in the afterlife.

The common folk had many informal means of appealing to their gods, outside the formal restraints of the temple bureaucracies. The focus of popular religion was the resolution of everyday complaints and cares.

## FURTHER READING

Allen, James P., *Genesis in Egypt: The Philosophy of Ancient Egypt Creation Accounts*. New Haven: Egyptian Seminar, Department of Near Eastern Languages and Civilizations, Yale University, 1988.

Assmann, Jan, *Egyptian Solar Religion in the New Kingdom: Re, Amun and the Crisis of Polytheism*. London: KPI, 1995.

Faulkner, R. (transl.), *et al.*, *The Egyptian Book of the Dead: The Book of Going Forth by Day*. San Francisco, Ca.: Chronicle Books, 1994.

Hornung, Erik, *Conceptions of God in Ancient Egypt: The One and the Many*. Ithaca, N.Y.: Cornell University Press, 1982.

Morenz, Sigfried, *Egyptian Religion*. Ithaca, N.Y.: Cornell University Press, 1973.

Quirke, Stephen, *Ancient Egyptian Religion*. London: The British Museum, 1992.

Teeter, Emily, "Popular Religion in Ancient Egypt," *KMT: A Modern Journal of Ancient Egypt,* Vol. 4, No. 2 (1993), 28–37.

*Chapter 7*

## SOCIETY AND ITS EXPECTATIONS

The nuclear family was the core of Egyptian society and many of the gods were even arranged into such groupings. There was tremendous pride in one's family, and lineage was traced through both the mother's and father's lines. Respect for one's parents was a cornerstone of morality, and the most fundamental duty of the eldest son (or occasionally daughter) was to care for his parents in their last days and to ensure that they received a proper burial.

Countless genealogical lists indicate how important family ties were, yet Egyptian kinship terms lacked specific words to identify blood relatives beyond the nuclear family. For example, the word used to designate "mother" was also used for "grandmother," and the word for "father" was the same as "grandfather"; likewise, the terms for "son," "grandson," and "nephew" (or "daughter," "granddaughter," and "niece") were identical. "Uncle" and "brother" (or "sister" and "aunt") were also designated by the same word. To make matters even more confusing for modern scholars, the term "sister" was often used for "wife," perhaps an indication of the strength of the bond between spouses.

### MARRIAGE

Once a young man was well into adolescence, it was appropriate for him to seek a partner and begin his own family. Females were probably thought to be ready for marriage after their first menses. The marrying age of males was probably a little older, perhaps 16 to 20 years of age, because they had to become established and be able to support a family.

Virginity was not a necessity for marriage; indeed, premarital sex, or any sex between unmarried people, was socially acceptable. Once married, however, couples were expected to be sexually faithful to each other. Egyptians (except the king) were, in theory, monogamous, and many records indicate that couples expressed true affection for each other. They were highly sensual people, and a major theme of their religion was fertility and procreation. This sensuality is reflected by two New Kingdom love poems: "Your hand is in my hand, my body trembles with joy, my heart is exalted because we walk together," and "She is more beautiful that any other girl, she is like a star rising . . . with beautiful eyes for looking and sweet lips for kissing" (after Lichtheim 1976: 182).

95

Marriage was purely a social arrangement that regulated property. Neither religious nor state doctrines entered into the marriage and, unlike other documents that related to economic matters (such as the so-called "marriage contracts"), marriages themselves were not registered. Apparently once a couple started living together, they were acknowledged to be married. As related in the story of Setne, "I was taken as a wife to the house of Naneferkaptah [that night, and pharaoh] sent me a present of silver and gold . . . He [her husband] slept with me that night and found me pleasing. He slept with me again and again and we loved each other" (Lichtheim 1980: 128*).

The ancient Egyptian terms for marriage (*meni*, "to moor [a boat]," and *grg pr*, "to found a house") convey the sense that the arrangement was about property. Texts indicate that the groom often gave the bride's family a gift, and he also gave his wife presents. Legal texts indicate that each spouse maintained control of the property that they brought to the marriage, while other property acquired during the union was jointly held. Ideally the new couple lived in their own house, but if that was impossible they would live with one of their parents. Considering the lack of effective contraceptives and the Egyptian's traditional desire to have a large family, most women probably became pregnant shortly after marriage.

Although the institution of marriage was taken seriously, divorce was not uncommon. Either partner could institute divorce for fault (adultery, inability to conceive, or abuse) or no fault (incompatibility). Divorce was, no doubt, a matter of disappointment but certainly not one of disgrace, and it was very common for divorced people to remarry.

Although in theory divorce was an easy matter, in reality it was probably an undertaking complicated enough to motivate couples to stay together, especially when property was involved. When a woman chose to divorce – if the divorce was uncontested – she could leave with what she had brought into the marriage plus a share (about one third to two thirds) of the marital joint property. One text (Ostracon Petrie 18), however, recounts the divorce of a woman who abandoned her sick husband, and in the resulting judgment she was forced to renounce all their joint property. If the husband left the marriage he was liable to a fine or payment of support (analogous to alimony), and in many cases he forfeited his share of the joint property.

Egyptian women had greater freedom of choice and more equality under social and civil law than their contemporaries in Mesopotamia or even the women of the later Greek and Roman civilizations. Her right to initiate divorce was one of the ways in which her full legal rights were manifested. Additionally, women could serve on juries, testify in trials, inherit real estate, and disinherit ungrateful children. It is interesting, however, that in contrast to modern Western societies, gender played an increasingly important role in determining female occupations in the upper classes than in the peasant and working classes. Women of the peasant class worked side by side with men in the fields; in higher levels of society, gender roles were more entrenched, and women were more likely to remain at home while their husbands plied their crafts or worked at civil jobs.

Through most of the Pharaonic Period, men and women inherited equally, and from each parent separately. The eldest son often, but not always, inherited his father's job and position (whether in workshop or temple), but to him also fell the onerous and costly responsibility of his parents' proper burial. Real estate generally was not divided among heirs but was held jointly by the family members. If a family member wished to leave property to a person other than the expected heirs, a document called an *imeyt-per* ("that which is in the house") would ensure the wishes of the deceased.

### CHILD-BEARING AND FAMILY LIFE

The relationship between coitus and pregnancy was clearly recognized by the ancient Egyptians. For example, the Late Period story of Setna relates, "She lay down beside her husband. She received [the fluid of] conception from him"; and a hymn to Khonsu relates, "the male member to beget; the female womb to conceive and increase generations in Egypt." Although the Egyptians understood the general functions of parts of the reproductive system, the relationships between parts was sometimes unclear. For example, they knew that the testicles were involved in procreation, but they thought the origin of semen was in the bones and that it simply passed through the testicles. Female internal anatomy was understood even less well. Anatomical naivety can be gleaned from the fact that, although the function of the womb was understood, it was erroneously thought to be directly connected to the alimentary canal. Thus, placing a clove of garlic in the vagina was supposed to test for fertility: if garlic could be detected on the breath of a woman then she was fertile; if not, then she was infertile.

In Egyptian households of all classes, children of both sexes were valued and wanted (there is no indication that female infanticide was practiced). In addition to fertility tests, tests for pregnancy and the determination of the gender of the child were devised. One test involved watering barley and emmer wheat with the urine of a hopeful mother-to-be. If the barley sprouted, the woman was pregnant with a male child; if the emmer wheat germinated, she was pregnant with a female child. If the urine had no effect, the woman was not pregnant. Though there actually may be some scientific basis for this test – a pregnant woman produces a variety of hormones, some of which can induce early flowering in particular plants – there is no known relationship between these plants and the determination of gender.

The birth of a child was a time of great joy as well as one of serious concern given the high rate of infant mortality and the stress of childbirth on the mother. Childbirth was viewed as a natural phenomenon and not an illness, so assistance in childbirth was usually carried out by a midwife.

Data collected from modern non-industrial societies suggest that infant mortality in ancient Egypt was undoubtedly high. One of the best ways to maintain a healthy infant under the less-than-sanitary conditions that prevailed in ancient times was by breast-feeding. In addition to the transfer of antibodies through mother's milk, breast-feeding also offered protection from food-born diseases. Gastrointestinal disorders are common under poor sanitary conditions, and because infant immunity is reduced during weaning, children's susceptibility to disease increases at this time. Indirect evidence for this occurring in ancient Egypt comes from a number of cemeteries where the child-hood death rate peaks at about age four, which correlates with an Egyptian child's introduction to solid foods. Prolonged lactation also offered a number of heath advan-tages to the mother. Primarily, it reduces the chance of conceiving another child too soon by hormonally suppressing ovulation, which allows the mother more time between pregnancies. The three-year period for suckling a child recommended in the "Instructions of Any" (New Kingdom) therefore struck an unconscious but evolution-arily important balance between the needs of procreation, the health of the mother, and the survival of the newborn child.

Egyptian children who successfully completed their fifth year could generally look forward to a full life, which in peasant society was about thirty-three years for men and twenty-nine years for women, based on skeletal evidence. Textual records indi-cate that for upper-class males, who were generally better fed and performed less stren-uous labor than the lower classes, life expectancy could reach well into the sixties and seventies and sometimes even the eighties and nineties. Upper-class women also looked forward to a longer life than women from the lower classes, but the arduous task of bearing many children resulted in a lower life expectancy compared to their male counterparts.

Dolls and toys indicate that children were allowed ample time to play, but once they matured past infancy (i.e., were weaned) they began training for adulthood. Young girls assisted their mothers with household tasks or worked with them in some capac-ity in the fields. Other female members of the mother's household would aid in the care of younger siblings. Similarly, young boys followed their fathers into their occupation, first carrying out simple chores, then later working and carrying out more important tasks. Parents also familiarized their children with ideas about the world, their relig-ious outlook, ethical principles, and correct behavior.

The end of childhood appears to have been marked by the onset of menses for girls and the ceremony of circumcision for boys. That circumcision was a ritual transition from boyhood to manhood is indicated by references such as "When I was a boy, before my foreskin was removed from me." As far as is known, in the Pharaonic Period only males were circumcised, but exactly how prevalent circumcision was through society is unclear. Some uncircumcised mummies, including King Ahmose and perhaps King Amunhotep I, indicate that the practice may have not been universal.

Young men did not usually choose their own careers. Herodotus and Diodorus refer explicitly to a hereditary calling in ancient Egypt. This was not a system of rigid inheritance but an endeavor to pass on a father's function to his children. A son was commonly referred to as "the staff of his father's old age," designated to assist the elder in the performance of his duties and finally to succeed him. The need for support in old age and to ensure inheritance made adoption quite common for childless couples; one New Kingdom ostracon relates, "As for him who has no children, he adopts an orphan instead [to] bring him up." There are examples of a man who "adopted" his brother and of a woman named Nau-nakht, who had other children, who adopted and reared the freed children of her female servant because of the kindness that they showed to her.

Although peasant children probably never entered any formal schooling, male children of scribes and the higher classes entered school at an early age. (Young girls were not formally schooled, but because some women knew how to read and write they must have had access to a learned family member or a private tutor.) Though we have no information about the location or organization of schools prior to the Middle Kingdom, we can tell that after that time they were attached to some administrative offices, temples (specifically the Ramesseum and the Temple of Mut), and the palace. In addition to "public" schooling, groups of nobles also hired private tutors to teach their children. Because education had not yet established itself as a separate discipline, teachers were drawn from the ranks of experienced or pedagogically gifted scribes who, as part of their duties and to ensure the supply of future scribes, taught either in the classroom or took apprentices in their offices.

Education consisted mainly of endless rote copying and recitation of texts, in order to perfect spelling and orthography. Gesso-covered boards with students' imperfect copies and their master's corrections attest to this type of training. Mathematics was also an important part of the young male's training. In addition, schooling included the memorization of proverbs and myths, by which pupils were educated in social propriety and religious doctrine. Not surprisingly, many of these texts stress how noble (and advantageous) the profession of scribe was: "Be a scribe for he is in control of everything; he who works in writing is not taxed, nor does he have to pay any dues."

Length of schooling differed widely. The high priest Bekenkhonsu recalls that he started school at five and attended four years followed by eleven years' apprenticeship in the stables of King Seti I. At about twenty he was appointed to a low level of the priesthood (*wab*). In another documented case, one scribe in training was thirty years of age, but this must have been an unusual case.

DRESS AND FASHION

Ancient Egyptians were extremely interested in fashion and its changes. This seems evident from trends seen in tomb scenes where the costumes and styles of the upper

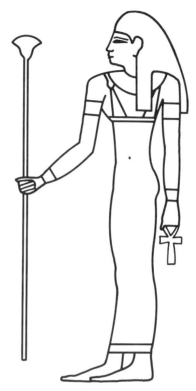

7.1  Woman's tight sheath dress.

classes were soon copied by the lower classes. The most common fabric for clothing (both women's and men's) was linen. Because linen is very hard to dye, most clothes were off-white, so color was added with heavy beaded collars and other jewelry.

The standard apparel of women from the Old Kingdom into the New Kingdom was the sheath dress, which could be worn strapless or with two broad shoulder straps. Most examples of these dresses reach the ankles (fig. 7.1). Most sources depict women wearing impossibly tight and impractical dresses, suggesting that the representations are idealized to emphasize the sensuality of the female body.

The most ancient garment worn by men was a kilt that was made of a rectangular piece of linen cloth wrapped rather loosely around the hips, leaving the knees uncovered (figs. 7.2 and 7.3). As a rule, it was wrapped around the body from right to left so that the edge of the skirt would be in the front. The upper edge was tucked behind the tie, or girdle, that held the kilt together. This garment was the standard male attire for all classes from peasants to royalty, though the quality of the linen and the exact style varied according to one's purchasing power. Some of the fancier, more expensive kilts had bias-cut edges, pleated decorative panels, or fringed edges, and were made of finer,

7.2 Man's kilt with triangular panel that represents the frontal view of an inverted box pleat. The man carries a folded handkerchief in one hand, and a slender staff, a mark of rank in his other hand. (Dynasty 5).

softer linen. By late Dynasty 4 and early Dynasty 5, it became fashionable to wear the kilt longer and wider or to wear it with an inverted box pleat that appeared as an erect triangular front piece (fig. 7.2). Though styles changed over time, the simple kilt remained the standard garb for scribes, servants, and peasants.

In the winter, the middle and upper classes wore a heavy cloak extending from neck to ankle, which could be wrapped around and folded or clasped in front. Depictions of such cloaks extend from Archaic to Ptolemaic times. Although sandals of rush and

7.3 Man's typical wrap-around kilt (Old Kingdom).

reeds are known, regardless of the occasion or social class, Egyptians apparently often went barefoot.

During the New Kingdom, when Egypt extended its political influence east into Asia, Egyptian fashion changed radically. With the influx of trade and ideas from the east, fashions became more varied, changed more quickly, and often took on an eastern flavor. Men and women of the upper classes, for example, wore layers of fine, nearly transparent kilts and long- or short sleeved shirts that tied at the neck, or draped themselves in billowing robes of fine linen that extended from neck to ankle and were drawn in at the waist by a sash (fig. 7.4). The better examples of these garments were heavily pleated, and some were ornamented with colored ball fringe.

For most of the Pharaonic Period, women wore their hair (or wigs) long and straight; after Dynasty 18 hairstyles became more elaborate. During all periods men wore their hair short, but they also wore wigs, the style befitting the occasion. These wigs were made of human hair or plant fiber. Both genders wore copious amounts of perfumes and cosmetics made of ground minerals and earth pigments. Fashion statements were made with accessories such as jewelry and ribbons. Men also carried staffs that marked status and social class.

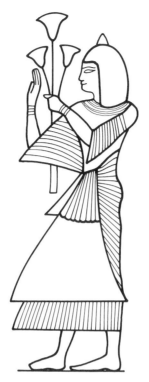

7.4  Classic New Kingdom clothing with elaborate pleating (Dynasty 19).

### ENTERTAINMENT

There is much evidence for the leisure activities of the ancient Egyptians. Men engaged in physical sports, such as hunting, fishing, archery, wrestling, boxing, and stick fencing. Long-distance races were organized to demonstrate physical prowess, and both men and women enjoyed swimming. Board games were popular, and games boards were constructed of a number of materials: wood, stone, clay, or simple drawings scratched on the ground. Moves on board games were determined by throw sticks, astragali (animal anklebones), or after the late New Kingdom, cubic dice that were usually marked in the same pattern used today. One of the most common games was *senet*, which was played on a board of thirty squares divided into three rows of ten squares (fig. 7.5). Like so many other aspects of Egyptian culture, *senet* had a religious significance, and the game was likened to passing through the underworld. The "twenty square game," which originated in Sumer and was known through the entire ancient Near East and Cyprus, was played on a rectangular board divided into three rows of four, twelve, and four squares, respectively. Both *senet* and twenty squares were played by two opponents. Another ancient games was *mehen*, played by several

7.5 The board game known as "senet" was played by two opponents. Moves were established by throwing marked sticks, knucklebones or dice (Dynasty 18).

players on a round board that looked like a coiled snake. The playing pieces, tiny lions and small balls, were moved from the tail of the snake to the goal on its head. Although this game was played in Egypt only during the Old Kingdom, it continued to be played in Cyprus for another 1,000 years.

Tomb paintings indicate that banquets were a popular form of relaxation, at least for the upper class. At such events food, alcoholic beverages, music, and dancing were common forms of entertainment. The organization of the tomb scenes may be misleading, it seems that proprieties of the times kept male and female guests seated in separate areas although men and women performed together.

The foundation of all daily or banquet meals, regardless of social class, was the same: bread, beer, and vegetables. The latter included leeks, onions, garlic, a number of pulses (beans, peas, lentils, etc.), and several varieties of melons. Wealthier Egyptians had more opportunities to enjoy red meat, fowl, honey-sweetened cakes and other delicacies. Lower-class Egyptians relied on fish and fowl for most of their meat proteins. The ready availability of wild fish and fowl made them inexpensive, while beef and, to a varying extent, other red meats were expensive and considered by many to be a luxury.

The national drink in ancient Egypt was beer, and all ancient Egyptians – rich and poor, male and female – drank great quantities of it. Wages were paid in grain, which was used to make two staples of the Egyptian diet: bread and beer. Beer was made from barley dough, so bread making and beer making are often shown together. Barley dough destined for beer making was partially baked and then crumbled into a large vat, where it was mixed with water and sometimes sweetened with date juice. This mixture was left to ferment, which it did quickly; the liquid was then strained into a pot that was sealed with a clay stopper. Ancient Egyptian beer had to be drunk soon after it was made because it went flat very quickly. Egyptians made a variety of beers of different strengths. Strength was calculated according to how many standard measures of the liquid was made from one *hekat* (4.54 liters) of barley; thus, beer of strength two was stronger than beer of strength ten.

In addition to beer, wine was also widely drunk. Jar labels with notations that the wine was from the "Vineyard of King Djet" indicate that wine production was well established as early as Dynasty 1. By Dynasty 5 and 6, grapevines and wine production were common motifs in decorated tombs, and records imply that some vineyards produced considerable amounts of wine. One vineyard, for example, is said to have delivered 1,200 jars of good wine and fifty jars of medium-quality wine in one year.

Wines in ancient Egypt, like wines today, were recognized by their vintage, often identified by the name of the village, town, district, or general geographic region where it was produced. At least fourteen different wine-producing areas existed in the Delta alone; although the extent of these regions cannot be defined, their general location can be identified – Upper Egyptian vintages were not as numerous as those of the Delta, but were said to be of excellent quality (e.g., Theban wines were known for their lightness and wholesomeness). Wines were also known to have been produced in the oases.

Wine jar labels normally specified the quality of wine, such as "good wine," "sweet wine," "very very good wine," or the variety, such as pomegranate wine. It is difficult to speculate about the taste of Egyptian wine compared to modern standards. Nevertheless, because of the climate, low acid (sweet) grapes probably predominated, which would have resulted in a sweet rather than dry wine. Alcohol content would have varied considerably from area to area and from vintage to vintage, but generally Egyptian wine would have had a lower alcohol content than modern table wines.

It has been suggested that the effects of drinking wine were sometimes enhanced by additives. For example, tomb paintings often depict wine jars wrapped or draped in lotus flowers, suggesting that the Egyptians may have been aware of the narcotic qualities of blue lotus petals when mixed with wine. There is much evidence for the excess consumption of both beer and wine, and King Menkaure (Dynasty 4) and King Amasis (Dynasty 26) figure in tales about drunkenness. Some ancient scenes are quite graphic in their depiction of over-indulgence (fig. 7.6). For instance, in the tomb of Paheri an

7.6  A woman who over-indulged (Dynasty 19).

elegant lady is shown presenting her empty cup to a servant and saying "give me eighteen measures of wine, behold I should love [to drink] to drunkenness."

Along with eating and drinking went dance and song. Dancing seems to have been a spectator sport in which professionals performed for the guests. As a rule, men danced with men and women with women. Singers, whether soloists or entire choruses accompanied by musical instruments, entertained guests in private homes and in the palace.

Ancient Egyptians played a variety of musical instruments. Of the wind instruments, one of the oldest was a flute made of reed or wood, and illustrated on Predynastic pieces of broken pottery (i.e., sherds) as well as on a slate palette from Hierakonpolis. By the Old Kingdom, single and double flutes were played. They could be side-blown (much like a modern flute), or end-blown (like a recorder) (fig. 7.7). The flute always remained popular among Egyptians and it has survived to this day as the Arabic nay and uffafa. Also popular during the Old Kingdom were large floor harps and various percussion instruments ranging from bone or ivory clappers to hand-rattles (*sistra*) and rectangular or round frame drums. Drums of all sizes were played using fingers and hands; sticks or batons were apparently not used.

During the New Kingdom, many new instruments were added to the instrumental ensemble, including small shoulder-held harps, trumpets, lutes, oboes, and seven-stringed lyres. Trumpets were generally restricted to the military. Egyptian lutes had a long slender neck and an elongated oval resonating chamber made of wood or tortoise shell (the sound emitted from these instruments would have been something

7.7 Musicians entertain at a banquet (Dynasty 18).

approximating a cross between a mandolin and the American banjo). The cylindrical drum, about 1 meter high with a leather skin laced on at each end, was also popular during the New Kingdom; it was used both by the military and civilian population. The long oboe, played with a double reed, was introduced to Egypt from Asia Minor, and during the Graeco-Roman period, a number of instruments of Greek origin were adopted by the Egyptians, including pan-pipes and a water organ with a keyboard.

Although the sound quality of the ancient instruments can in some cases be recreated, no evidence exists that the Egyptians ever developed a system of musical notation; thus the ancient melodies, rhythms, and keys remain unknown. Some scholars believe, however, that vestiges of the ancient music may be found in the music of the peoples now living in Western Desert oases, and these songs are being scrutinized for their possible origins.

In contrast to the banquets of the rich and the organized meetings of the lower classes, a different type of entertainment was provided by inns and beer houses where drinking often led to singing, dancing, and gaming, and men and women were free to interact with each other. Taverns stayed open late into the night, and patrons drank beer in such quantities that intoxication was not uncommon. In one ancient text a teacher at a school of scribes chastens a student for his night activities: "I have heard that you abandoned writing and that you whirl around in pleasures, that you go from street to street and it reeks of beer. Beer makes him cease being a man. It causes your soul to wander . . . Now you stumble and fall upon your belly, being anointed with dirt" (Caminos 1954: 182).

The streets of larger towns no doubt had a number of "beer halls," and the same text as just quoted refers to the "harlots" who could be found there. Proverbs warning young men to avoid fraternization with "a woman who has no house" indicate that some form of prostitution existed in ancient Egyptian society. For instance, the "Instructions of Ankhsheshenqy" admonish, "He who makes love to a woman of the street will have his purse cut open on its side" (Lichtheim 1980: 176). During the Graeco-Roman period, brothels were known to exist near town harbors and could be identified by an erect phallus over the door, and tax records refer to houses that were leased for the purpose of prostitution. Prostitution was not, however, associated with temples or religious cults in Egypt.


## SUMMARY

The nuclear family was the core of Egyptian society. Marriage was largely a way of regulating the transfer of property, and, with the exception of the royal family, marriage was monogamous. Children were a valued part of the society, and there is no evidence that daughters were less desirable than sons. The eldest son generally followed his hereditary calling, filling his father's post and presiding over his parents' burials.

Women's legal rights were equal to that of men. They had a right to divorce, a right to a portion of the marital property, and a right to bequeath their earthly belongings to whomever they chose.

Ancient Egyptians were offered a number of social outlets. Music, song and dance, and recreational games, as well as the consumption of alcoholic beverages, were integral parts of social occasions. Although temperance was advocated and a number of textual references allude to society's moral standards, drinking to excess was apparently not uncommon.


## FURTHER READING

Baines, John, "Society, Morality and Religious Practice," in *Religion in Ancient Egypt* (B. E. Shafer, ed.,) pp. 123–200. Ithaca, N.Y.: Cornell University Press, 1991.

Decker, Wolfgang, *Sports and Games of Ancient Egypt*. New Haven: Yale University Press, 1992.

Erman, Adolf, *Life in Ancient Egypt*. New York: Dover Books, 1971.

James, T. G. H., *Pharaoh's People*. Chicago: University of Chicago Press, 1984.

Janssen, Rosalind M. and Jack J. Janssen, *Getting Old in Ancient Egypt*. London: Rubicon Press, 1996. *Growing Up in Ancient Egypt*, London: Rubicon Press, 1980.

Johnson, Janet H., "The Legal Status of Women in Ancient Egypt," in *Mistress of the House, Mistress of Heaven: Women in Ancient Egypt* (Ann Capel and Glenn Markoe, eds.), pp. 175–185, 215–217. Cincinnati: Cincinnati Art Museum, 1997.

Manniche, Lise, *Music and Musicians in Ancient Egypt*. London: The British Museum, 1991.

Robins, Gay, *Women in Ancient Egypt*. London: The British Museum, 1993.

Strouhal, Eugene, *Life of the Ancient Egyptians*. Norman, Okla.: University of Oklahoma Press, 1992.

Teeter, Emily, "Female Musicians in Pharaonic Egypt," in *Rediscovering the Muses: Women's Musical Traditions* (K. Marshall, ed.), pp. 68–91. Boston: Northeastern University, 1993.

Vogelsang-Eastwood, Gillian, *Egyptian Pharaonic Clothing*. Leiden: E. J. Brill, 1993.

Watson, Phillip, *Costumes of Ancient Egypt*. New York: Chelsea House, 1987.

Williams, Ronald J., "Scribal Training in Ancient Egypt," *Journal of the American Oriental Society* 92 (1972), 214–221.

*Chapter 8*

# LANGUAGE AND WRITING

Egyptian is grouped in the Afro-Asiatic (also known as Hamito-Semitic) language family, which consists of six branches: ancient Egyptian, Semitic (including Hebrew and Arabic), Berber (spoken to the west of Egypt), Chadic (spoken near Lake Chad), Cushitic (spoken in parts of Ethiopia, Somalia, and the Sudan), and Omotic (spoken in southwest Ethiopia). Egyptian, or Coptic, as the last stage of the language is called, was superseded by Arabic in the seventh century AD. It is now a dead language, although it is used for the liturgy of the Coptic Church of Egypt, much like Latin is used in the Catholic Church. The ancient Egyptian language is technically related to modern Egyptian Arabic, but the two languages are, for practical purposes, completely different.

According to Egyptian tradition, Thoth, the god of wisdom and learning, was the first to recognize that the sounds of speech could be conveyed through writing; some time in the primordial era when gods lived on earth, this knowledge of writing (called *medjut netcher,* "words of the god") was passed on to humankind. In actuality, the ancient Egyptian language is the second-oldest recorded language (after Sumerian). Traditionally, the advent of writing in Egypt has been placed in Dynasty 1 but excavations at Abydos in the 1990s have recovered ivory labels that indicate that the system dates to at least Dynasty 0. Since the last stage of the language – Coptic – is still used as the liturgical language of the Coptic Church, the Egyptian language can claim to have been used for more than 5,000 years, which is longer than any other.

The question of whether writing was introduced into Egypt or was an indigenous development remains open. Because the Egyptian and Sumerian systems are similar in some respects – namely the use of phonetic writing conveyed by pictographic scripts and the use of determinatives – and because other features of Mesopotamian culture are present in Egypt in the Late Predynastic and Archaic Periods, it has been argued that Sumerian was the original inspiration for the Egyptian written language. In spite of the fundamental similarities, however, most other details of the languages are different, especially the absence of vowels in written Egyptian.

## DECIPHERMENT OF HIEROGLYPHS

The last known written text in hieroglyphs dates to AD 394. The decimation of the priestly class (which was the last group to use hieroglyphic writing), the spread of

Christianity into Egypt, and the development of a simpler form of the written language (Coptic) brought about the extinction of this ancient script. When Horapollo, a native Egyptian, authored (in Greek) a work called the *Hieroglyphica* at the end of the fifth century AD, it is clear that the true nature of the writing system was already misunderstood. Horapollo combined dimly remembered and partly correct notions about sign values with outlandish and erroneous explanations involving alleged symbolic associations of the hieroglyphs. For example, he claimed that the hare hieroglyph was employed in the writing of the word "open," because a rabbit was ever alert and open-eyed. These totally false connections between the form of the hieroglyphs and their meaning were espoused and fostered by neo-Platonic philosophy. The idea that the hieroglyphs conveyed ancient and hidden wisdom prevailed throughout Roman antiquity and the Middle Ages to mystics of today, to the detriment of correct decipherment.

Although the knowledge of reading the hieroglyphic script was lost in antiquity, progress was gradually made in its decipherment. In 1636 Athanasius Kircher, a German priest and linguist, published his findings that Coptic, the liturgical language of the Christian Egyptian Church, was related to ancient Egyptian. In 1761 Jean Jacques Barthélemy suggested that the oval rings (cartouches) found in hieroglyphic texts enclosed the names of kings. These were important clues, but substantial work was not achieved until the discovery of the Rosetta Stone by the French in 1799 (see chapter 1). This granite slab measures 118 centimeters high, 77 centimeters wide, 30 centimeters thick and weighs 762 kilograms (fig. 8.1). It originally extended an additional 50 centimeters in height, but was broken in antiquity. On the stone's face is a text incised in three different scripts: hieroglyphs (referred to in the text as the "words of the gods") at the top, demotic ("the script of the documents") in the middle; and Greek ("the script of the islands," used by the ruling elite at the time of the inscription) at the bottom. The Greek section revealed that the text was a decree dated to year 9 of the reign of Ptolemy V (196 BC) dealing with the re-establishment of lands and holdings of Egyptian temples. The importance of the stone as a key to deciphering the hieroglyphs was immediately apparent, for the French correctly assumed that the three scripts all recorded the same text.

In 1802 two important contributions appeared, the first by a French scholar, Sylvestre de Sacy, and the second by de Sacy's student, a Swedish diplomat, Johan Åkerbald. Because most scholars assumed that the hieroglyphic text was purely symbolic (i.e., a picture represented a word) while the demotic text was phonetic (i.e., a picture represented a sound), de Sacy concentrated on the demotic section, trying to identify personal names known from the Greek text by searching for repeated groups of signs. He believed that this would enable him to identify the sound values of the demotic letters, which could ultimately reveal the signs of the alphabet. Though he was able to isolate the names Ptolemy and Alexander in demotic, he was unable to identify the phonetic values of the individual characters.

8.1 The Rosetta Stone. The surface is incised in three scripts; hieroglyphs (top); demotic (center); and Greek (bottom). The text is a decree of Ptolemy V (196 BC) regarding temple endowments.

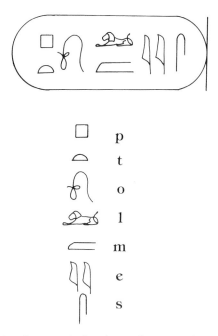

8.2a  The name Ptolemaios on the Rosetta Stone.

Åkerbald, following de Sacy's lead, managed to identify several proper names in the demotic, including Ptolemy, Alexander, Arsinoe, and Berenice. Furthermore, he was able to determine individual phonetic signs, eventually identifying twenty-nine "letters," of which approximately half were correct. Using those phonetic values, he was able to read several words whose phonetic values were known from Coptic. His success was limited by his false assumption that demotic was "alphabetic," when indeed, like hieroglyphic, it is a combination of systems.

The next major step in the decipherment of the hieroglyphs was made by the British linguist Thomas Young in 1814. Young is credited with definitely establishing that the hieroglyphs were not purely symbolic, but rather that they were related to demotic in that some signs were phonetic; indeed, he correctly surmised that demotic is essentially a cursive form of hieroglyphic. With this new assumption, Young was able to determine the phonetic values of the signs that appeared within the cartouches (fig. 8.2a), correctly reading the name Ptolemy.

Credit for the final decipherment of hieroglyphic Egyptian goes to the French linguist Jean-François Champollion. He worked on the same premise as Young, but he had an advantage in having access to additional sources with which to test the proposed phonetic values. In 1815 an obelisk inscribed in Greek and hieroglyphs had been discovered at Philae near Aswan. Using the texts from the obelisk, which contained the names Ptolemy and Cleopatra (fig. 8.2b), Champollion was able to verify and expand

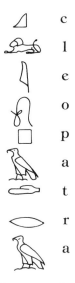

8.2b The name Cleopatra on the Rosetta Stone.

upon his list of phonetic values. This list of established phonemes increased even more through his work on cartouches at Abu Simbel, and by 1824 Champollion published his *Précis du Système Hiéroglyphique*, unequivocally establishing the phonetic character of the language.

Today, through the efforts of generations of Egyptologists and linguists, there are few texts that cannot be read with certainty, and scholarly discussions now tend to focus on the fine points of grammar and lexical questions.

## THE WRITTEN LANGUAGE

The ancient Egyptian written language is divided into five stages of development: Old Egyptian (2650–2135 BC), Middle Egyptian (2000–1750 BC), Late Egyptian (1550–700 BC), demotic (600 BC-AD 500) and Coptic (*ca.* AD 300 to the present). Greek was the language of the ruling elite during the Ptolemaic Period (332–30 BC), and it gradually became the standard for general administrative and daily purposes, though hieroglyphs continued to be used for religious purposes. It was superseded by Arabic after the conversion of Egypt to Islam in the seventh century. These stages of the language are based on the distinctive grammatical forms and orthography of each period. Middle Egyptian is considered to be the "classical" stage of the language, and it was employed for literary compositions long after it was replaced by Late Egyptian and even demotic. By the Late Period it was clearly anachronistic and would have sounded even more archaic than Chaucer's English sounds to modern English speakers. Late Egyptian included adaptations for recording words and sounds of foreign origin, such as the introduction of the "L" sound. Late Egyptian also expressed more of the colloquial language than the earlier stages, such as the use of the definite article. Hieroglyphic writing of the Ptolemaic Period was very distinctive in its orthography and grammar. Despite retaining many features of the archaic classical Middle Egyptian, it was characterized by cryptographic puns, the development of many new signs, and the use of acrophony (in which signs were combined and the phonetic value of the word was taken from each sign's first consonant). This more esoteric use of signs contributed to later assumptions that the ancient written language was entirely symbolic.

Old, Middle, and Late Egyptian were written in hieroglyphs. (The term "hieroglyph" comes from the Greek words *hiero*, meaning "sacred," and *glyphika*, meaning "carvings," because the ancient Egyptian script was closely associated with temples and religious structures.) Though several thousand individual signs are known, only about 800 were commonly used. Most of the pictographs were derived from the environment or daily life (e.g., animals, architectural elements, plants, and tools). There was no word division and virtually no punctuation. Hieroglyphs could be written horizontally or vertically, from right to left or left to right. In rare cases, they were written "retrograde," that is, in reverse order from bottom to top. The orientation of the signs depended upon their placement and use. One can determine sign direction most easily by observing the animal and human signs, all of which will face the beginning of the line (fig. 8.3).

Because the elaborate hieroglyphs were time-consuming to draw, Old, Middle, and Late Egyptian were usually written in a cursive script known as *hieratic* (fig. 8.4), from the Greek word *hieratikos,* "priestly." Hieratic was written in ink from right to left in either horizontal or vertical columns. Texts that refer to scribal schools indicate that scribes learned hieratic before progressing to hieroglyphs. Although it was often highly cursive and employed abbreviated combinations of signs (ligatures), the form of the script was firmly rooted in the more explicit hieroglyphs. The earliest extensive hieratic document extant dates to Dynasty 5 (*ca.* 2600 BC), and the latest to the third century AD.

From Dynasty 26 on, the demotic script was used for daily legal, administrative, and commercial purposes, while the formal hieroglyphs continued to be used in religious contexts such as in temple reliefs. (The name demotic is derived from the ancient Greek

8.3 A brief hieroglyphic text written (top) from left to right; (bottom) from right to left.

8.4 Hieratic script with hieroglyphic equivalent. The text is read right to left. It is part of a letter instructing the recipient to be very attentive to a business matter.

word *demotiks,* meaning "of the people.") A highly cursive script (fig. 8.5), demotic was written in horizontal lines from right to left. Based on hieratic, it was characterized by ligatures, abbreviations, and fewer determinatives. It was used almost exclusively on papyri and *ostraca*, although it was occasionally used in formal contexts on stone (e.g., the Rosetta Stone and Ptolemaic funerary stelae).

Coptic is the Egyptian language written in twenty-four Greek letters with the addition of six demotic signs which supply phonetic values not present in Greek (fig. 8.5). The term Coptic was derived from "gubti," an Arabic corruption of the Greek word for Egyptian, *Aiguptios*. Coptic is always written left to right in horizontal lines. Because vowels are written in Coptic, this script provides important clues to the vocalization of the earlier stages of the language. Coptic, being purely alphabetic, may have replaced demotic because it was an easier system and so was a more appropriate vehicle to record religious texts that were ultimately destined for the lay audience. Another factor that may have contributed to the replacement of demotic by Coptic during the Christian period was that demotic was associated with the pagan religious tradition.

On the basis of textual evidence modern scholars know that the earlier stages of Egyptian also had dialects. For example, a reference in Papyrus Anastasi I (Dynasty 19) alludes to dialects as "like a Delta man's conversation with a man of Elephantine." Yet the origins and real differences between dialects are hard to discern because the written language did not express the colloquial, and no vowels were written to help modern scholars reconstruct the pronunciation.

### THE PRINCIPLES OF WRITING

Ancient Egyptian combined phonetic signs with ideographic signs (ideograms), which convey their meaning through their form, and with determinatives, which have no phonetic value yet give an indication of the meaning of the word.

Phonetic signs can be alphabetic, conveying a single sound, such as 𓏤 (*b*) or 𓅓 (*m*); biliteral, the combination of two phonemes, such as 𓏠 (*mn*); or triliteral, the combination of three phonemes, such as 𓄤 (*nfr*). In ancient Egyptian there were twenty-four

*Egypt and the Egyptians*

## STANDARD EGYPTIAN SCRIPTS

| Hieroglyph | Sign | Phonetic value | Hieratic | Demotic | Coptic |
|---|---|---|---|---|---|
| | vulture | glottal stop | | | |
| | reed | I | | | |
| | forearm | ayin | | | omitted |
| | quail chick | w | | | |
| | foot | b | | | Π or ß |
| | stool | p | | | Π or ß |
| | horned viper | f | | | |
| | owl | m | | or | |
| | water | n | | | |
| | mouth | r | | [ ] | P or λ |
| | reed shelter | h | | | |
| | twisted flax | ḥ (heavily aspirated h) | | | or omitted |
| | placenta | ḫ (unvoiced laryngeal) | | | or |
| | animal's belly | ẖ (uncertain; laryngeal with no corresponding sound in English) | | | |
| | door bolt | s | | | |
| | folded cloth | s | | | |
| | pool | sh | | | |
| | hill | q | | | K, |
| | handled basket | k | | | K, |
| | jar stand | g | | | |
| | loaf | t | | | T, |
| | tethering rope | tj | | | , T |
| | hand | d | | ( ) | T |
| | snake | dj | | | |

8.5 Chart with the alphabetic hieroglyphic signs, their phonetic values and the hieratic, demotic, and Coptic equivalents. Note that hieratic and demotic are always written and read from right to left. The hieroglyph signs on this chart are also read from right to left.

alphabetic signs (fig. 8.5) and hundreds of bi-, tri-, and even quadriliteral signs. In many cases, the bi- and triliterals were accompanied by an alphabetic sign known as a phonetic complement that repeated some of the phonetic values of the complex sign. This led to some flexibility in how a word could be written; for example ☥ (*ankh*, "life") could also be written, ☥⁓ with the ⁓ (*n*) and ⊖ (*kh*) values being repeated.

Egyptian ideograms which could represent a complete word, also had a phonetic value (☉ *ra*, "sun," ⬚ *pr*, "house"). Some of these logograms could also be used as determinatives, which have no phonetic value but were used to distinguish between words of similar sounds. For example, in English the words "pair" and "pear" are homophones; an ancient Egyptian might have distinguished between the two by following the first with two strokes and the second with a drawing of a fruit. Determinatives were also helpful for refining the meaning of related words. To distinguish a scribe (the person) from a scribal document, the figure of a man ( 🪑 ) would be placed after the scribal palette to designate the former while a picture of a papyrus role ( ⟺ ) after the palette would designate the latter. The distinctive complexity of the determinatives also allowed them to function as word dividers.

The Egyptian script functioned according to the rebus principle, whereby symbols representing the sounds of actual objects that can be drawn were combined to form the pronunciation of abstract words that could not be conveyed by a picture. In other words, by utilizing this principle the English word "belief" might be conveyed by picturing a bee and a leaf. Because this system is essentially phonetic, the signs employed to spell many Egyptian words bear no meaningful relationship to their original use, having been employed solely for their phonetic value.

Hieroglyphic signs were always considered to have an aesthetic appeal, and they were regarded as small-scale art. As a result, balance and symmetry of inscriptions affected the way in which texts were written. Efforts were made to avoid unsightly gaps between signs, leading to the common practice of transposing signs. When an inscription framed a doorway, the signs to the left of the doorway faced the doorway (right to left), while those to the right side faced to the left (fig. 8.6). When used in conjunction with relief, inscriptions were always arranged according to their context and use. Thus, when used as dialogue or an identifying label for a figure who faced to the left, the signs would likewise face to the left. In other cases, a large-scale figure in a relief could substitute for the small seated man or women determinative that normally followed the writing of a personal name. Decorum also affected the way in which things were written – for instance, the names of gods would be written before other words to indicate the relative importance of the deity. This "honorific transposition" is very evident in royal names. For example, the name Tutankhamun ("living image of Amun") was written Amun-tut-ankh because the god Amun had precedence over the other elements of the name even though the correct pronunciation, indicated by its translation into other languages, was Tut-ankh-amun.

8.6 Hieroglyphic signs arranged symmetrically around a doorway at Medinet Habu. The signs to the left of the doorway are read from right to left; those on the right side are read from left to right. The text on the lintel is arranged symmetrically from a central hieroglyph (Dynasty 20).

## LITERACY

It is clear from the quantity and range of extant documents that writing played an important role in ancient Egyptian society, but it is highly unlikely that literacy was widespread among the general population. Scholars estimate that literacy averaged less than 1 percent during most of the Pharaonic Period and peaked at about 10 percent during the Graeco-Roman Period, when Greek was the official language of Egypt. Nevertheless, Egyptian texts on the subject indicate that literacy was desirable because it conferred status and provided a means of advancement to even the highest offices. In fact, a thorough training in scribal skills was considered an essential prerequisite for anyone with professional or political aspirations.

Basic reading and writing skills were taught in schools attached to temples, palaces, and government offices; more advanced training was obtained on the job in a system akin to an apprenticeship. School texts of the New Kingdom, which form the bulk of evidence on Egyptian education methods, indicate that reading and writing were learned by copying excerpts from classic works. The iconic/phonetic mixture of the writing system probably had much to do with how it was taught; because there was no alphabet to learn, long hours had to be spent memorizing many characters and entire phrases. Reading aloud and then copying the enunciated texts were a common way of learning – even pupils and scribes working alone would first call out the words then turn their attention to writing. This system of oral transmission of the language is indicated clearly in surviving texts filled with variant or erroneous spelling and botched or omitted phrases.

Like today, literacy in ancient Egypt covered a range of proficiency levels, from those who could only read and write their names to professional scribes. Scribal mistakes in texts on temple and tomb walls, and especially in cases where workmen were ordered to erase specific names, gives interesting insight that some artisans were fully literate, while others could only, with apparent difficulty, recognize certain words or groups of signs.

## WRITING, RELIGION, AND SECULAR LITERATURE

The ancient Egyptian script was far more than a means of communication. It had a religious potency unknown for any other writing system, for it had the capability to transcend the boundary of life and death. The best evidence for the Egyptian belief in this power are the pleas or requests – the so-called "letters to the dead" – from the living to a deceased family member or friend.

Representations in ancient Egypt had the ability to function as the object that they represented, hence a painting of a man bringing food to the tomb served to provide the deceased with eternal sustenance (see chapter 10). Because hieroglyphs were tiny

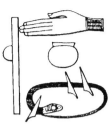

8.7 The serpent in this text has been "killed" with three knives (Dynasty 18).

pictures, they also had the ability to substitute for the material item. Thus, to erase a personal name was to erase the memory, and hence the eternal existence, of the deceased. Hieroglyphs of animals that were considered to be dangerous to the deceased, such as snakes or quail – which might bite or eat the offerings – could be rendered harmless by immobilizing them with representations of knives or drawing them without legs (fig. 8.7).

Although writing and religion were inextricably entwined, religious texts did not totally dominate the ancient literature. The genre that gives Egyptian writing its distinctive flair is tales: romantic poems and so-called instruction and wisdom texts. Stories were elaborate affairs, often culminating in an instructional or moral message. The Egyptians themselves acknowledged the intrinsic value of these works and looked upon them as creative endeavors. For modern scholars, the works are not only interesting in their own right but provide a window on the Egyptian psyche. As the texts show, the ancient Egyptians had a passion for fair play and a great capacity for humor and love.

## VOCALIZATION

Our knowledge of the original pronunciation of Egyptian is incomplete. Like Arabic and other Afro-Asiatic languages, written Egyptian was a purely consonantal system; that is, there were no signs to represent vowels. In such systems, written words are made up of a string of consonants and can only be pronounced properly by someone who knows the language. For example, when reading the classified advertisements in a newspaper, anyone who has shopped for an automobile can recognize and read the seller's abbreviation: 1993 Ford, red, 2dr, exc. cond., v-6, lw ml, ask. 4K obo, will neg. Although not strictly lacking in vowels, the abbreviations used are easily readable by anyone familiar with the English language and basic automobile terminology. In the same way, an Arabic speaker can read Arabic and an ancient Egyptian could read hieroglyphs, for knowledge of the spoken language allows the native speaker to insert the proper vowels even though they are not written. Obviously, such a system poses a problem for scholars trying to vocalize ancient Egyptian words written in hieroglyphs because no one knows with certainty how they were pronounced.

Coptic, the latest stage of Egyptian, provides some clues about how the ancient language was vocalized and how it sounded. Similarly, the transcription of Egyptian names in other foreign languages that can be vocalized (e.g., Greek, Akkadian) also help reconstruct the vocalic structure of the language. For example, the official names of Ramesses II, which in our modern pidgin are pronounced "Ramesses-mery-Amun, User-Maat-re Setepenre," were more likely pronounced "Riamesesa mai-amána Wasmú`re`a."

For many ancient words, however, there are no known referents to their pronunciation. Egyptologists, therefore, have adopted a simple rule to make the consonantal groups pronounceable: they insert a vowel (usually an "a" or an "e") between each consonant. Through this method *snb* would be pronounced seneb. Additionally, it has been agreed to pronounce certain consonants that have vowel-like qualities as a, i, and u. For example 𓇋 is pronounced "i" or "ee", the chick (𓅱) as "w," and the vulture (𓄿) is pronounced like an "a." These pronunciations are totally artificial, and in all probability an ancient Egyptian would not be able to understand a modern scholar speaking the ancient language, even though they could communicate effortlessly in writing.

An inevitable problem associated with vocalizing a non-vocalic written language is that different scholars spell the ancient words differently. Despite the existence of rough conventions, scholars whose native languages differ will emphasize different pronunciations. For example, Queen *Nfrt-ity* is usually vocalized as Nefertiti in English, while Germans say Nofretete. An example of the potential variety of spellings/pronunciations that exist can be gleaned from looking at the name of King Djoser's vizier, *Iim htp* (Imhotep), which has thirty-four different modern documented spellings.

## SUMMARY

Ancient Egyptian in its written form is among the oldest recorded languages in our history. An offshoot of Egyptian art, it appeared in an embryonic form during the late Predynastic Period and continued to be used for 3,000 years until it was superseded (for other than liturgical uses) by Greek during the Ptolemaic Period. Philologists have divided the long history of the language into five stages that are roughly equivalent to Egypt's political history: Old, Middle, and Late Egyptian, demotic, and Coptic.

Much of the difficulty in deciphering Egyptian stems from the fact that the system combined phonetic and non-phonetic signs. Although fundamentally different from our own written language, ancient Egyptian possessed a highly evolved grammar that was capable of expressing a full range of tense and aspect, grammatical features that are poorly expressed even in English. Originally limited to matters of business and state (including religion), writing expanded to fill all niches of society from personal letters to religious, legal, and business documents. Today, the ancient language is well understood and virtually all texts can be read with certainty.

## FURTHER READING

Baines, John, "Literacy and Ancient Egyptian Society," *Man* 18 (1983), 572–599.

Davies, W. Vivian, *Egyptian Hieroglyphs*. Berkeley/Los Angeles, Ca.: University of California Press, 1987.

Foreman, Werner and Stephen Quirke, *Hieroglyphs and the Afterlife in Ancient Egypt*. Norman, Okla.: University of Oklahoma Press, 1996.

Gardiner, Alan, *Egyptian Grammar*. Oxford: The Griffith Institute/ Oxford University Press, 1957.

Harris, James R. (ed.), *The Legacy of Egypt*. Oxford: Oxford University Press, 1971.

Hawkins, Jacquetta D., "The Origin and Dissemination of Writing in Western Asia," in *The Origins of Civilization* (P. R. S. Moorey, ed.), pp. 128–166. Oxford: The Clarendon Press, 1979.

Loprieno, Antonio, *Ancient Egyptian: A Linguistic Introduction*. Cambridge: Cambridge University Press, 1995.

Parkinson, Richard and Stephen, Quirke, *Papyrus*. Austin, Tex.: University of Texas Press, 1995.

Quirke, Stephen and Carol Andrews, *The Rosetta Stone*. New York: Harry Abrams, 1988.

Ray, John D., "The Emergence of Writing in Egypt," *World Archaeology* 17 (1986), 307–316.

    "The Mesopotamian Influence on Ancient Egyptian Writing," in *Egypt in Africa* (T. Celenko, ed.), pp. 38–39. Indianapolis: Indianapolis Museum of Art, 1995.

Zauzich, Karl-Theodor, *Hieroglyphs without Mystery* (transl. A. Roth). Austin, Tex.: University of Texas Press, 1992.

## Chapter 9

# HOMES FOR THE PEOPLE, THE PHARAOH, AND THE GODS

Egypt was one of the first cultures to develop an identifiable architectural style. Egyptian architecture evolved over several millennia to meet the physical, religious, and aesthetic needs of the people. Yet although there were stylistic and technical developments in architecture during the 3,000-year span of pharaonic history, these developments were balanced against the natural conservatism of the ancient Egyptians, and many of the same decorative forms are seen in the architecture from the Predynastic Period to the New Kingdom.

## BUILDING TECHNIQUES AND MATERIALS

The simplest structures were made of woven reed mats stretched between tamarisk wood poles or reed bundles. The mats that formed the walls were gathered and bound at the corners, making a characteristic rounded edge; copied later in stone, this decorative form is known as *"torus molding."* Frayed ends of the reed mats extended from the top of the structure. When left loose, they became the antecedent of the *cavetto cornice*; bound, they probably became the antecedent of the *khekeru* frieze (fig. 9.1). Roofs of reed structures were either flat, made of thin poles covered with mats and mud, or arched, built of bundles of reeds much like the large reed houses (*mudif*) of the marsh Arabs in southern Iraq.

Egypt had abundant sources of water, alluvial soil, and straw from which to make mud-brick, which was the dominant building material of the late Predynastic through the Dynastic Period. Because of their insulating capacity, mud-brick structures were well adapted to the local environment: interior rooms stayed cool in the summer and warm in the winter. The method of making bricks is shown in several Middle Kingdom tomb scenes and in the Dynasty 18 tomb of Rekhmire (fig. 9.2). First, the hard earth was broken up with a hoe and made into mud by adding water. Straw and sand were added to increase cohesiveness, and the mixture was kneaded with the feet until it was of the right consistency. The mud was then placed in a wooden, rectangular mold without a top or bottom. Once the mud had set, the mold was lifted off, leaving the brick on the ground to dry in the sun. Bricks were dried on one side for three days, then turned over and dried for a week. Dried bricks were amazingly strong; bricks containing only fine sand, for example, could withstand stress loads up to 52 kilograms per square centimeter. Bricks made of straw and coarser sand were not as strong, but

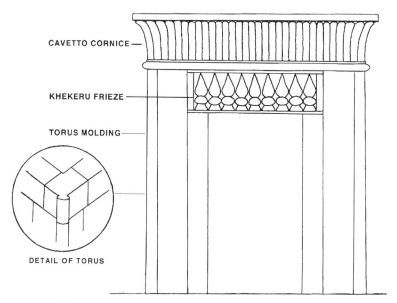

CAVETTO CORNICE ——

KHEKERU FRIEZE ——

TORUS MOLDING ——

DETAIL OF TORUS

9.1 Architectural features: torus molding; *khekeru* frieze and cavetto cornice.

could still withstand a considerable stress load. Over time, various techniques were developed to increase the stability of mud-brick construction. Walls could be stabilized by projecting pillars alternating with concave recesses creating a niched pattern that was employed on the exterior of early private and royal tombs (fig. 9.3). The mammoth brick walls that surrounded cities and temple precincts (those surrounding the temple precinct at El Kab are 566 by 548 meters and 11.3 meters thick) were built in sections, usually in alternating courses of headers and stretchers, and stabilized by layers of mats placed under every few courses of brick.

Perhaps the earliest example of stone architecture comes from the Dynasty 1 tomb of King Den at Abydos where granite and limestone were used for floors and roofing supports. The first large-scale use of stone dates to the Dynasty 3 pyramid complex of King Djoser (see fig. 10.8). In that monument, stone was used in direct imitation of mud-brick, for the limestone blocks employed at the Djoser complex are small, much like mud-bricks. It was not until the early Dynasty 4 pyramids of Snefru at Meidum and Dashur that stone of monumental proportions was quarried and employed.

Stone was extracted from mines or open quarries that were cut back in stepped patterns. Limestone was the favored building stone of the Old Kingdom, but in the New Kingdom sandstone quarries in Upper Egypt were exploited, leading to greater use of that stone. Granite, being much harder to quarry and work, was used more sparingly, primarily for thresholds, lintels, sarcophagi, and for the portcullis and lining of the interior passages of the Old Kingdom pyramids. The choice of tools and techniques for extracting stone from quarries depended upon the type of stone. Limestone and

9.2 Brick-making, tomb of Rekhmire at Thebes. To the left, men draw water from the pond to mix with earth (center) to form the mud bricks. To the upper center and right of the scene, men form the bricks in a rectangular mold, stacking them to dry in the sun (center). To the right, the dried bricks are stacked to be transported to the building site (Dynasty 18).

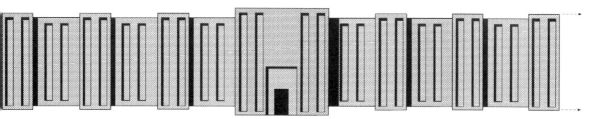

9.3 Niched "palace façade" wall treatment on the enclosure wall of the Stepped Pyramid complex at Saqqara (Dynasty 3).

sandstone, which are relatively soft, were cut with saws aided by abrasive quartz sand or chisels driven with hardwood hammers. Copper tools were used until the late New Kingdom when bronze gradually began to replace copper as the material of choice. Iron was never extensively employed during the Pharaonic Period for tools. Hard stone (e.g., granite, diorite, quartzite) was worked with dolerite pounders (which weighed up to 5 kilograms), for copper was ineffective against such stone. Fire was banked against hard stone to help fracture its surface, but the use of wetted wooden wedges to break hard stone is not documented before the Late Period (500 BC). Stone surfaces were finished with progressively finer chisels and finally by rubbing the surface with a hard polishing stone until it was smooth.

### DOMESTIC ARCHITECTURE

Compared to funerary architecture, comparatively little is known of ancient Egyptian domestic architecture of any period. One of the main problems in recovering information about houses is that they were built of perishable materials; additionally, until recent years there was little emphasis upon excavation of domestic – as opposed to monumental – architecture. Our best sources come from the remains of houses at Kahun (Lahun), Tell el Daba, Amarna, and Deir el Medina, none of which were typical towns.

Other than their dimensions and roughly oval shape, little is known of the earliest houses that date to the Acheulean Period (100,000 years BP), yet they remain among the earliest constructed human shelters: only the house rings at Olduvai are older. Evidence of house structures in the Middle and Upper Paleolithic is meager, but the remains of light reed shelters daubed with mud have been recovered from a number of Neolithic and early Predynastic sites. These structures, found at Merimde, Omari, Badari, and elsewhere, were round or oval and made of poles of pliable tree branches, palm ribs, or thick reeds. Floors were often slightly subterranean, excavated to a depth of about 30 to 40 centimeters and roughly circular in shape. The poles were often stuck in the earth around the edge of the pit wall, which was used as support to help bend the poles or bundles of reeds into a dome or vault. In at least some instances, rather than tapering inward to form a dome, the poles were left standing straight and cut at even lengths, creating vertical walls. A tall center pole was used to support a conical roof that was thatched from the center down to the walls. At the early Predynastic site of Hememieh, the lower half of the house walls were made of packed mud. The Hememieh structures, called "hut circles" by the excavators, had 35 centimeter-thick mud walls that stood slightly less than 1 meter tall. On the basis of impressions found in the dried mud, it is postulated that traditional thatching or woven matting was affixed atop the mud hut circle foundation (fig. 9.4).

Shelters at the early Predynastic site of Mahasna (Naqada I) are the earliest-known rectangular houses. Like the traditional circular houses, they appear to have been built of posts and interlaced branches plastered with mud, although their walls intersected at right angles. It is difficult to know, however, if these rectangular structures represent houses, enclosures for animals, or storage facilities. Evidence from Maadi, for example, suggests that although the people lived in round houses, animals were kept in rectangular corrals or pens.

Documented by clay models recovered from late Naqada II/early Naqada III burials at El Amrah, the earliest mud-brick domestic architecture was in the form of rectangular homes with flat roofs. These structures resemble the later Dynastic houses and, in many ways, the peasant houses of modern rural Egypt.

Excavations of Archaic and Old Kingdom domestic deposits are extremely rare, so the design of early Dynastic houses has been inferred from clay models recovered from First Intermediate Period tombs. These so-called "soul houses," thought to represent homes for the soul, are in all probability based on actual houses, and archaeological excavations of Middle and New Kingdom residential sites have tended to support this conclusion. These models represent various house types, ranging from a simple rectangular structures to more elaborate two-storied structures with porches (fig 9.5).

9.4 Hememieh hut circle.

Perhaps as early as the late Archaic Period, but certainly by the Old Kingdom, the standard Egyptian house type was a multi-roomed, rectangular, mud-brick home. Reminiscent of a temple layout, the main entrance of the standard house led to a reception area; private quarters were located in the back, shielded from prying eyes and ears. Based on excavations at Tell el Amarna, this design was still in general use by the middle and upper classes of society during the New Kingdom.

The small size and simple design of the average Egyptian home can be explained by factors related to Egyptian culture as much as economics. Unlike Euro-American culture, the ancient Egyptian concept of living space extended beyond the confines of the house walls. In ancient Egypt, like in modern peasant villages, many activities were carried out in the streets, on the roof, or in the general vicinity of the house. Spinning, weaving, playing games, eating, and any number of other domestic activities all occurred outside the home. In short, the ancient Egyptians' concept of private and public living space differed from that of our own, a difference reflected in the space requirements deemed essential for a home.

Middle Kingdom domestic architecture has been elucidated by excavations at the site of Kahun, a government-controlled community located at the entrance to the Fayum. Here, workers of the pyramid of Senwosert II were supplied homes and wages

(*a*)

(*b*)

9.5 Egyptian soul houses and offering trays showing types of domestic architecture: 9.5a simple hut enclosure 9.5b house with roof terrace 9.5c multiple storied home with stairs and portico (Dynasties 11–12).

(c)

9.5 (*cont.*)

in exchange for their labor. The village (fig. 9.6) was constructed on a grid system, with 200 houses set alongside designated streets and the entire complex walled and guarded. Granaries of varying size were located around the house, and sometimes additional rooms for servants were present either on the roof or main floor. In the eastern section of the town were a dozen extremely large houses; most encompassed an area of 1,000 square meters, and one house actually exceeded 2,400 square meters! Comprised of sixty to seventy rooms, these houses most likely belonged to the social elite of the community. In the center of each was a large open courtyard with a shady portico leading to one or more reception rooms with ceilings supported by two to four wooden pillars. Other exits led to the kitchen, a row of storage rooms, and servant's quarters. At the end of a long hall were the owner's private rooms and those reserved for guests.

The best archaeological evidence for New Kingdom domiciles comes from Tell el

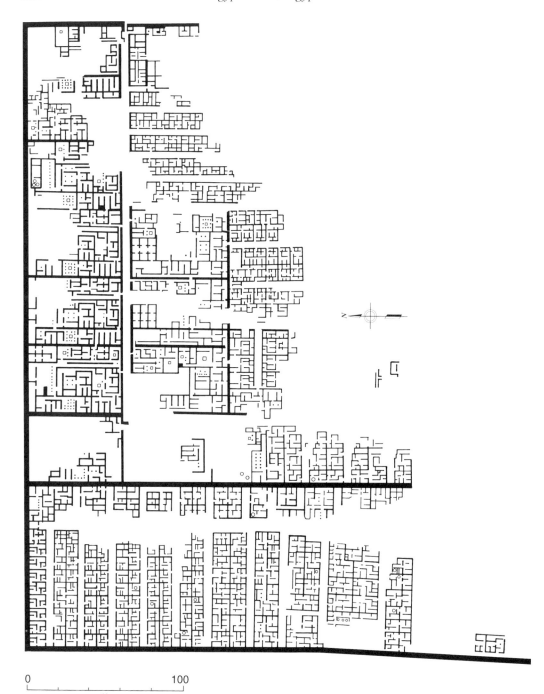

0                100

m

9.6  Plan of residential quarter at Kahun. Smaller houses are arranged in rows (bottom) while a group of larger "mansions" are grouped to the upper left (Dynasty 12).

Amarna, the capital city of King Akhenaten (Dynasty 18). It is difficult to assess how representative of the rest of Egypt the Amarna houses are, for Amarna was a planned community that was occupied for only about twenty years. Nevertheless, it does not seem likely that new building methods or styles of domestic architecture would have been created just for this site; indeed, images of houses that occur in Amarna tombs and in the tombs at Thebes show many similarities.

Although it would be difficult to find two identical Amarna houses, the same elements are repeated throughout all homes albeit in slightly different metrical proportions and combinations (fig. 9.7). The main feature was a square, central reception or living room. At one end of this room was a low brick divan or dais used by the owners of the house when receiving guests; at the other end was an area lined with stone or plaster, presumably used for washing. The ceiling of the reception room was usually supported by one or more columns, and small openings high up on the walls were designed to catch any outside breeze and circulate the room's air. Adjacent to the central room were storage areas and the more private domestic quarters, principally the bedrooms. Remains of walls and floors painted with motifs such as birds, marshes, and flowers indicate that the interior of house was, at least in some cases, painted. In many, if not most, houses a stairway led to the roof where a light structure for summer sleeping was sometimes located. Because bread and beer were dietary staples, most houses, even modest ones, had granaries, usually simple dome- or beehive-like structures or larger cylindrical towers covered with a cupola and built on a platform in rows on both sides of the house or on the roof.

Private quarters, particularly bathing areas and lavatories, are exceptionally well preserved at Amarna, allowing modern researchers an unusual glimpse into the daily life of the ancient Egyptians. In the larger houses a bathing area and a separate lavatory were often located next to the bedroom. The mud-brick walls of the bathroom were faced with thin limestone slabs, and the floor immediately below the facing usually had a slight depression to hold water that was poured over the person bathing. A drain at one side emptied the water either through the wall of the house to the outside or into a large pot set into the floor of the bathroom. (In one house of moderate size the outlet through the wall was a tubular ceramic vessel with the bottom knocked out; the water then flowed into a conduit that led to a large pottery vessel containing a small dish probably used to bail out the collected water.) Lavatories consisted of a wood or stone seat supported on low walls over a pottery receptacle. Some lavatories were equipped with a small box of sand to throw onto the waste material.

The houses at Deir el Medina are another source of information on domestic architecture of the New Kingdom. Like Amarna, this village was atypical, for it was a company town built expressly for housing the men who worked in the Valley of the Kings. Although the town plan was changed several times, by the Ramesside Period

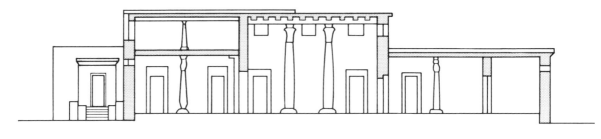

SECTION

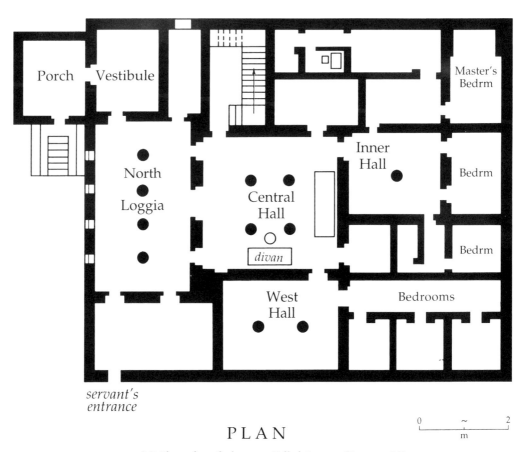

PLAN

9.7  Floor plan of a house at Tell el Amarna (Dynasty 18).

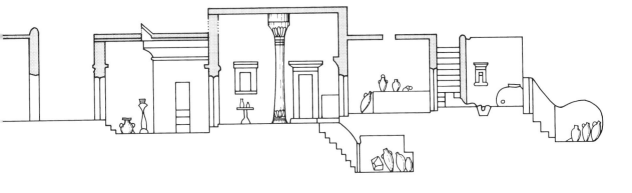

SECTION

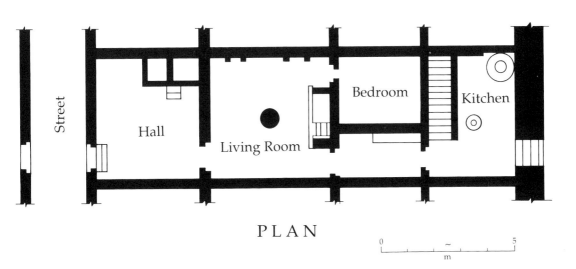

PLAN

9.8 Plan of a house at Deir el Medina, Thebes (Dynasty 19).

the settlement contained seventy houses, most of which were row houses with common walls. The houses (fig. 9.8), which measure approximately 5 by 15 meters, had four rooms: an entrance hall, a central roofed room with a ceiling supported by one or two columns, and back storage rooms. Additional storage areas were located in the cellar, and cooking was done in a walled enclosure behind the house. A stairway gave access to the roof, which may have been used for sleeping in fair weather or for additional storage.

Although no actual examples of multiple-story domiciles have survived from the New Kingdom, representations and models of houses (fig. 9.9) indicate that they could be two or even three stories, presumably in areas where land was at a premium. One

9.9 A three-story townhouse, as shown in the tomb of Dheutynef at Thebes. The house sheltered a variety of people and occupations related to the household. Weavers work in the basement; the major family and reception rooms were on the ground floor and upper floors. Rounded granaries were located on the roof. Slender columns in the form of lotus and papyrus flowers support the ceilings. (Dynasty 18).

such depiction shows that the first floor had a number of rooms for receiving guests and conducting business for the estate, while the second floor was devoted to family activities, a dining room, and bedrooms. A staircase led from the first to second floor and onto the roof, where servants' quarters and granaries were located and fuel was stored.

THE PALACE: HOUSE OF THE KING

In spite of the prominence of the king in Egyptian society, there are tremendous difficulties in discussing the form of the royal palace. One of the biggest problems is the definition of "palace," for there were a variety of structures associated with the king: large complexes that seem to have housed the royal family and their retainers; administrative centers that do not have residential quarters; and ceremonial palaces that were attached to the cult or funerary/royal temples and which may have never actually been used by the living king (see chapter 10). Determining which form (or forms) was the actual residence is extremely difficult – even the fundamental question of whether the New Kingdom royal domicile at Thebes stood on the east or the west bank has yet to be definitively answered.

Much of our information about the appearance of the earliest royal residences comes from funerary architecture (the false door of chapels, tomb superstructures, and sarcophagi) that, according to texts, are said to have imitated the royal residence. These structures are rectangular, with the so-called "palace façade" (fig. 9.3). According to the representations the lower section of the facade was hung with colored mats, and the door posts were surmounted by a drum lintel. The doorway was closed with double doors or by a rolled mat that descended like a window shade.

The Malkata complex in western Thebes, built by Amunhotep III (Dynasty 18), is generally considered to have been a residential palace for it comprises a sprawling group of buildings that could easily accommodate the king and his entire retinue. The buildings at Malkata were built of mud-brick, and the interior walls and floors of many of the rooms were once covered with brightly painted plaster. The rooms were roofed with wooden beams supported by wooden columns. Stone was used sparingly, mainly for column bases, thresholds, and the dais of the king. The site is dominated by the Palace of the King, located to the south of a large, open-air audience hall. The Palace of the King (fig. 9.10) consists of a long, narrow, columned hall flanked by a series of smaller rooms, perhaps for the king's family. The palace was equipped with three audience halls (A–C) of varying size, identified by a raised dais for the throne of the king and emplacements for columns that supported a canopy over the throne. The Malkata complex included three other large buildings designated as "palaces," each perhaps associated with the reception rooms of the king's major wives. Residential rooms and service areas were separate from the state/residential buildings. The absence of strict zoning is evidenced by a group of modest private houses that stood between the open air audience hall and the Palace of the King.

Like Malkata, the city of Amarna built by Akhenaten (Dynasty 18) contained several palaces and a sprawling complex of buildings and private houses. Five structures at Amarna have been identified as palaces, although the distinction in their function is not clear. The Northern Palace (fig. 9.11) was a walled structure of approximately

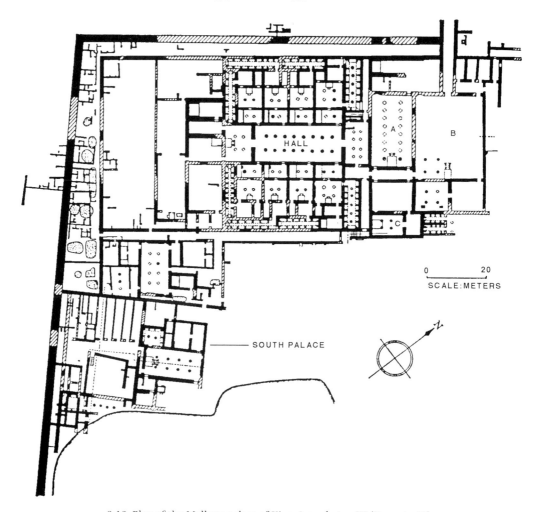

9.10 Plan of the Malkata palace of King Amunhotep III (Dynasty 18).

16,675 square meters built around a central pool. This huge structure did not contain living apartments, hence it may have been an administrative rather than a residential palace. The throne room was centrally located on the east side of the palace, in imitation of a temple sanctuary (see below). The Northern Palace also included animal stalls, an aviary, and open air chapels for the worship of the Aten. Like most administrative buildings, the structure was built of mud-brick and stone was employed only for column bases and thresholds. As at Malkata, the floors and walls were covered with painted plaster.

The palace of Merneptah (Dynasty 19) at Memphis was located within a temple complex. It combined features of the Malkata structures and the Northern Palace at

THRONE ROOM

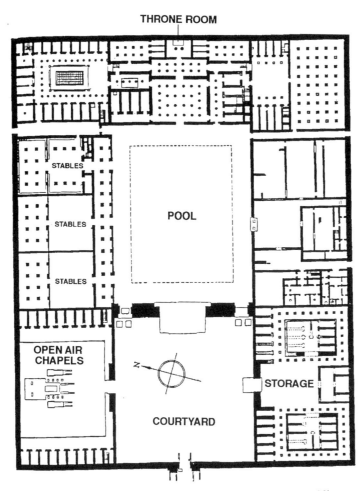

STABLES

STABLES

POOL

STABLES

OPEN AIR
CHAPELS

N

STORAGE

COURTYARD

9.11  Plan of the North Palace at Tell el Amarna (Dynasty 18).

Amarna in that it is clearly ceremonial, yet it includes an abbreviated version of a residence. This structure (fig. 9.12), built of mud-brick with stone thresholds and column
bases, was over 3,000 square meters in size. The central court led into a pillared vesti-
bule and throne room. The walls were painted in bright primary colors, and some areas
were inlaid with faience tiles and covered with gold leaf. The throne room (fig. 9.13),
measuring 12 by 19 meters, was furnished with a richly decorated dais. Like the throne
room at Amarna and like the sanctuary of the god in a temple (see below), the throne
room in Merneptah's palace was located in the back of the structure. Behind the throne
room were the private chambers of the king, including a sleeping room, a lavatory, and
an elaborate bathing chamber. Adjacent to the palace's main entrance was a window-
like balcony reached by a short flight of steps. This architectural feature is well known

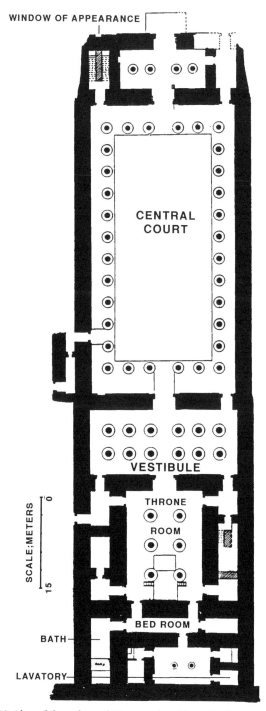

9.12 Plan of the palace of Merneptah at Memphis (Dynasty 19).

9.13 Reconstruction of the throne room in the palace of Merneptah at Memphis (Dynasty 19). Drawn and restored by Mary Louise Baker, 1920.

from representations in tombs and from funerary palaces – it was the "window of appearance" from which the king would be viewed by his subjects.

## TEMPLES: HOUSES OF THE GODS

Egyptian temples were built to house the gods, and the architectural forms employed in temples were intended to reflect the cosmos and the idea of eternal regeneration. The sanctuary of the god represented the mound of creation from which all life developed. Ceilings were decorated with stars of the vault of heaven or with constellations. Monumental columns represented the pillars that supported the heavens, and the column shafts mimicked the aquatic plants (lotus or papyrus) that grew from the watery abyss from which all life began. The enormous double gateways (*pylons*) that formed the entrance to the temples were symbolic of the horizon, evoking the idea of eternal rebirth with the rising sun. The alternation of open and closed spaces created a rhythm of darkness and light, eliciting ideas of birth, death, and rebirth.

Temples were built as acts of royal patronage in which the king demonstrated his devotion to the god. Temples were usually rebuilt, enlarged, and modified over thousands of years, and each act of pious construction was incised with the name of the pharaoh who commissioned the work. The sacred nature of temple precincts was enduring, and it is very common for one temple to overlay another. At the site of Hierakonpolis, for example, a New Kingdom wall stands atop a Middle Kingdom temple that was built on the ruins of an Old Kingdom temple, which in turn had been built on the ruins of a Predynastic temple.

Every town or settlement in Egypt had its own temples or shrines. Even though certain gods were often more popular in one region or another, deities were not strictly geographically designated, and temples of a specific god could be found in many areas of Egypt. It is not always possible to determine why temples were located in specific locations, other than the fact that, once established, the area was generally revered and maintained. Each temple or part of a complex temple had a specific name; the Luxor Temple was referred to as the "Southern Enclosure of the God Amun," while the temple of Thutmose III at Karnak was "Splendid is the Monument."

The earliest temples were constructed of mud-brick, thatching, and other light materials, so their remains are not well preserved. Hieroglyphic depictions record several different forms, most of them simple, open tent-like shrines with vaulted roofs. Texts and later representations suggest that there were two main forms of shrines, one associated with the north ( 𓉐 ) and one with the south ( 𓉔 ). The temples in the *heb sed* courtyard of the Dynasty 3 pyramid complex of Djoser (figs. 9.3, 9.14, 10.11) are some of the best evidence for these early forms. Although stone, the Djoser temples appear to have copied the design of the earlier perishable temples, suggesting that the walls of the early temples were mats stretched on poles and that the characteristic features of later architecture (torus molding and cavetto cornices) were well established quite early.

Chapels of the Old Kingdom often have three sanctuaries arranged side by side in the back of the structure. The multiple chapels may have been to accommodate statues of triads of gods which imitated the nuclear family of mankind.

Middle Kingdom temples that have been identified and excavated are relatively few. Those at Ezbet Rushdi (Amunemhet I) and Medinet Maadi (Amunemhet III) retained the three chapels of the Old Kingdom temple but added a forecourt or columned hall in front of the triple sanctuary. The Middle Kingdom temple at Tod (Senwosert I) included a sanctuary for a sacred boat, a feature that became standard during the New Kingdom and later.

9.14 Detail of a shrine with arched roof line symbolizing Upper Egypt in the jubilee courtyard of the Stepped Pyramid complex at Saqqara (Dynasty 3).

Our evidence for temples of the New Kingdom is much fuller. There is much variation in temple plan, mainly because many temples were built over a long period of time, with successive kings making additions. Hence the "front" of the temple was periodically absorbed into the temple proper as new façades were constructed. The best and largest example of this process of augmentation is the Temple of Amun at Karnak, with a central enclosure measuring 550 by 520 meters (fig. 9.15). The gateway, or pylon, of New Kingdom temples symbolized the horizon. Closed with two enormous wood doors, the pylon was usually decorated in sunk relief and carved and painted with scenes of the king slaughtering his enemies, thereby mythically ensuring those victories for eternity. Tall cedar flagpoles, topped by colored pennants, were inset into recesses in the façade. The exterior of New Kingdom temples was also typically ornamented with a pair of obelisks. Progressing through the pylon, one usually entered an open court, the walls of which were decorated with scenes of the king making offerings to the gods, with special emphasis given to scenes of the god who resided in the temple. Courts were sometimes ringed by a *portico* (rows of columns) or filled with columns (*hypostyle hall*). A series of pylons, courts, and hypostyle halls led to the

9.15 Reconstruction of the Karnak complex at Thebes. The temple of Amun surrounds the rectangular sacred lake (center). The temple of Khonsu is located in the right corner of the Amun enclosure while the Temple of Mut (far right) is connected to the Amun temple by an avenue of sphinxes. The smaller temple of Montu is in its own enclosure to the north (far left). Each temple is composed of a series of gateways (pylons) and open or closed courtyards. Each temple was considered to be the abode of the particular god. The hundreds of priests who worked in the temples attending to the needs of the deity lived in small houses within and outside the walls.

entrance of the sanctuary. As one approached this "bedroom" of the god, the levels of the floor rose, the ceilings became lower, and the light levels dropped, creating an atmosphere of sanctity appropriate to the god's private chambers. The actual statue of the god resided in a shrine (*naos*) that was closed with double wooden doors. The naos, whose roof was, at least in some temples, in the form of a pyramid ( 🏛 ), was symbolic of the primeval mound from which all life sprang.

Some temples were connected by processional walkways lined with sphinxes. The temple of Amun at Karnak was linked to the temple of Mut and the Temple of Luxor – two and a half kilometers away – by such processional walkways. Most temples, even those some distance from the Nile, were connected to the river by a system of canals. A quay at the front of the temple allowed provisions for the temple to be unloaded and enabled the procession of the god to travel by water.

### SUMMARY

Architecture is one of the most distinctive features of Egyptian civilization. Unfortunately, relatively little is known about domestic architecture – even royal palaces – because such structures were made of perishable materials (reed or mud-brick). In contrast, temples are well documented because they, as the eternal homes of the god, were normally built of stone.

The standard Egyptian house type in most periods was a multi-roomed, rectangular mud-brick structure. By modern Western standards, ancient domiciles were generally small and simple, although some were multi-storied. Many daily activities, such as weaving, eating, and cooking, were performed outside the house, often in a courtyard behind the main building. Larger homes were self-contained estates with granaries, stables, and rooms for house staff.

Royal "palaces" took various forms: sprawling residential centers for the king and his entire court; smaller administrative centers where the king did not actually reside; and ceremonial structures associated with the king's cult. Palace architecture was closely related to that of the cult temples; for example the king's throne room mimicked the god's naos, reinforcing the divinity of the king.

Temples were built to house the cult statues of the gods. Composed of a series of standard architectural features (pylons, columns, and sanctuary), temples evoked the mythical conception of the creation of the world. The king was a patron of the temple, and temple building was a sign of piety. Most existing temples do not follow a single unified plan, but rather they were modified and expanded as successive kings added to the structure.

FURTHER READING

Arnold, Dieter, *Building in Egypt: Pharaonic Stone Masonry*. Oxford: Oxford University Press, 1991.

Arnold, Felix, "A Study of Egyptian Domestic Architecture," *Varia Aegyptiaca* 5 (1989), 75–93.

Bietak, Manfred (ed.), *Haus und Palast im alten Ägypten*. Vienna: Vienna der Österreichischen Akademie der Wissenschaften, vol. 14, 1996.

Fischer, Clarence S., "The Eckley B. Coxe Jr Expedition," *The Museum Journal, The University Museum, Philadelphia* 8(7) (1917), 211–225.

Frankfort, Henri and John D. S. Pendlebury, *The City of Akhenaten, Part II: The North Suburb and the Desert Altars* (with a contribution by H. Fairman), 40th Excavation Memoir. London: The Egypt Exploration Society, 1933.

Kemp, Barry J., *Ancient Egypt: Anatomy of a Civilization*. London: KPI, 1991.

"The Early Development of Towns in Egypt," *Antiquity* 51 (1977), 185–200.

"The City of el-Amarna as a Source for the Study of Urban Society in Ancient Egypt," *World Archaeology* 9 (1977), 123–139.

"Temple and Town in Ancient Egypt," in *Man, Settlement and Urbanism: Proceedings of a Meeting at the Research Seminar in Archaeology and Related Subjects at the Institute of Archaeology, London University* (P. Ucko, R. Tringham, and G. W. Dimbleby, eds.), pp. 657–680. London: Duckworth Press, 1972.

O'Connor, David, "Mirror of the Cosmos: The Palace of Merenptah," in *Fragments of a Shattered Visage: The Proceedings of the International Symposium on Ramesses the Great* (Edward Bleiberg and Rita Freed, eds.), pp. 167–198. Memphis, Tenn.: Institute of Egyptian Art and Archaeology, 1991.

Schafer, Byron (ed.), *Temples of Ancient Egypt*. Ithaca, N.Y.: Cornell University Press, 1997.

Spencer, A. Jeffrey, *Brick Architecture in Ancient Egypt*. Warminster: Aris and Phillips, 1979.

*Early Egypt: The Rise of Civilization in the Nile Valley*. Norman, Okla.: University of Oklahoma Press, 1993.

Uphill, Eric P. , *Egyptian Towns and Cities*. Aylesbury: Shire, 1988.

## Chapter 10

## THE QUEST FOR ETERNITY

One of the most characteristic features of ancient Egyptian culture is the awareness of death and the preparations that were made for the end of life. The attention and resources that the Egyptians lavished upon death might lead one to assume that they were obsessed with death and lived only to die. On the contrary, texts such as the Old Kingdom autobiography of Hordjedef relates "depressing for us is death, it is life that we hold in esteem" (Morenz 1973: 187), and the biography of Taimehotep (*ca.* 35 BC) clearly states that death was not welcomed:

> As for death "Come" is its name,
> All those that he calls to him come to him immediately;
> Their hearts afraid through dread of him.
> He snatches the son from his mother
> Frightened, they all plead before him,
> But he does not listen to them

> (Lichtheim 1980: 63).

The Egyptians' solution to the frightening prospect of death was to transform the end of life into something understandable – death became a simple transition from the life they knew to eternal existence in a realm that was a mirror image of the living.

The Egyptian conception of the mechanics of this transition between life and death was complex. They believed that the soul was composed of different aspects. One part was the *ka*, the life energy of the individual and essentially a physical double of the person. It was depicted in the same form as the living person, in some cases with the hieroglyph for *ka* (⊔) on the head of the figure. Although believed to be created at the time of birth and present throughout the person's lifetime, most discussions of the *ka* were in reference to life after death; indeed the phrase "to go to one's *ka*" was a euphemism for "to die." As a physical double of the deceased, the *ka* had material needs such as food and drink even after death. In fact, the most common funerary inscription invoked "a thousand of bread, a thousand of beer, oxen, and fowl for the *ka* of the deceased." The *ba*, another division of the soul, was portrayed as a bird with a human head (fig. 10.1). It represented the aspect of the deceased that was able to maintain communication between the land of the living and the afterlife. The *ba* was believed to stay with the mummy in the dark, subterranean tomb during the night, but during the day it left to spend time in the sunshine. In some texts, the chirping of birds is equated

10.1 The soul (*ba*) of Userhat and his wife in the form of birds with a human head, sitting in a garden. Tomb of Userhat at Thebes (Dynasty 19).

with the chatter of the dead, serving as a reminder to those still alive of the eternal presence of the souls of the departed. The third aspect, the *akh,* was the transfigured blessed spirit that survived death. It was a luminous element that after death conferred *akh*-hood; it was the power, the spirit of the deceased. The *akh* was represented as the person him or herself and was thought, in its transfigured form, to mingle with the gods.

In order for an individual to live again after death there were several requirements. First, the body had to be preserved as a home or anchor for the *ka* and *ba,* hence the practice of mummification as a means of preserving the physical remains. Furthermore, the body had to be recognizable so that the *ba* would know where to return each night. Therefore, not only was the body mummified but the identity of the body was ensured by various means such as modeling the features of the mummy in plaster, encasing it in an anthropoid coffin, and supplying an extra head or pair of feet made of *cartonnage* (a substance like papier-mâché).

The process of mummification – essentially the removal of moisture from the body

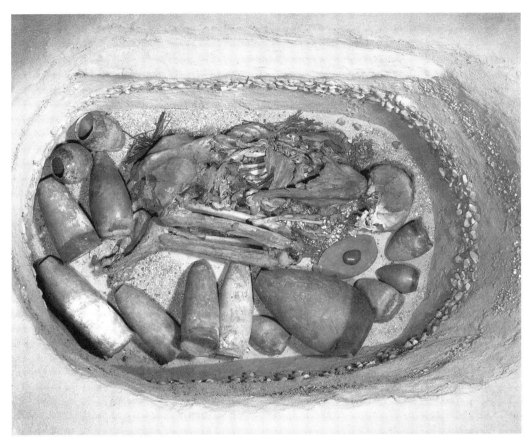

10.2 Predynastic pit burial, *ca.* 3500 B.C. The body, in a flexed position on a piece of matting, is surrounded by grave goods including a cosmetic palette and pottery vessels that held food offerings.

– underwent many changes during the 3,000-year span of its use. The earliest mummies were Predynastic bodies most of which were simply laid in oval pits in the sand, and which were naturally desiccated by contact with the hot sand (fig. 10.2). Some of the Predynastic burials at Hierakonpolis attest to what may be the first use of linen wrappings and resin. When the Egyptians began placing the bodies of the deceased in coffins, the remains could no longer naturally mummify and more elaborate artificial means of preservation began to develop. During the Archaic Period there is evidence that bodies were more commonly wrapped in linen, but no evidence of evisceration or the practice of desiccating the body exist. By Dynasty 3, artificial mummification was practiced. Herodotus' claim that there were several different styles of mummification, ranging from very modest to elaborate and expensive, has been confirmed by modern archaeology. In most cases, the soft internal organs (stomach, liver, lungs, and intestines) were removed through an incision made with a flint knife

10.3  Alabaster canopic jars in which the viscera were stored. The gods represented are (left to right) Hapi (who protected the lungs); Imsety (liver); Duamutef (stomach); and Qebehsenuef (intestines) (Dynasty 25).

on the left side, and the brain was removed through an opening broken in the ethmoid sinus. The body was then packed with dry *natron* (sodium carbonate), a natural salt found in the Egyptian desert. Once the moisture had been drawn out of the corpse by the *natron*, the body was anointed and wrapped with linen bandages and sheets. Magical protection was afforded by *amulets* placed on specific parts of the body.

The soft organs were mummified separately and usually placed in the tomb in receptacles called *canopic jars* (fig. 10.3). Although the preservation of the organs in order to theoretically restore their function to the deceased in the afterlife was emphasized, there was inconsistency in this practice. The brain was discarded, perhaps because it could not be removed intact or because the Egyptians were uncertain of its function. The lack of information concerning the fate of smaller organs (e.g., kidneys, gall bladder, and internal reproductive organs) suggests that they were treated in various ways, either discarded or left in place. The heart, which was considered to be the seat of intellect and emotions, was often left in the thorax. Sometimes it was reinforced or completely replaced by a large *scarab*, often inscribed with Spell 30B of the "Book of the Dead" that referred to the judgment of the deceased before the tribunal of the gods (in hieroglyphs a scarab means "to come into being" or "to exist"). We are told in the Late Period tale of Setne that the entire mummification process required seventy days.

Because the *ka* of the deceased had to be sustained with food, beverages, and the things that the individual had during his lifetime, tombs – referred to as "houses of eternity" – became virtual storehouses, stocked with everything the deceased required

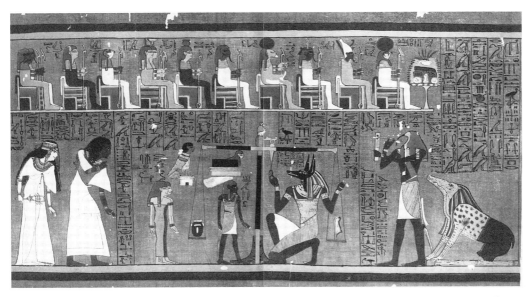

10.4 Scene from the "Book of the Dead" showing the heart of the deceased being weighed against the feather of truth. The deceased stands to the left of the scale with his wife. Anubis crouches beneath the scale. Ibis-headed Thoth, pen case in hand, records the judgment while the monster Ammet stands ready to devour the heart of the unworthy. Papyrus of Ani (Dynasty 19).

in the afterlife. The Egyptians believed that a written reference or picture of an object could substitute for the actual object (see chapter 11), so the walls of tombs were decorated with scenes of offering-bearers and the preparation of food. Tomb walls were also decorated with scenes of family life and the activities that the deceased enjoyed, or hoped to enjoy, in the afterlife. Because these representations could substitute for the actual people depicted, after Dynasty 1 there was no tradition of sacrificing people to accompany their lord into the afterlife (see below). Indeed, from the Old Kingdom onward, many tombs were stocked with statues of workers (*shabtis*) and entire workshops that would supply any need, allowing the deceased to spend eternity in luxury and ease.

In addition to meeting the requirements of life after death, rebirth also depended upon the deceased being a moral person. From the end of the Old Kingdom through the Late Period, Egyptians believed that the soul of the deceased was judged by a tribunal of the gods in the "Hall of Two Truths." The deceased's heart, which was thought to be the seat of the soul and intelligence, was placed in a balance and weighed against the feather symbolizing Maat, or Truth (see chapter 6) (fig. 10.4). The dead person then recited the liturgy known from Spell 125 of the "Book of the Dead" to attest to his character:

I gave bread to the hungry, beer to the thirsty, clothes to the naked, and a boat to him who was boatless. I have not deprived the orphan of his property; I have not killed; I have not commanded to kill. I have given god's offerings to the gods, and invocation offerings to the spirits. . . . I am pure of mouth and pure of hands . . . I have done what is right for the Possessor of Truth. I am pure, my brow is clean, my hindparts are clean . . .

(Faulkner 1994: pl. 31)

If the confession was truthful, the deceased's heart would be lighter than the feather of Maat, and he or she would be allowed to pass into the afterlife. From that time on, the dead person's name was compounded with Osiris, the god of the afterlife, and he became a transfigured *akh*, one of the blessed dead who could spend a pleasant eternal life.

## NON-ROYAL TOMBS

Building a proper tomb was one of an individual's most important accomplishments, and great resources were lavished upon their construction. Probably upon reaching young adulthood, people started planning and building their tomb. In most cases, tombs were planned for a single individual or for a husband and wife. Throughout Egyptian history private tombs became increasingly complex, developing into bipartite structures composed of a superstructure and an underground burial chamber that was blocked and made inaccessible after the mummy was deposited (fig. 10.5).

The earliest private (non-royal) tombs were oval pits, sometimes lined with mats. The body was placed in a contracted position, accompanied by a few pots of beer and food and perhaps a palette upon which to grind cosmetics (fig. 10.2). No superstructures have survived from these earliest tombs, but it is assumed that the pit was covered with a mound of earth that symbolized the mound of creation from which all life sprang, thereby ensuring the individual's rebirth.

By Dynasty 2 or 3, the simple mound superstructure that covered private tombs evolved into a rectangular stone structure called a mastaba (from the Arabic for "bench"). Mastabas could be of many sizes, and examples in the Giza necropolis range from several square meters to over 5,000 square meters. On the east side of most mastabas were two niches. The one to the south was decorated with a paneled recess called a false door that was thought to grant the *ba* and the *ka* access from the burial chamber to the mastaba's offering chamber (fig. 10.6). Through the course of the Old Kingdom this southern niche was enlarged until it developed into a series of rooms within the superstructure of the mastaba. These rooms, usually decorated with scenes of daily life and offerings, served as memorial chapels where family and friends could come and pray for the deceased and leave funerary offerings to sustain the *ka*. Elsewhere in the mastaba, a sealed room, or *serdab*, contained a stone or wood statue of the deceased,

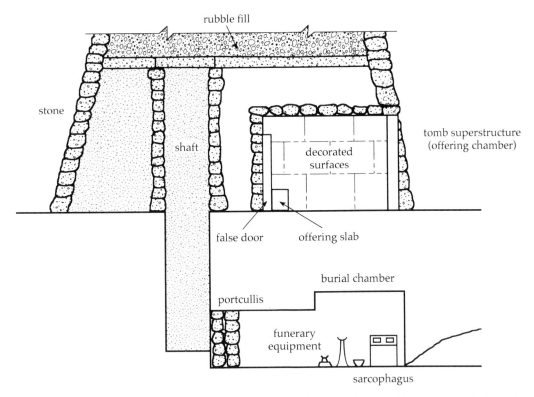

rubble fill

stone

shaft

decorated
surfaces

tomb superstructure
(offering chamber)

false door

offering slab

burial chamber

portcullis

funerary
equipment

sarcophagus

10.5 Section of mastaba tomb consisting of an offering chapel equipped with a false door and offering slab. The mummy was placed in the subterranean burial chamber. After the burial was deposited, the doorway to the burial chamber was blocked and the shaft was filled with rubble.

which, like the cult statue of the god in the temple (see chapters 6 and 9), was thought to be enlivened by the *ka* force of the deceased and to provide a resting place for the soul of the deceased.

In theory, tombs in the Nile Valley were to be located on the west bank of the river, the land of the setting sun and of the dead. In practice, tombs were located on either side of the river but on the desert edge, away from the valuable cultivable land. During Dynasties 4 and 5, a period of great state centralization, courtiers were buried in vast necropolises near the pyramid tombs of their king. The pyramids at Giza are surrounded by hundreds of tombs of the officials and bureaucrats who served the kings. Many of these tombs were granted as rewards from the crown in thanks for government service.

Private tombs could also be rock-hewn rather than built. Depending upon the terrain, they were cut into the rocky escarpment on the desert edge or carved down into the stony plain. The bipartite nature of the tombs was retained, with the burial chamber located under the offering chamber and blocked after the burial. Many tombs

10.6 View of the interior of the mastaba of Mereruka (Dynasty 6) at Saqqara showing the false door with Mereruka emerging from the darkness of the subterranean burial chamber. The walls of the chamber are carved and painted with images of the deceased, his family and activities of daily life.

had small open forecourts, often with a tree planted to provide shade to visitors to the tombs and perhaps a resting place for the *ba* (fig. 10.1), which is often shown sitting in a tree.

By the early New Kingdom (Dynasty 18), the rock-cut tombs at Thebes attest to the special attention given to the decoration of their chapels, which were ornamented with brightly painted scenes of daily life. By Dynasty 19, tomb decoration changed to images of mummification and scenes from the "Book of the Dead," emphasizing the fate of the deceased after death and the confrontation with the gods. By the Third Intermediate Period, many private tombs were small, and group tombs (shared by generations of the same family or by members of one profession) became common. Scenes that once decorated the walls of tombs were scaled down and transferred to individual coffins. Dynasties 25 and 26, a period of relative prosperity, again witnessed the building of large private tombs with walls carved and painted in a combination of Old and New Kingdom themes. The most elaborate of these tombs, exemplified by the Theban tombs of Montuemhet, Shoshenq, and Pabasa, are enormous underground complexes with hypostyle halls, multiple chambers, and large courts cut up to the ground level to admit sunlight.

ROYAL TOMBS

Because the architecture of the tombs of the first kings did not differ significantly from the early tombs of high officials, there has been some confusion about the actual location of the royal tombs. The general consensus now is that most of the kings of Dynasty 1 and 2 were buried at Abydos, probably the ancestral home of the earliest kings and also the center of the cult of the god Osiris. For reasons that are still unclear, the tombs of the first several kings of Dynasty 2 were located at Saqqara; by the end of the following dynasty and for the rest of the Old Kingdom, royal tombs were always located at Meidum, Dashur, Giza, Abu Sir, and Abu Roash, near the northern administrative center of Memphis. Despite this move, Abydos, by virtue of its association with Osiris, never completely lost its ritual importance. This is indicated by the fact that kings and other high officials buried elsewhere often elected to erect a commemorative tomb, or *cenotaph*, at Abydos.

Like the early private tombs, the first royal tombs were composed of compartmented subterranean chambers (presumably for the burial of the king and for the storage of grave goods) (fig. 10.7), and a mud-brick superstructure. The sides of the mastabas were niched in imitation of the royal palace, emphasizing the concept that the tomb was the eternal home of the deceased. Two stelae carved with the name of the king stood to the east of the mastaba, presumably marking where funerary offerings were left. No mastaba roofs have been preserved, but it has been assumed that they were slightly vaulted in imitation of the mound of creation. Even in this very early period, it is clear

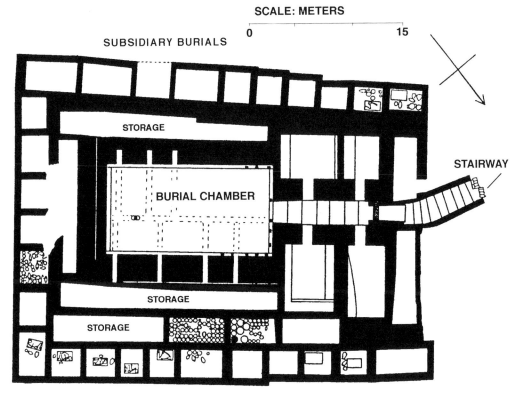

10.7  Tomb of King Qa'a (Dynasty 1) at Abydos. The tomb is a simple rectangle surrounded by a niched
mud-brick façade. A stairway gave access to the subterranean burial chamber. The burial chamber is
surrounded by storage rooms and square compartments in which the king's retainers were buried.

that the royal tomb was only a single part of a funerary complex. Other features of the
earliest royal complexes found at Abydos include huge mud-brick enclosures located
away from the tomb near the river that may have been massive offering chapels. The
best preserved is the massive 122 by 65 meter enclosure of Khasekhemwy, formerly
identified as a "fort." The complexes also include a niched enclosure wall around the
tomb, like that which surrounds the tomb of Queen Merneit, and ritual boats, either
real or stone imitations. All of these features were retained and further developed in
the Old Kingdom royal tomb complexes. One feature found only with Dynasty 1 tombs
are subsidiary burials of courtiers, indicating that at this early date retainers of the
king were sacrificed to accompany their king into the afterlife. For example, the tomb
of Qa'a (see fig. 10.7) was ringed by a series of mud-brick compartments that contained
twenty-six subsidiary burials, while that of Djer was accompanied by more than 150.

The best preserved early tomb is that of King Djoser, the second king of Dynasty 3

10.8  The Stepped Pyramid of Djoser at Saqqara (Dynasty 3).

(*ca.* 2687–2667 BC) (fig. 10.8). Its exceptional preservation is because it was built of stone – the first large-scale use of that material. Djoser's complex is tremendously important for our understanding of early architecture and the royal mortuary cult. Perhaps most interesting is that the stone structure was built to mimic perishable materials (mud-brick, reeds) that were originally used to build the early tombs. The stone blocks are very small, and even the stone slabs forming the ceilings of passageways were carved in imitation of rounded log beams.

The complex also provides information about the various components of the early royal mortuary complex, many aspects of which were retained in the next centuries. The focus of the complex is the pyramid tomb superstructure that rises in six steps to a height of 60 meters. This superstructure was initially designed as a traditional flat mastaba, but for unknown reasons it was extended to the west and then converted from a flat mastaba to a stepped pyramid (fig. 10.9). The royal burial chamber is located 28 meters below ground level amid a warren of hallways and rooms, some of which are decorated with bright blue-green faience tiles in imitation of mats and carved niches

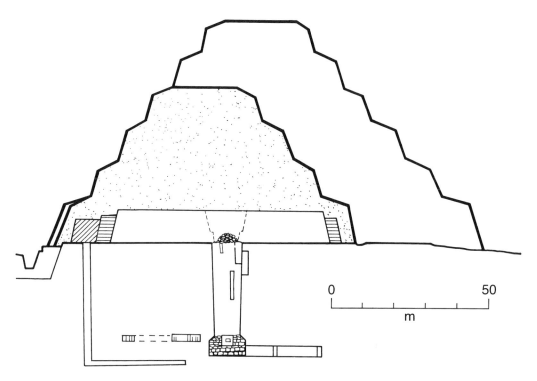

10.9 Elevation of the Stepped Pyramid showing the gradual extension of the mastaba and its conversion to a pyramid and the structure's subterranean passages and burial chamber.

depicting the king performing rituals of the jubilee festival (see chapter 6). The burial chamber itself is lined with granite slabs quarried from Aswan – more than 950 km to the south. The body of the king was carried into the subterranean passages through a descending entrance on the north side of the pyramid. The burial chamber itself was entered through a hole in its ceiling that was blocked with a granite plug more than 1 by 2 meters. No body or coffin contemporary with the tomb was discovered, and it is assumed that, like virtually all royal burials, the tomb was robbed in antiquity. More than 40,000 stone vessels were discovered in the adjacent chambers of the substructure that once housed the burials of Djoser's family. To the south of the pyramid was a second elaborate substructure, now referred to as the South Tomb (figs. 10.10a, 10.10b). The function of the South Tomb is unknown, but the energy expended upon it's construction (its shaft is 7 meters square and 28 meters deep) indicates that it was of great importance to the mortuary cult. The entire complex was enclosed by a niched wall about 19 meters tall that enclosed an area 560 by 280 meters, much like the walls around the earliest tombs at Abydos. The enclosure wall is decorated with fourteen false gates carved as if they were eternally open, perhaps emulative of the walls of the

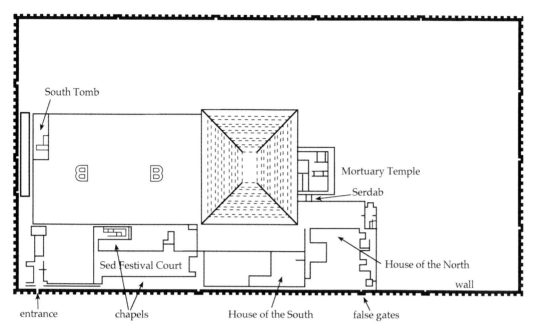

10.10a  Plan of the Stepped Pyramid enclosure at Saqqara (Dynasty 3).

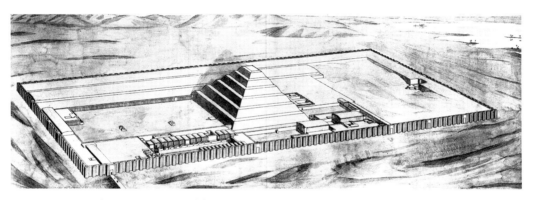

10.10b  Reconstruction of the Stepped Pyramid enclosure at Saqqara (Dynasty 3).

ancient city of Memphis. A single functional door, 27 meters from the southeast corner and carved in the eternally open position, is the only access into the complex.

The pyramid, its entrance, an offering chapel adjacent to the pyramid, the South Tomb, and the enclosure wall were all standard features of later pyramid complexes. Yet the Djoser complex is unique because of its great emphasis upon the jubilee festival. The courtyard south of the stepped pyramid has two B-shaped platforms which, as indicated by representations of the jubilee festival, were the turning marks for the

10.11  The jubilee (*Sed*) festival court of the Stepped Pyramid complex at Saqqara showing the various forms of shrines (Dynasty 3).

king's ritual run. Further to the east stands the jubilee court, lined on the east and west with chapels of three different designs emblematic of shrines of the north, the south, and a combined form (fig. 10.11). These buildings are extraordinary reminders of what the now-vanished Predynastic shrines made of mats and wood must have looked like. One type of chapel has a flat roof with cavetto cornice and torus molding, while another has an arched roof that is supported by imitations of reed bundles with umbels drooping from their tops. The third type has an arched roof with cavetto cornice. All of these ornate chapels are counterfeit buildings built only for the soul of the deceased king to enact the jubilee ceremony; the doors, carved in an eternally open position, lead to blank walls – there is no interior space in the chapels.

Dynasty 4 was the apogee of royal pyramid construction. The "Great Pyramid" of Khufu at Giza (fig. 10.12), built less than a century after Djoser's stepped pyramid, is tremendously refined, yet also retains many of the features of the earlier building. A primary difference between the two is the construction method. Rather than the small blocks used for Djoser's pyramid, Khufu's architect – probably his nephew Hemiunu – used an estimated 2.3 million blocks of limestone that range from 2.5 to 15 tons. The

10.12 The pyramids at Giza looking north. Left to right: Menkaure, Khafra, and Khufu. The "queen's pyramids" of Menkaure are in the foreground (Dynasty 4).

resulting pyramid, which was 140 meters tall and 230 meters on each baseline, was built during Khufu's twenty-three-year reign. The Great Pyramid, like the other pyramids at Giza and those of Snefru at Dashur, are composed of multiple components (fig. 10.13): the main pyramid; a mortuary temple to the east; a satellite, or subsidiary, pyramid to the south (which had developed from the earlier south tomb); and a covered causeway connecting the mortuary temple to a valley temple. The core of the complex (the main pyramid, the satellite pyramid, and the mortuary temple) were usually surrounded by an enclosure wall. Additionally, some pyramids have three so-called "queen's pyramids" to the southeast of the main tomb.

No bodies contemporary with the pyramids have ever been recovered, but sarcophagi and contemporary texts attest to their function as tombs. The pyramid shape may represent the mound of creation from which all life sprung or the descending rays of the life-giving sun. Evidence from pyramids of late Dynasties 3 and 5, as well as the "queen's pyramids" at Giza, suggest that the "true" pyramids are actually stepped

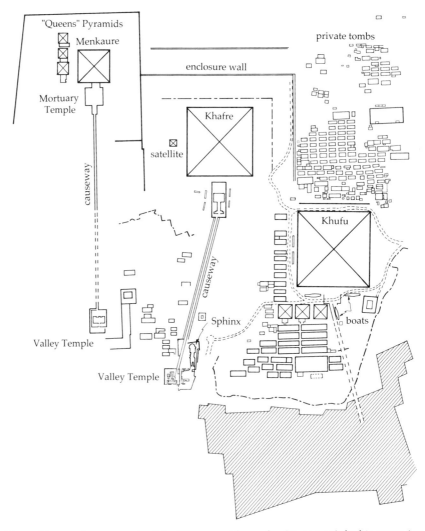

10.13 The architectural components of the Giza pyramid complex (Dynasty 4), looking west (top of page).

pyramids that have been encased, thereby combining the ideas of the mound and the rays of the sun. With a few exceptions (the Bent Pyramid of Snefru, and Userkaf's pyramid), the pyramid entrance is on the north side, probably in reference to the theological concept that the dead king merged with the north circumpolar star, which never vanishes below the horizon and therefore "lives" eternally.

The function of the other individual elements that make up the classic pyramid complex is not entirely clear. The mortuary temple on the east side of the pyramid was perhaps where the priests of the royal cult left offerings to sustain the *ka* of the king.

The valley temple has been identified as the "tent of purification" in which the mummification and purification of the body was performed. It has also been suggested that the fragments of the many statues discovered in Khafra's valley temple were likely to have served as doubles of the king and were part of the cult for the revivification of the king. An alternate suggestion is that the cult of the king in his earthly form of Horus was celebrated in the valley temple, while in the mortuary temple he was venerated in his celestial aspect of Re. The ritual boats found in association with the royal tombs were either used in the funerary ceremonies or, more likely, were employed by the spirit of the deceased king to cross the heaven in his eternal form of Re. The best-preserved boat, that of Khufu, discovered in 1954, is 43 meters in length and was made of huge planks of cedar imported from Lebanon.

The pyramids were built by free men who worked for the state. Estimates of the number of men who actually labored on the Great Pyramid has recently been reduced from Herodotus' 100,000 to about 20,000 people. Building sites were active year round, with gangs of workmen serving in rotation just as priests served part-time in the temples. Located about a kilometer south of Khufu's pyramid complex, bakeries, food-processing installations, and a modest cemetery clearly associated with Dynasties 4 and 5, provide evidence for a workmen's village. Although the exact arrangement of ramps and techniques used to build the pyramids is still unknown, it seems likely that a combination of methods was applied to each project depending upon the topography of the site and the size of the monument.

Pyramid-shaped tombs were employed for the burial of almost all the kings of the Old and Middle Kingdoms, but the quality and size of the monuments declined dramatically after Dynasty 4. For example, the pyramid at Saqqara of Pepi II, who is credited with ninety-five years of rule, has a baseline of approximately 80 meters, far smaller than the three pyramids at Giza, that have baselines of 233, 218, and 110 meters – and all built during much shorter reigns. Yet even though the general quality of building declined, such as the use of smaller blocks of stone, the use of rubble rather than block cores, and the use of mud-brick, there was still considerable innovation. The burial chamber of Unis, the last king of Dynasty 5, is decorated with the oldest hieroglyphic texts of the funerary theology of the king. These "Pyramid Texts," which were employed in most late Old Kingdom royal burial chambers thereafter, detailed the transformation of the king, his association with the imperishable circumpolar stars, and his ascension to heaven.

By the New Kingdom the style of royal tombs changed dramatically. From early Dynasty 18 (Thutmose I) to the end of Dynasty 20, the royal tombs were clustered in limestone cliffs in the Valley of the Kings in western Thebes. Rather than a visible pyramid accompanied by mortuary and valley temples, the New Kingdom royal tombs were separated from the other parts of the complex. Cut into the rock, sometimes extending more than 100 meters into the floor of the valley in alternating pillared chambers and hallways, each tomb culminated in a burial chamber that held the sarcophagus of the king. Once the burial was placed in the tomb, the tomb was made inaccessible by filling in the entrance passages (Dynasty 18) or sealing the great double doors (Ramesside tombs). The cult of the king was celebrated in royal temples (also known as mortuary temples) that were built on the west bank along the edges of the cultivation. Surrounding these great temples was an extensive cemetery of noblemen who, just as in the Old Kingdom necropolis at Giza, wished to be buried next to their king. The rock-cut tombs of many of the queens and royal children were located in a southern wadi called the Valley of the Queens.

Because the cluster of royal tombs in the Valley of the Kings could be easily guarded, the separation of the tomb and temple during the New Kingdom may have been a response to the need for increased security. Only one royal tomb has been discovered substantially intact (that of Tutankhamun), but the furnishings of that tomb, as well as contemporary records and artifacts that can be assumed to have been plundered from other royal tombs, suggest that the New Kingdom royal tombs were richly appointed with furniture, jewelry, royal insignia, ritual objects, food, and drink – everything that the king would need for eternity.

Like earlier royal tombs, the decoration and architecture of New Kingdom had ritual significance. Tombs stressed the association of the king with the sun god, for through his participation in the unending solar cycle the king would eternally be reborn. The walls are decorated with funerary texts – the Amduat ("That which is in the Underworld"), the "Book of Gates," the "Book of the Heavenly Cow," and the "Litany of Re" – all of which have instructions about the perilous journey of the king as sun god through the twelve dark hours of the night until his rebirth at dawn (fig. 10.14). Sarcophagi were normally placed in a recess chiseled in the floor – an allusion to the watery abyss of Nun from which all life began. Most of the floor plans of the Dynasty 18 tombs incorporated a 90° angle that symbolizes the separation of day (birth) and night (death), while the Ramesside tombs have a straight axis (fig. 10.15) that evokes the idea of the life-giving rays of the sun penetrating to the burial of the king and awakening him from his eternal slumber.

The New Kingdom version of the mortuary temple on the east side of the pyramid was known as the mortuary (or royal) temple (fig. 10.16). These structures were built in imitation of Amun Re's cult temples, thereby stressing the divinity of the deceased kings, especially their association with the god in his Theban forms. Just as the god's temples had a sanctuary located axially in the back of the temple, the royal temples had such an area for the king in his guise of Amun. The New Kingdom royal temples contain other standard elements: an open-air shrine to Re, the celestial god of eternity; a covered chapel of Osiris; and a chapel for the veneration of the king's father or ancestors. One of the most puzzling aspects of the Ramesside royal temples is the presence of a "palace" located on the south side (the best preserved are at the Ramesseum and

10.14 The tomb of Amunhotep II showing a wall decorated with the Amduat, a religious text that describes the king's journey through the dark hours of the night. Valley of the Kings (Thebes) (Dynasty 18).

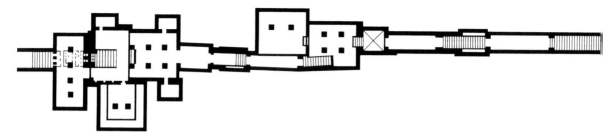

10.15 Plan of the tomb of Seti I in the Valley of the Kings showing the axial plan (Dynasty 19).

10.16 Artist's reconstruction of the eastern façade of the mortuary (royal) temple of Ramesses III at Thebes (Medinet Habu). The temple was surrounded by a great fortified wall. A basin and dock (foreground) to receive boats from the Nile were constructed to the east of the temple entry (Dynasty 20).

Medinet Habu). These structures have characteristics of residential palaces, such as a raised dais for the king's throne (symbolic of the mound of creation), storerooms, and even bathing rooms. One very distinctive architectural feature is the "window of appearance" that allowed the king to display himself to the throng gathered within the first court of the temple. The traditional interpretation of these structures is that they were palaces used by the king while he was in Thebes. This scenario now seems unlikely, for the buildings are very small and lack rooms for retainers and the members of the family. Instead, they were probably symbolic palaces for the spirit of the king in which a cult statue of the king – attended by the cult priests – prevailed over the complex.

10.17 Royal tombs at Tanis. The small tombs are built of reused architectural elements such as column drums and architraves. Left to right: Pseusennes I, Osorkon II, and two inscribed tombs (Dynasty 21).

The royal temples, like the god's temples, had a variety of uses. Medinet Habu, the royal temple of Ramesses III (fig. 10.16), and the Ramesseum, the royal temple of Ramesses II, appear to have been intimately linked to the functioning of the state. After the death of Ramesses III, Medinet Habu became the administrative seat of western Thebes, while the Ramesseum is surrounded by vaulted storerooms in which the income from the temple's domain was stored for distribution. Thus these "funerary" structures played an important role in the land of the living as well.

Some royal temples continued in use long after the death of their patron king. The temple of Hatshepsut at Deir el Bahari (*ca.* 1500 BC), renovated by Ramesses II (*ca.* 1250 BC), and again by the Ptolemies, played an important role in funerary rituals more than 1,500 years after it was built. In contrast, Amunhotep III's huge temple (of which the Colossi of Memnon are the main remaining feature) fell out of favor, and within a century and a half the temple stones were carried away for reuse in the temple of Merneptah.

The tombs of the Third Intermediate Period kings are located at Tanis in small, cramped structures built of recycled architectural elements (fig. 10.17). Like the New Kingdom tombs, their walls are decorated with scenes that associate the king with the sun god. Little is known of the royal tombs of the period after Dynasty 22. The kings of Dynasty 25 were buried in their homeland in Nubia; those of Dynasty 26 were buried at Sais in the Delta. The tombs of many of the later kings have yet to be located.

## SUMMARY

Like many peoples, a fundamental goal of the ancient Egyptians was to transcend death. They achieved this goal by believing in eternal life in a realm that was a mirror image of their life on earth. The successful transition of the deceased from one realm to another depended upon maintaining the physical remains in a lifelike appearance, upon passing a judgment by the gods, and upon the soul of the deceased being supplied with the sustenance and objects which he had enjoyed during his lifetime. These requirements led to the process of artificial preservation of the body (mummification) and the building of tombs ("houses of eternity"), which became vast repositories for the goods that would sustain the deceased for eternity.

Private tombs ranged from early oval graves with few offerings to elaborate mastaba tombs similar to those of the early kings. Royal tombs developed from mud-brick mastabas to stone pyramids to rock-cut subterranean tombs. Although there was great development in form, many of the underlying features such as the presence of a false door and subsidiary temples were used for nearly 3,000 years. The architecture and funerary texts (following the appearance of decorated burial chambers in Dynasty 5) all strove to ensure that the king was equipped with the knowledge to navigate the dangers of the darkness of night and to emerge reborn as the sun god at dawn, and the stockpiling of food and furnishings insured that life in the next world would be one of comfort and prosperity.

## FURTHER READING

Edwards, I. E. S., *The Pyramids of Egypt*. Harmondsworth: Penguin, 1985.
Emery, Walter B., *Archaic Egypt*. Harmondsworth: Penguin, 1961.
Fakhry, Ahmed, *The Pyramids*. Chicago: University of Chicago Press, 1961.
Foreman, Werner and Stephen Quirke, *Hieroglyphs and the Afterlife in Ancient Egypt*. Norman, Okla.: University of Oklahoma Press, 1996.
Hawass, Zahi and Mark Lehner, "Builders of the Pyramids," *Archaeology Magazine* (1997), 30–38.
Hornung, Erik, *The Valley of the Kings: Horizon of Eternity*. New York: Timken Press, 1990.
Morenz, Sigfried, *Egyptian Religion*. Ithaca, N.Y.: Cornell University Press, 1973.
O'Connor, David, "The Earliest Royal Boat Graves," *Egyptian Archaeology* 6 (1995), 3–7.
Quirke, Stephen, *Ancient Egyptian Religion*. London: The British Museum, 1992.
Spencer, A. Jeffrey, *Early Egypt: The Rise of Civilization in the Nile Valley*. Norman, Okla.: University of Oklahoma Press, 1993.

*Chapter 11*

# EGYPTIAN ART:
## CRAFTSMEN, TECHNIQUES, AND CONVENTIONS

Egyptian civilization lasted for more than 3,000 years, yet art from any period during that long timespan can instantly be identified as being from Egypt. Even though there was considerable variation in style, Egyptian art seems relatively static in comparison to the radical changes in Western art over a much shorter period. This conservatism of artistic style is due to the fact that art was a function and tool of a religious system striving to maintain perfect order in the universe. The creation of the universe was considered to be a state of initial perfection that should be emulated and preserved; thus, there was little value placed upon dramatic innovation in art, for modification moved art away from perfection. This reverence for the past is apparent in the Late Period, when artisans carefully studied and copied the then 2,000-year-old scenes in Old Kingdom tombs.

In contrast to the art of the Western world, which is valued primarily for aesthetics ("art for art's sake"), artistic skill, or viewer appreciation, Egyptian art was produced to fulfill the religious function of substitution through which a representation of a thing or a person could function as the object depicted (see chapters 6 and 10). Therefore, though the ancient artists were highly skilled and certainly appreciated art for its sheer beauty, paintings and reliefs in tombs and temples were more than simple decorations – they represented events and people in a timeless, idealized world independent of time and space. For example, a statue of a person was believed to be a permanent abode for the spirit of that individual and guaranteed his or her eternal life after death. Thus a sculptor was considered to "give birth to" a statue or "to cause the statue to live." Similarly, scenes depicting the king smiting his enemies were potent guarantors of the ability of that king, or any subsequent king, to defeat the enemies of Egypt. Many seemingly simple scenes, such as fishing and fowling in the marshes, are in fact elaborate allegories that refer to the maintenance of order in the cosmos. Virtually all Egyptian art is an allusion to timeless order and the stability of the world.

### ARTISANS, TOOLS, AND TECHNIQUES

Artists were members of the craftsman class, generally holding no special status and plying their trade in the towns and villages of Upper and Lower Egypt. Artists of exceptional skill might fall under the patronage of the king and work for the palace, while other craftsmen, considered to be under the patronage of the creator god Ptah, worked for the temples producing ritual objects and embellishing temple walls. Individual artisans were specialists (e.g., draughtsman, relief carver, painter) who worked with other artisans as a team to complete a single project. Unlike modern works of art that reflect the personal tastes and inspiration of a single individual, the products of the Egyptian atelier bear the imprint of many, and therefore very few works of art are signed. Indeed, only a few artists are known by name.

The type of Egyptian art probably most familiar to us today is the painted or carved walls of tombs and temples. For both painted and carved scenes, preparation of the wall surface was the same. First the wall, whether excavated or built of stone blocks, was flattened with ever finer chisels. Flaws in the stone were patched with plaster to provide a smooth surface. If the surface was of particularly poor quality it was coated with a thick layer of mud mixed with chopped straw and covered with a wash of plaster. After the surface was prepared, a series of lines were marked on the wall to assist in positioning and drawing the figures. These guidelines and grids were either ruled on the wall or made by laying a length of string dipped into red pigment across the surface at the appropriate level and snapping it against the wall. (In many unfinished tombs, these lines are still visible.) A draughtsman then made a preliminary sketch of the scene on the wall in red pigment. These sketches were sometimes executed by a team of artists working on different parts of the composition under the supervision of the master draughtsman. Once the outline was done, the master draughtsman corrected and finalized the designs in black.

If the scene was to be painted, color was applied with coarse brushes made from bundles of palm fibers, grass doubled over and lashed together at the doubled end to make a handle, or pieces of fibrous wood chewed or beaten at one end. Finally, the entire scene was finished by redrawing the outlines and the details within them with narrow reed brushes similar to those used by scribes.

Dry pigments were prepared by crushing various substances in a mortar or on a grinding palette with a stone pestle. Reds and yellows were obtained from ochre, a mineral of clay and iron oxide that ranges in color from light yellow to brown or red. White was made from gypsum (calcium sulfate) or calcium carbonate, which, like ochre, occurred naturally in Egypt. Some blue came from azurite, a carbonate of copper present in Sinai and the Eastern Desert, but more often was made from a compound of silica, copper, and calcium. Malachite, a copper carbonate also found in Sinai and the Eastern Desert, produced bright greens, while black was made from soot. To make paint, the dry pigments were mixed with an adhesive compound, normally a water-soluble gum or egg white. Artists generally worked with these colors, but there was considerable variation, and intermediate shades could be obtained by laying one pigment over another. During the New Kingdom subtle tints were not uncommon, and there are examples of shading. By Roman times, Egyptian artists had developed the technique of encaustic (pigmented wax) painting, which allowed for a larger range of pastel hues. Some tomb paintings and paintings on wood surfaces such as coffins were often covered with a transparent varnish of diluted resin.

If the scene was to be carved in relief before being painted, the outlines of the figures were incised with a sharp tool. Two main kinds of relief, raised (*bas relief*) and sunk (*intaglio*), were employed by the Egyptians. In raised relief, the background was cut back leaving the figures standing out from the surface of the stone. In sunk relief, on the other hand, the surface of the figure was cut into the stone. Because sunk relief involved cutting away only the figures rather than the entire background area, it was preferred for hard stones such as granite and quartzite that are more laborious to work than limestone and sandstone. Even on softer stones sunk relief was often employed when there were large areas to decorate because it was quicker to execute than raised relief. Because shadows tend to flatten the contours of sunken relief, it was particularly suitable for use in the bright sunlight of exterior surfaces, while raised reliefs were often reserved for scenes within a temple or tomb. In both techniques, the figures were often carved in great detail. After the carving was completed, the surface was covered with another thin layer of plaster and the background and the figures themselves were painted. To complete the scene, the fine details on the figures together with their final outline were touched up with a fine brush.

Sculpture in the round also followed a process of several steps. After the block was delivered from the quarry, the general outline of the statue was marked in red, and apprentices roughly cut the block to size with saws and chisels. The block was then turned over to more experienced stonemasons to define the shape. Progressively more fine work and detail was added with fine picks, and the final polish was done with smoothing stones (fig. 11.1). The tools of sculptors were similar to those used by stonemasons: copper chisels of various sizes, saws, drills, and stone pounders. Bronze tools were gradually added to the repertoire in the first millennium BC.

Like reliefs, most statues were originally painted in bright hues of red, yellow, blue, green, black, and white. In addition to paint, sculptures – both relief and in the round – were often decorated with other materials. Startling life-like eyes made of rock crystal, obsidian, and quartz were added to some statues, especially during the Old Kingdom, and sections of stone relief were sometimes hollowed out and filled with bright *faience* inlay. A precursor of this technique appears in the Dynasty 4 tomb of Nefermaat, in which the deeply cut sunk relief scenes were filled with brightly colored paste.

Although people are most familiar with stone statuary that was commissioned by the state and by members of the elite, the common people made and commissioned figurines and statuettes of baked clay or wood (fig. 11.2). Wood was also used for reliefs and architectural elements such as doors, and was worked chiefly with adzes, drills, and chisels. The native timbers of Egypt (sycamore, tamarisk, and acacia) did not produce large planks suitable for statuary and they were too fibrous for fine joinery,

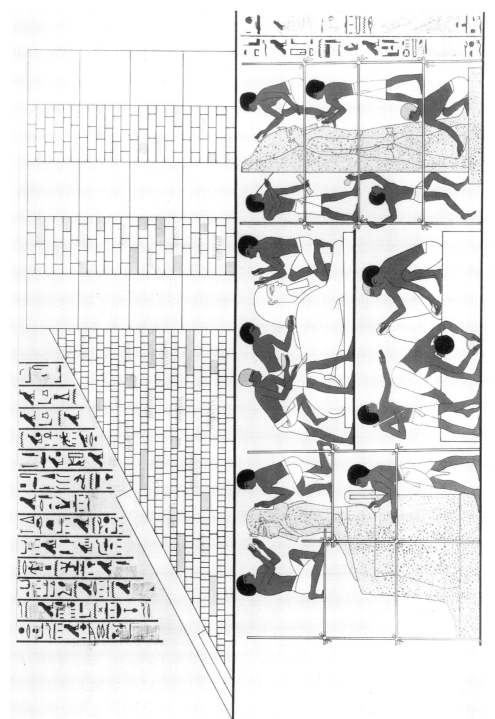

11.1 Artisans finishing granite statues of the king and a limestone sphinx and offering table with rubbing stones. An artist, standing on a scaffold, inscribes the back pillar of the king. The upper register shows a pillared hallway with brick fill to act as a building scaffold. Tomb of Rekhmire, Thebes (Dynasty 18).

11.2 Baked clay figurine of a king. In contrast to the stone statues of the elite, the bulk of the population made simple baked clay figures (Dynasties 21–24).

so high-quality wooden objects were usually made of pine and cedar imported from Lebanon or of ebony from Nubia.

Decorating or creating entire works with various metals dates to the Old Kingdom. Rough surfaces on some statues indicate that they were originally covered with gold leaf. Statues made of sheets of beaten copper appear in the late Old Kingdom, the most famous example being the life-size statue of Pepi I (Dynasty 6) which was probably beaten over a wooden core. The earliest examples of bronze statues date to Dynasty 18 (Thutmose III), but they do not become common until the Third Intermediate Period, at which time thousands of bronze statues of gods were made using the *lost wax process*. Metal was also used for ornamentation of architecture. Scenes from the New Kingdom tomb of Rekhmire show that large objects such as doors were sometimes cast in a single piece. Small holes in New Kingdom reliefs indicate that they were covered with gold or bronze sheets, and the tips of obelisks were likewise encased with sheets of gold.

Egyptian jewelers of the Middle and New Kingdoms were able to produce highly

11.3 Stone and glass pectoral from the tomb of Sithathoryunet at Dashur. The pectoral combines
hieroglyphs in a decorative motif that spells out the wish "May the Horus, Kha-kheper-Re (Senwosert II)
have millions of years of life." Reign of Senwosert II (Dynasty 12).

refined and beautiful products for the luxury trade. Gold, electrum, and sometimes
silver were employed to make elaborate jewelry, especially pectorals, some of which
were suspended from finely braided chain. Gold pieces were often encrusted with tiny
gold granules – a technique that would challenge even today's finest craftsmen. The
lapidary arts were highly developed, and craftsmen worked carnelian, jasper, rock
crystal, agate, lapis lazuli (from Asia), and turquoise (imported from Sinai), as well as
glass (called "melted stone") or faience substitutes into colorful inlays for elaborate
jewelry (fig. 11.3).

## PRINCIPLES OF REPRESENTATION

In contrast to the "perceptual" art of the Graeco-Roman tradition, the art of ancient
Egypt is "conceptual." In perceptual art, which is characterized by the conventions of
single-point perspective and foreshortening to create the illusion of three dimensions,
the subject is portrayed from the viewpoint of the artist. Conceptual art, on the other
hand, attempts to portray the subject from its own perspective rather the viewpoint
of the artist, because the goal is to communicate essential information about the object
itself, not how it appears to the viewer. Complex compositions reflect multiple viewpoints, for each object is shown as if isolated from surrounding objects. In the effort

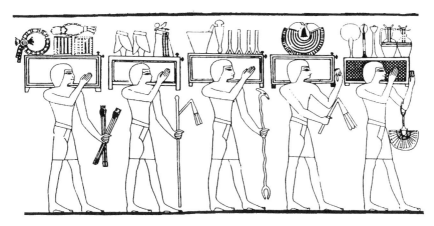

11.4  Procession of offering bearers from the tomb of Rekhmire at Thebes (Dynasty 18).

to relay the essential characteristics of the object, conceptual art tends to combine lateral and plan views to produce a composite diagram. In other words, if both the top and the side of an object are considered to be especially important for its identification, they are shown simultaneously.

The development of the complex conceptual conventions inherent in Egyptian art are tied to its religious function. Because representations were intended to substitute for the actual objects portrayed, each individual object was important in its own right; thus, the artist attempted to give the maximum amount of data about his subject without restoring to the "distortions" of overlapping, single-point perspective, or foreshortening.

The conceptual basis of ancient Egyptian art is best understood by looking at actual examples. That the ancient artist attempted to convey information about objects rather than portray them in three dimensions is shown by figure 11.4, which shows a procession of men carrying boxes of funerary offerings. Each box is shown as a simple rectangle because that was its distinctive form. There is no attempt to show the boxes in perspective by depicting them as trapezoids (fig. 11.5), for the Egyptians would have considered this a distortion of the boxes' true shape. Furthermore, in this scene (fig. 11.4) the contents of each box are shown above the container rather than inside, to avoid having to "tip" the boxes for the viewer. Each object within the box is shown in its most characteristic and recognizable form, even if this means combining various views. Hence the beaded collars, kilts, and hand mirror are depicted from above, while the jars are depicted from the side. Each object is shown as if in isolation – there is no overlapping that would mask characteristic features of individual objects – and each is in its correct relative size so that the artist could convey the maximum information about the object with the least amount of distortion. The tendency to combine plan

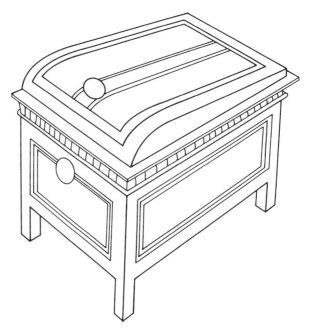

11.5 Drawing of a box employing Western perspective. Note how the rules of perspective have rendered the side of the box as a trapezoid.

and lateral views can also be observed in a typical pond and garden scene (fig. 11.6). The pond is rectangular as if viewed from above, while the trees are drawn in profile on the surface of the pond. The viewer's common sense plays a role in translating the message: trees, although portrayed lying flat so as not to mask the pond, are understood by the viewer to be standing around the edge of the pond. The entire scene, once interpreted, provides an accurate picture of a garden pond.

Although the ancient Egyptians did not attempt to create the illusion of three dimensions the way artists in the Western tradition do, they did try to express the idea of depth within a scene. Depth within a composition was conveyed not by diminishing the size of the object (foreshortening), but occasionally by overlapping or, more commonly, by placing a more distant object above a closer object. Placing an object above another to indicate distance is best illustrated by a standard scene of boats on the Nile (fig. 11.7). Two ships appear, one above each other, yet each is positioned on its own separate aquatic baseline to indicate that each is on the Nile, one behind the other. This sort of convention allowed the ancient artist to convey the relative size of each ship and to give full details of the hull and rigging, for none of the boats overlaps or masks the others.

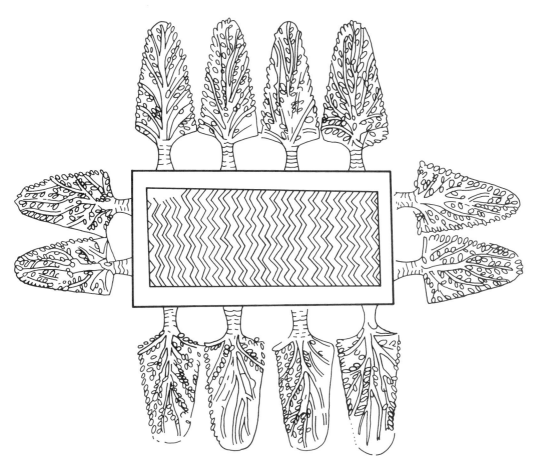

11.6 Scene of a garden and pond. This image combines various viewpoints (frontal and aerial) to give the maximum information about the scene (Dynasty 18).

## REPRESENTATION OF THE HUMAN FORM

Ancient Egyptian representations of the human form are recognizable because of their tremendous uniformity. This uniformity was ensured by the use of a grid system, which first appeared as simple guidelines during Dynasty 5 (*ca.* 2500 BC) and provided standard proportions to fixed points of the human body so that figures were relatively standard. This system developed into a series of squared grid lines during the Middle Kingdom, with each square perhaps based on the width of a closed fist. Standing male figures were divided into eighteen equal squares from the hairline to the sole of the foot (fig. 11.8). (It is thought that the measurement stopped at the hairline rather than at the crown of the head to allow for the addition of various headdresses.) Distinctive parts of the body were measured in multiples of the grid square; for example, the knee

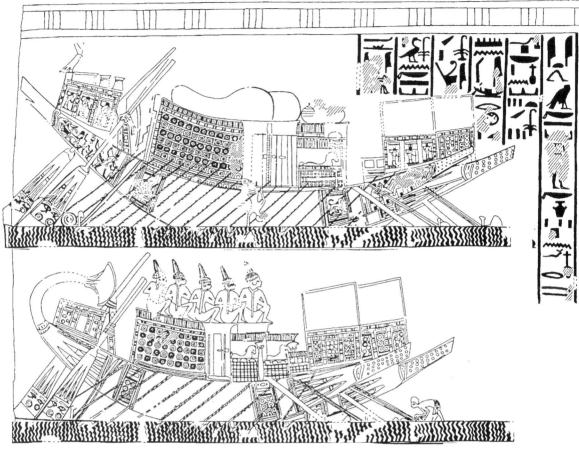

11.7 Boats on the Nile as shown in the tomb of Huy at Thebes. Note how the upper boat, which is supposed to be behind the lower boat, sails on a duplicate ground line hatched to indicate it represents the Nile (Dynasty 18).

was at the sixth square (the height of six fists) from the baseline, the bottom of the hip at the ninth; and the neck the sixteenth. Standing figures of women (fig. 11.9) were also drawn on eighteen squares from soles to hairline, but they were usually depicted as more slender than their male counterparts and the small of the back was positioned higher. The grid system also accommodated figures in postures other than standing, such as seated figures that were apportioned over a fourteen-square grid. This canon of proportions changed during the Late Third Intermediate Period when the human figure was elongated with the use of a twenty-one square grid. This modification is very evident in Ptolemaic reliefs in which the figures appear to be very high-waisted (fig. 11.10).

Parts of the human body, like inanimate objects, were depicted in its most

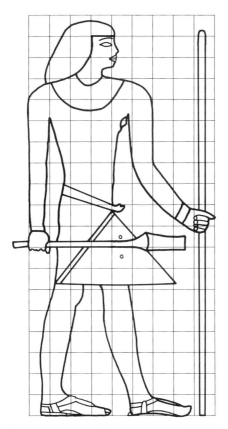

11.8  Male figure superimposed over proportional eighteen-square grid.

characteristic and identifiable form (fig. 11.11). Hence the face was shown in profile to express its contour, but the eye was shown in its unabstracted, frontal, almond-like shape rather than a profile wedge. Shoulders were portrayed frontally to express their width, while the rest of the torso was three-quarters turned, and the contour of the buttock, calf, and arch of the foot were in profile. Although the Egyptian artist almost always conformed to the traditional canon of human representation, he certainly had the skill to portray the human form in other ways. For example, the faces of certain genre figures, such as musicians and horses, as well as the common hieroglyphs of the human face (☙) and the forward-looking owl (🦉), are shown frontally, belying the idea that the Egyptian artist was unable to draw such forms.

The desire of the artist to communicate the most essential features of the human form in two dimensions is especially apparent in the rendering of women, who were normally portrayed with the profile of a single high, rounded, breast. Even though these female figures may be clothed in a dress with broad shoulder straps, the breast – as a

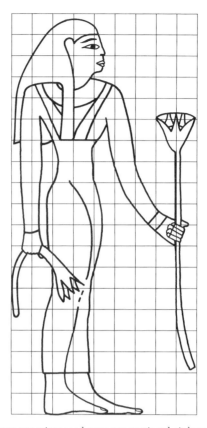

11.9 Female figure superimposed over proportional eighteen-square grid.

characteristic part of the female – in two dimensions is shown exposed (fig. 11.12a), yet three-dimensional statues of women dressed in the same garb show that the straps cover the breasts (fig. 11.12b).

The same concern with the essential characteristics of the human form can be seen in the rendering of the human hand. In the effort to depict all the fingers, the hand nearer the viewer was shown in the same form as the far hand – essentially upside down – otherwise the distinctive part of the hand – the thumb – would have been obscured (fig. 11.13). Likewise, for much of Egyptian history, the human foot was represented with the arch visible in both and near and far feet, presumably because the arch was a characteristic feature of the foot. Accurate rendering of left and right feet showing all five toes on the near foot was experimented with during the reigns of Thutmose IV and Amunhotep III and became common during the Amarna period. It continued to appear sporadically during the New Kingdom and finally became a common mode of representation during the Ptolemaic Period.

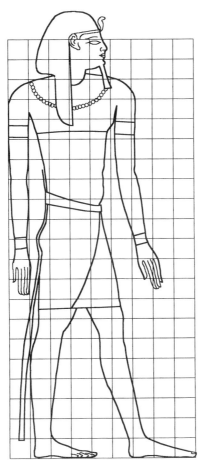

11.10 Figure from Ptolemaic relief (third century BC) superimposed over twenty-one-square grid, resulting in elongated proportions.

Status and role were also expressed through artistic conventions such as size, color, pose, and placement. In general, importance was expressed by relative size. Hence, in scenes of estate owners surveying workers or of the king inspecting his troops, the superior figure is much larger than the subordinates. Statues and two-dimensional representations of men were painted reddish-brown while women were colored yellow, a difference that some scholars see as supporting differences in gender roles – men became tanned because they had to work in fields, but women, at least ideally, did not. Placement of figures is especially important in portrayals of husband and wife. In both seated and standing pairs, the woman is usually to the male's left (the viewer's right). In standing compositions, the women almost always has her arm around her husband's shoulder or waist, but it is very rare for the man to be represented embracing his wife.

11.11 Standard representation of the human figure. Note how the man, named Akhethotep, is portrayed in a combination of views; his face in profile, his eye frontally; and his body in combination of profile, frontal, and oblique views (Dynasty 3–4).

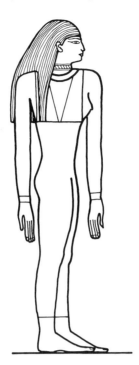

11.12a. Woman with v-neck dress shown in relief. The identification of the figure as female is emphasized by showing the breast bared.

In balanced compositions of a man and woman seated at either side of a table of offerings, the man is normally on the viewer's left facing right, which was apparently the dominant position. Ironically, in a tomb belonging to a married woman, the husband usually is not shown, perhaps because if he were, the rules of decorum would force the woman into the secondary position in monuments that were supposed to commemorate her.

## PORTRAITURE AND IDEALIZATION

Images of people were intended to substitute for them for eternity, so representations rarely show an individual in any state other than the prime of health and life. This symbolic aspect of Egyptian art precludes the existence of real portraiture, for the goal of the artist was to show the individual as he or she wished to be, not as they actually were. Men are shown with broad muscular chests and narrow hips while women are shown impossibly thin and long-legged. Age, physical infirmity, or deviations from the cosmetic ideal are rarely portrayed in the main figures, generally being restricted to field-hands, laborers, and subservient figures. Age is so seldom indicated in art that in most cases the captions that accompany group scenes are the only way to distinguish

11.12b. Statue of a woman wearing a v-neck dress similar to that depicted in figure 11.12a, showing how the
straps actually cover her breasts (Chicago Oriental Institute 10618) (Dynasty 5).

between a tomb-owner's wife and his mother. That there was little attempt to portray
people as they actually appeared is also confirmed by the fact that many statues were
made without a particular purchaser in mind, and the statue was matched to its owner
merely by the addition of a hieroglyphic label. Likewise, the identity of a statue could
be changed by effacing the label and substituting another name without altering the
features.

   The only substantial – and, indeed, tremendous – variation from the traditional
forms of human representation appeared during the reign of Amunhotep IV/Akhenaten
(Dynasty 18) (see chapters 3 and 6). The most prominent change was in the representation of the king and his family. Over the course of Akhenaten's seventeen-year reign,
the depictions, which appeared in both temple and domestic contexts, ranged from
naturalistic to highly abstracted and grotesque (figs. 11.14a, 11.14b). The most extreme
variation from the standard canon, which appeared early in the reign, shows the king

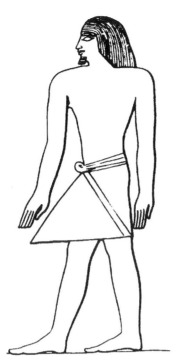

11.13 Classic representation of the human figure showing an arch in both feet and identical hands. Tomb of Mereruka at Saqqara (Dynasty 6).

with an elongated neck, drooping jaw, and fleshy feminine body. The emphasis upon scenes of nature, with animals frolicking, and informal scenes of the royal family and courtiers, have led some to suggest that the representations were an effort to portray the king and his family as they actually appeared. However, the inconsistency of the portrayals suggests that the change in style was purely artistic, motivated by the changing religious program of the king. Furthermore, religious texts that refer to king as the agent of creation suggest that the representations of the king are a reference to him in his role of androgynous creator god.

In contrast to the idealization of the human form, Egyptian artists depicted animals with great attention to detail. Scenes of fishing and fowling incorporate images of the fauna which can be precisely identified by modern scholars.

## SUMMARY

Egyptian art served a religious function rather than a purely aesthetic one. Representations were thought to substitute eternally for what was portrayed, so objects were shown in a manner which was thought to give the fullest and least

11.14a  Differing representations of Nefertiti (Dynasty 18) emphasizing the symbolic nature of Egyptian art:
the idealized form.

abstracted information, combining multiple viewpoints, plan, and profile views into a
composite, highly symbolic diagram. Foreshortening and other elements of single-
point perspective were generally avoided because they were considered to be distortions.

The fundamental characteristics of Egyptian art were established during the early
Old Kingdom and survived with minor variations throughout the Pharaonic Period.
The relatively static style was associated with the idea that the state of the world was
perfect at its creation, and therefore innovation was not necessarily valued because it
moved the cosmos away from the earlier state of perfection. The use of standard proportions for the human form maintained by a system of grid and guide lines, as well
as the organization of artists into teams working together on a single work, ensured
that the art was standardized and did not reflect the inspiration of a single craftsman.

Human figures were portrayed in an idealized form because the representations were

11.14b Differing representations of Nefertiti (Dynasty 18) emphasizing the symbolic nature of Egyptian art:
the radical style.

intended to depict individuals as they wished to remain, and how they wished to be remembered, for eternity. Thus, idiosyncratic features such as age, obesity, or infirmity were usually avoided by the ancient artists.

## FURTHER READING

Aldred, Cyril, *Egyptian Art*. New York: Thames and Hudson, 1985.
Arnold, Dorothea, *The Royal Women of Amarna*. New York: The Metropolitan Museum of Art, 1996.
Iversen, Erik, *Canon and Proportions in Egyptian Art*. London: Sedgwick and Jackson, 1955.
Lucas, Alfred, *Ancient Egyptian Materials and Industries*. London: Edward Arnold and Co., 1926.
Robins, Gay, *The Art of Ancient Egypt*. Cambridge, Mass.: Harvard University Press, 1997.
    *Proportion and Style in Ancient Egyptian Art*. Austin, Tex.: University of Texas Press, 1994.
Schäfer, Heinrich, *Principles of Egyptian Art* (trans. J. Baines). Oxford: Oxford University Press, 1974.

*Chapter 12*

# CULTURAL DEATH OR TRANSFORMATION OF A CIVILIZATION?

Although it is common to refer to the "death" of the pharaonic civilization, there is no consensus as to what point in history it "died" or whether it was merely transformed. A basic problem with such a discussion is the definition of exactly what constitutes the death of a civilization. As defined by Redfield and Singer (1954), civilization refers to the great traditions of a state; thus, "death" must refer to the loss of these great traditions.

On the one hand, the great traditions of the Egyptian culture – its elaborate polytheistic religion, sovereignty, system of writing, the creation of monumental art and architecture – had all vanished by the Late Antique Period (early Christian period) or shortly afterward. On the other hand, however, many aspects of ancient Egypt lived on. Economically, Egypt did not collapse. The annual inundation of the Nile ensured a renewable supply of rich arable land, and irrigation works were dependent upon local rather than central governmental power. Natural resources were never exhausted as they were in the case of the states of Mesopotamia. In addition, the basic infrastructure of the Egyptian state was relatively inexpensive to maintain – there was no great system of dikes or roads, and no standing army to exhaust the national treasury. Politically, there was no fragmentation of the Egyptian state that can be compared to the "fall" of a state such as Rome or the Inca empire. Pharaonic Egypt withstood periods of decentralization (the Intermediate Periods), foreign conquest, and occupation by Hyksos, Persians, Assyrians, Greeks, and Romans, yet the borders of the country remained largely unchanged even into the Christian and Islamic periods. Indeed, the borders of the modern state of Egypt are not appreciably different today from those that existed in the third millennium BC, so one cannot properly speak of the physical fragmentation of the state.

In terms of religion, the ancient theology continued to exert a strong influence. Greeks and Romans became adherents of the cult of Isis. Christians built their churches within pagan temples, such as Medinet Habu, and reconsecrated others, such as Philae, for their new monotheistic religion. Even today the pharaonic temples continue to play a part in folk religion of rural Egypt, with Coptic Christians and Muslims alike visiting the temples to gather sand that has been ground from the ancient pillars to use as a remedy for barrenness. One of the clearest surviving rituals is the annual festival of the Islamic saint Abu Haggag, which is celebrated by a procession of boats around the temple of Luxor in imitation of the ancient festival of Opet.

Finally, the influence of Egyptian art and architectural style is clearly visible in early Greek sculpture (the kouroi) and Roman monuments. The Romans also collected Egyptian art and disseminated it throughout their vast empire. The Neoplatonists (fifth century AD) and, much later, the Freemasons (eighteenth century) studied Egyptian iconography in their search for enlightenment, while Neoclassical artists and designers such as Piranesi and Robert Adam inspired a mania for all things Egyptian that swept through Western Europe during the late 1770s and early 1800s. Centers of Christian piety and learning, such as St Peter's in Rome, were embellished with obelisks, a pagan symbol of sun worship. The plazas of great cities – London, Paris, Rome, Istanbul, New York – likewise imported and raised Egyptian obelisks in homage to the ancient Egyptians. Today, Egyptian motifs decorate myriad objects of daily life, from fabrics and furniture to beer cans and dishware.

It is clear that the concept of "death" does not take into account the many aspects of Egyptian culture that continued, even to the present day. Therefore, it is argued that it is more productive to consider that the culture was transformed. But how was it transformed and what factors were involved? Was there a single cause, such as military conquest or poor leadership? Surveying the 3,000 years of Egypt's history suggests that a single cause is too simplistic, and that the modification of Egyptian civilization resulted from the complex culmination of evolutionary processes.

Although perhaps not dramatic enough to constitute true demise, one cannot deny that there were changes in Egypt's economic and political systems. The Romans heavily taxed Egypt, to the extent that farms in Lower Egypt were depopulated as farmers fled to Upper Egypt or Nubia to escape their obligation to the state. Even more damaging to the long-term health of the Egyptian state was that the Romans increasingly exported the resources received through taxation to help support Roman imperial expansion instead of redistributing the goods to state workers within Egypt, as had been done in former times. Politically, Egypt did lose her sovereignty. With the rule of the Persians, Romans, Byzantines, Arabs, and, to a lesser degree, Ptolemaic, Macedonian Greeks who considered Egypt their own kingdom, Egypt was ruled by powers outside the Nile Valley and was drawn into the status of a client state. Yet the nature of each of these periods of foreign rule shared basic characteristics: each was autocratic, and each had a definite theocratic basis – the divine Roman emperor, the Byzantine emperor, the caliph of Islam – so these political changes were easily comprehended by the majority of the Egyptian populace. One theocratic autocracy simply replaced another, and daily life continued much the same as before. Even today, life in Upper Egypt among the peasants has not changed appreciably from ancient times.

Perhaps the most obvious source of cultural transformation was the belief system, which influenced all aspects of the Egyptian culture and served as the medium through which new elements of society were introduced. Although the Greeks greatly respected Egyptian religious beliefs and, as indicated by the Ptolemaic temples whose walls are covered with liturgies, made valiant efforts to preserve the cult, their Roman successors had little interest in the native beliefs. With the conversion of Emperor Constantine (AD 306–337) to Christianity, the Egyptian civilization underwent a major change. Egypt's king had always served as the focus of the religious cult: the walls of the temples were covered with timeless images of the pharaoh making offerings to the gods, and it was he who functioned as the intermediary between humankind and the deities, and who ensured the protection of the land and her people. Without the king – the core of the religious system – ancient Egyptian culture was irrevocably altered. Finally, in AD 392 the Roman Emperor Theodosius ordered the pagan temples closed and a 3,000-year tradition came to an end.

## SUMMARY

Although the ancient Egyptian civilization is traditionally considered to have "died" (its death placed variously at the end of the Ramesside Period, or at the Persian, Greek, or Roman conquests), many aspects of the culture were simply transformed. The political boundaries of the land are largely unchanged from 4,500 years ago, and, for much of the modern era, Egypt continued to be a theocracy as the rule of the semi-divine pharaoh was replaced by the Roman and Byzantine emperors and by the caliph of Islam. Indeed, life for the Egyptian peasant class has not changed significantly in the last few millennia, and even today popular folk traditions contain an echo of the pharaonic past.

An indication of the endurance of Egyptian culture – its transformation rather than true demise – is seen in the fascination that modern cultures have for the ancient past, and in the ways other cultures have incorporated many aspects of Egyptian civilization into their own.

## FURTHER READING

Redfield, Robert and Milton Singer, "The Cultural Role of Cities," *Economic Development and Cultural Change* 3 (1954), 53–73.
Service, Elman R., *Origins of the State and Civilization*. New York: W. W. Norton, 1975.
Yoffee, Norman and George L. Cowgill (eds.), *The Collapse of States and Civilizations*. Tucson, Ariz.: University of Arizona Press, 1988.

# BIBLIOGRAPHY

Adams, Robert McC. (1966) *The Evolution of Urban Society: Early Mesopotamia and Prehistoric Mexico*. Chicago: Aldine Publishing Co.

(1981) *Heartland of Cities: Surveys of Ancient Settlement and Land Use on the Central Floodplain of the Euphrates*. Chicago: University of Chicago Press.

Aldred, Cyril (1973) *Akhenaten and Nefertiti*. New York: Viking Books.

(1979) *Tutankhamun: Craftsmanship in Gold in the Reign of the King*. New York: The Metropolitan Museum of Art.

(1984) *Egypt to the End of the Old Kingdom*. New York: McGraw and Hill.

(1985) *Egyptian Art*. New York: Thames and Hudson.

(1987) *The Egyptians*. London: Thames and Hudson.

(1988) *Akhenaten, King of Egypt*. New York: Thames and Hudson.

Allen, James P. (1988) *Genesis in Egypt: The Philosophy of Ancient Egypt Creation Accounts*. New Haven: Egyptian Seminar, Department of Near Eastern Languages and Civilizations, Yale University.

Andreev, Y. V. (1989) "Urbanization as a Phenomenon of Social History," *Oxford Journal of Archaeology* 8, 167–177.

Andrews, Carol (1981) *The Rosetta Stone*. London: The British Museum.

(1984) *Egyptian Mummies*, Cambridge, Mass.: Harvard University Press.

Anthes, Rudolf (1961) "Mythology in Ancient Egypt," in *Mythologies of the Ancient World* (S. N. Kramer, ed.), pp. 15–92. New York: Doubleday.

Arnold, Dieter (1977) "Rituale und pyramidentempel," *Mitteilungen des Deutschen Archäologischen Instituts Abteilung Kairo* 33, 1–14.

(1991) *Building in Egypt: Pharaonic Stone Masonry*. Oxford: Oxford University Press.

Arnold, Dorothea (1996) *The Royal Women of Amarna*. New York: The Metropolitan Museum of Art.

Arnold, Felix (1989) "A Study of Egyptian Domestic Architecture," *Varia Aegyptiaca* 5, 75–93.

Assmann, Jan (1984) *Ägypten: Theologie und Frömmigkeit einer frühen Hochkultur*. Stuttgart/Berlin/Köln/Mainz: Kohlhammer.

(1995) *Egyptian Solar Religion in the New Kingdom: Re, Amun and the Crisis of Polytheism*. London: KPI.

Aufrère, Sidney, Jean-Claude Golvin, and Jean-Claude Goyon (1991) *L'Egypte Restituée: Sites et temples de Haute Egypte*. Paris: Editions Errance.

Badawy, Alexander (1954) *A History of Egyptian Architecture I: From the Earliest Times to the End of the Old Kingdom*. Cairo: Sh. Studio Misr.

(1966) *A History of Egyptian Architecture II: The First Intermediate Period, the Middle Kingdom and the Second Intermediate Period*. Berkeley, Ca.: University of California Press.

Baer, Klaus (1960) *Rank and Title in the Old Kingdom*. Chicago: University of Chicago Press.

(1962) "The Low Price of Land in Ancient Egypt," *Journal of the American Research Center in Egypt* 1, 25–42.

Bagnell, Roger (1993) *Egypt in Late Antiquity*, Princeton: Princeton University Press.

Baines, John (1983) "Literacy and Ancient Egyptian Society," *Man* 18, 572–599.

(1991) "Society, Morality and Religious Practice," in *Religion in Ancient Egypt* (B. E. Shafer, ed.), pp. 123–200. Ithaca, N.Y.: Cornell University Press.

Baines, John and Jaromir Málek (1980) *Atlas of Ancient Egypt*. New York: Facts on File.

Bascom, William (1955) "Urbanization among the Yoruba," *The American Journal of Sociology* 60, 446–454.

Bell, Harold Idris (1948) *Egypt from Alexander the Great to the Arab Conquest: A Study in the Diffussion and Decay of Hellenism*. Oxford: Clarendon Press.

Bell, Lanny (1985) "Luxor Temple and the Cult of the Royal *Ka*," *JNES* 44(4), 251–294.

Bevan, Edwyn (1968) *The House of Ptolemy*. Chicago: Ares,

Bierbrier, Morris (1982) *The Tomb-Builders of the Pharaohs*. London: The British Museum.

(1995) *Who Was Who in Egyptology*. London: Egypt Exploration Society.

Bietak, Manfred (ed.) (1996) *Haus und Palast im alten Ägypten*. Vienna: Vienna der Österreichischen Akademie der Wissenschaften vol. 14.

Boas, George (trans.) (1950) *The Hieroglyphics of Horapollo*. Princeton: Princeton University Press.

Breasted, James Henry (1906) *Ancient Records of Egypt*. 5 Vols. Chicago: University of Chicago Press.

Brewer, Douglas J. (1991) Temperature in Predynastic Egypt inferred from the Remains of the Nile Perch. *World Archaeology* 22, 228–303.

Brewer, Douglas J. and Renée Friedman (1991) *Fish and Fishing in Ancient Egypt*. Warminster: Aris & Phillips Ltd.

Brewer, Douglas J., Donald Redford and Susan Redford (1995) *Domestic Plants and Animals: The Egyptian Origins*. Warminster: Aris & Phillips Ltd.

Brovarski, Edward, Susan Doll, and Rita Freed (eds.) (1982) *Egypt's Golden Age: The Art of Living in the New Kingdom 1558–1085 B.C.* Boston: Museum of Fine Arts.

Bryan, Betsy (1996) "In Women, Good and Bad Fortune are upon Earth: Status and Roles of Women in Egyptian Culture," in *Mistress of the House, Mistress of Heaven* (A. Capel and G. Markoe, eds.), pp. 25–46, 189–191. Cincinnati: Cincinatti Musuem of Art.

Butzer, Karl W. (1976) *Early Hydraulic Civilization in Egypt: A Study in Cultural Ecology*. Chicago: University of Chicago Press.

Caminos, Ricardo (1954) *Late Egyptian Miscellanies*. Oxford: Oxford University Press.

Carneiro, Robert (1970) "A Theory of the Origin of the State," *Science* 169, 733–738.

Caton-Thompson, Gertrude (1929) "Hememeih," in *The Badarian Civilisation* (G. Brunton and G. Caton-Thompson), British School in Archaeology in Egypt and Egyptian Research Account publication 46. London: British School in Archaeology in Egypt and Egyptian Research Account.

Ceram, C. W. (1951) *Gods, Graves and Scholars*. New York: Alfred Knopf.

Černý, Jaroslav (1940) "Consanguineous Marriages in Pharaonic Egypt," *Journal of Egyptian Archaeology* 40, 23–29.

Childe, V. Gordon (1948) *The Dawn of European Civilization*. New York: Knopf.

(1950) "The Urban Revolution," *Town Planning Review* 21, 3–17.

(1952) *New Light on the Most Ancient East*. New York: Grove.

Chimielewski, Waldemar (1968) "Early and Middle Paleolithic Sites near Arkin, Sudan," in *The Prehistory of Nubia I* (Fred Wendorf, ed.), pp. 110–147. Dallas, Tex.: Southern Methodist University Press.

Clark, David (1979) "Towns in the Development of Early Civilization," in *Analytical Archaeologist* (edited by "His Colleagues"), pp. 435–444. London.

Clark, R. T. Rundle (1960) *Myth and Symbol in Ancient Egypt*. New York: Grove.

Clayton, Peter. A. (n.d.) D*avid Robert's Egypt*. London.

Curl, James S. (1994) *Egyptomania: The Egyptian Revival: A Recurring Theme in the History of Taste*. Manchester: Manchester University Press.

Daniel, G. (1968) *The First Civilizations*. London: Thames and Hudson.

David, Rosalie (1986) *The Pyramid Builders of Ancient Egypt: A Modern Investigation of Pharaoh's Workforce*. London/Boston: Routledge and Kegan Paul.

Davies, Nina de Garis (1926) *The Tomb of Huy,* Theban Tomb Series, Vol. 4. London: The Egypt Exploration Society.

Davies, Norman de Garis (1944) *The Tomb of Rekh-Mi-Re' at Thebes.* New York: The Metropolian Museum of Art.

Davies, W. Vivian (1987) *Egyptian Hieroglyphs.* Berkeley/Los Angeles: University of California Press.

Decker, Wolfgang (1992) *Sports and Games of Ancient Egypt.* New Haven: Yale University Press.

Deuel, Leo (1961) *The Treasures of Time.* New York: World Publishing Co.

Diodorus, *Diodorus of Sicily* (trans. by C. H. Oldfather) (1976). New York: Putnum.

Dixon, David M. (1972) "The Disposal of Certain Personal, Household and Town Waste in Ancient Egypt," in *Man, Settlement and Urbanism*: *Proceedings of a Meeting at the Research Seminar in Archaeology and Related Subjects at the Institute of Archaeology, London University* (P. Ucko, R. Tringham, and G. W. Dimbleby, eds.), pp. 635–650, London: Duckworth Press.

Dodson, Aidan (1991) *Rock-cut Tombs.* Princes Risborough, Buckinghamshire: Shire.

Donadoni, Sergio (ed.) (1997) *The Egyptians.* Chicago: University of Chicago Press.

Drower, Margaret S. (1985) *Flinders Petrie: A Life in Archaeology.* London: Gollancz.

Edwards, Iorwerth E. S. (1985) *The Pyramids of Egypt.* Harmondsworth: Penguin.

Edwards, Iorwerth E. S., C. J. Gadd, N. C. L. Hammond (eds.) (1970) *The Cambridge Ancient History, Vol. 1/1: Prolegomena and Prehistory.* Cambridge: Cambridge University Press.

(eds.) (1971) *The Cambridge Ancient History, Vol. 1/2: Early History of the Middle East.* Cambridge: Cambridge University Press.

Edwards, Iorwerth E. S., C. J. Gadd, E. Sollberger (eds.) (1973) *The Cambridge Ancient History, Vol. 2/1: Middle East and Aegean Region, c. 1800–1380 B.C.* Cambridge: Cambridge University Press.

(eds.) (1975) *The Cambridge Ancient History, vol. 2/2: Middle East and Aegean Region, c. 1380–1000 B.C.* Cambridge: Cambridge University Press.

Emery, Walter B. (1949) *Great Tombs of the First Dynasty I.* Cairo: Government Press.

(1958) *Great Tombs of the First Dynasty at Saqqara III.* 47th Excavation Memoir, London: Egypt Exploration Society.

(1961) *Archaic Egypt.* Harmondsworth: Penguin.

Emery, Walter B. and L. P. Kirwan (1935) *The Excavations and Survey between Wadi es-Sebua and Adindan, 1929–31,* Vol. I-II. Service des Antiquities de l'Egypte. Cairo: Government Printing Office.

Erman, Adolf (1971) *Life in Ancient Egypt.* New York: Dover Books.

Eyre, Chris. J. (1987) "Work and the Organization of Work in the Old Kingdom," in *Labor in the Ancient Near East* (M. Powell. ed.), pp. 5–47. New Haven: American Oriental Society.

Fagan, Brian (1977) *The Rape of the Nile.* New York: Charles Scribner's Sons.

Fairman, Walker B. (1949) "Town Planning in Pharaonic Egypt," *Town Planning Review* 20, 32–51.

Fakhry, Ahmed (1961) *The Pyramids.* Chicago: University of Chicago Press.

(1973) *Siwa Oasis.* Cairo: American University in Cairo Press.

Faulkner, Raymond. (trans.), *et al.* (1994) *The Egyptian Book of the Dead: The Book of Going Forth by Day.* San Francisco: Chronicle Books.

Firth, Cecil M. (1912) *The Archaeological Survey of Nubia. Report for 1908–09,* Vols. I, II. Cairo: Government Press.

(1927) *The Archaeological Survey of Nubia. Report for 1910–11.* Cairo: Government Press.

Fischer, Clarence S. (1917) "The Eckley B. Coxe Jr Expedition," *The Museum Journal The University Museum, Philadelphia,* vol. VIII, no. 7, 211–225.

Fischer, Henry G. (1976) *Varia. Egyptian Studies I.* New York: The Metropolitan Museum of Art.

(1977) "Gaufürst," in *Lexikon de Ägyptologie II,* cols. 407–417. Wiesbaden: Otto Harrassowitz.

Foreman, Werner and Stephen Quirke (1996) *Hieroglyphs and the Afterlife in Ancient Egypt.* Norman, Okla.: University of Oklahoma Press.

Fox, Richard G. (1977) *Urban Anthropology: Cities in their Cultural Settings*. Englewood Cliffs, N.J.: Prentice Hall.

Frankfort, Henri and John D. S. Pendlebury (1933) *The City of Akhenaten, Part II: The North Suburb and the Desert Altars* (with a contribution by H. Fairman), 40th Excavation Memoir. London: The Egypt Exploration Society.

Gardiner, Alan (1948) *The Wilbour Papyrus*. 4 Vols. Oxford: Oxford University Press.

(1957) *Egyptian Grammar*. Oxford: The Griffith Institute/Oxford University Press.

(1961) *Egypt of the Pharaohs*. Oxford: Oxford University Press.

Gilead, David (1970) "Handaxe Industries in Israel and the Near East," *World Archaeology* 2, 1–11.

Grant, Michael (1972) *Cleopatra*. New York: Dorset Press.

Greener, Leslie (1966) *The Discovery of Egypt*. New York: Dorset Press.

Grimal, Nicolas (1992) *A History of Ancient Egypt*. Oxford: Blackwell.

Haarmann, Ulrich (1980) "Regional Settlement in Medieval Islamic Cairo," *Bulletin of the School of Oriental and African Studies* (University of London) 43, 55–66.

Harris, James R. (ed.) (1971) *The Legacy of Egypt*. Oxford: Oxford University Press.

Hart, George (1990) *Egyptian Myths*. London: The British Museum.

Hassan, Fekri (1981) *The Predynastic of Egypt: Subsistence-Settlement Studies in the Naqada-Khattara Region*, Final Report to the National Science Foundation.

(1985) "Radiocarbon Chronology of Neolithic and Predynastic Sites in Upper Egypt and the Delta," *The African Archaeological Review* 3, 95–116.

(1988) "The Predynastic of Egypt," *Journal of World Prehistory* 2, 135–185.

(1993) "Town and Village in Ancient Egypt: Ecology, Society and Urbanization," in *The Archaeology of Africa: Food, Metals and Towns* (Thurstan Shaw, Paul Sinclair, Bassey Andah and Alex Okpoki, eds.), pp 551–569. London/New York: Routledge.

Hawass, Zahi (1995) "Programs of Royal Funerary Complexes of the Fourth Dynasty," in *Ancient Egyptian Kingship*, Probleme der Ägyptologie 9 (David O'Connor and David Silverman, eds.), pp. 221–262. Leiden: E. J. Brill.

Hawass, Zahi and Mark Lehner (1997) "Builders of the Pyramids," *Archaeology Magazine*, 30–38.

Hawkins, Jacquetta D. (1979) "The Origin and Dissemination of Writing in Western Asia," in *The Origins of Civilization* (P. R. S. Moorey, ed.), pp. 128–166. Oxford: The Clarendon Press, 1979.

Hayes, William (1955) *A Papyrus of the Late Middle Kingdom in the Brooklyn Museum*. Brooklyn, N.Y.: The Brooklyn Museum.

Helck, Wolfgang (1977) "Gau," in *Lexikon der Ägyptologie II*, cols. 385–407. Wiesbaden: Otto Harrassowitz.

Hamdan, Gamal (1961) "Evolution of Irrigation Agriculture in Egypt," *Arid Zone Research* 17, 119–142.

(1964) "Egypt – The Land and People," in *Guidebook to the Geology and Archaeology of Egypt* (Frank Riley, ed.). Amsterdam: Elsevier.

Herodotus, *Books I-II* (trans. A. D. Godley). Cambridge, Mass.: Harvard University Press, 1920.

*The Histories* (II) (trans Aubrey de Sélincourt; and revised A. R. Burn). London: Penguin Books, 1972.

Herold, J. Christopher (1992) *Bonaparte in Egypt*. New York: Harper and Row.

Hoffman, Michael A. (1982) *The Predynastic of Hierakonpolis: An Interim Report*. Cairo: Egyptian Studies Association.

(1984) *Egypt Before the Pharaohs*. London: Ark Paperbacks.

Holmes, Diane L. (1992) "Recent Investigations in the Badari Region," in *Interregional Contacts in the Later Prehistory of North Africa* (Lech Kryzaniak, ed.), pp. 301–316. Pozan: Pozan Archaeological Museum.

Hornung, Erik (1982) *Conceptions of God in Ancient Egypt: The One and the Many*. Ithaca, N.Y.: Cornell University Press.

(1990) *The Valley of the Kings: Horizon of Eternity*. New York: Timken Press.

(1992) *Idea into Image: Essays on Ancient Egyptian Thought*. New York: Timkin Press.

Hume, William F. (1925) *The Geology of Egypt, Vol. I.* Cairo: Government Press.

Hutflies, Ann, (1995) "Politics and Potsherds," MS thesis on file, Dept of Anthropology, University of Illinois.

Issawi, Bahay (1976) "An Introduction to the Physiography of the Nile Valley," in *Prehistory of the Nile Valley* (F. Wendorf and R. Schild, eds.), pp. 3–22. New York: Academic Press.

Iversen, Erik (1955) *Canon and Proportions in Egyptian Art.* London: Sedgwick and Jackson.

James, T. G. H. (1962) *The Hekanakhte Papers and other Early Middle Kingdom Documents,* Publication of the Metropolitan Museum of Art. Expedition 19. New York: The Metropolitan Museum of Art.

(1979) *An Introduction to Ancient Egypt.* London: The British Museum.

(1984) *Pharaoh's People.* Chicago: University of Chicago Press.

(1988) *Ancient Egypt: The Land and its Legacy.* Austin, Tex.: University of Texas Press.

James, T. G. H. (ed.) (1982) *Excavating in Egypt.* Chicago: University of Chicago Press.

Janssen, Jac J. (1975) *Commodity Prices from the Ramesside Period.* Leiden: E. J. Brill.

(1978) "The Early State in Egypt," in *The Early State* (H. Claessen and P. Skalnick, eds.), pp. 213–234. The Hague: Mouton.

Janssen, Rosalind M. and Jac J. Janssen (1980) *Growing up in Ancient Egypt.* London: Rubicon Press.

(1996) *Getting Old in Ancient Egypt.* London: Rubicon Press.

Johnson, Janet H. (1997) "The Legal Status of Women in Ancient Egypt," in *Mistress of the House, Mistress of Heaven: Women in Ancient Egypt* (Ann Capel and Glenn Markoe, eds.), pp. 175–185, 215–217. Cincinnati: Cincinnati Art Museum.

Johnson, W. Raymond (1996) "Amunhotep III and Amarna: Some New Considerations," *Journal of Egyptian Archaeology* 82, 65–82.

Kanawati, Naguib (1977) *The Egyptian Administration in the Old Kingdom: Evidence on its Economic Decline.* Warminster: Aris and Philips.

Kees, Hermann (1961) *Ancient Egypt: A Geographical History of the Nile.* Chicago: University of Chicago Press.

Keller, Kathleen. A. (1994) "Speculations Concerning the Interconnections between the Royal Policy and the Reputation of Ramesses IV" in *For His Ka: Essays Offered in Memory of Klaus Baer* (David Silverman, ed.), pp. 145–157. Studies in Ancient Oriental Civilizations 55, Chicago: The Oriental Institute.

Kemp, Barry J. (1972a) "Fortified Towns in Nubia," in *Man, Settlement and Urbanism: Proceedings of a Meeting at the Research Seminar in Archaeology and Related Subjects at the Institute of Archaeology, London University* (P. Ucko, R. Tringham, and G. W. Dimbleby, eds.), pp. 651–656. London: Duckworth Press.

(1972b) "Temple and Town in Ancient Egypt," in *Man, Settlement and Urbanism: Proceedings of a Meeting at the Research Seminar in Archaeology and Related Subjects at the Institute of Archaeology, London University* (P. Ucko, R. Tringham and G. W. Dimbleby, eds.), pp. 657–680. London: Duckworth Press.

(1976) "The Window of Appearance at Amarna and the Basic Structure of the City," *Journal of Egyptian Archaeology* 62, 81–99.

(1977a) "The City of el Amarna as a Source for the Study of Urban Society in Ancient Egypt," *World Archaeology* 9, 123–139.

(1977b) "The Early Development of Towns in Egypt," *Antiquity* 51, 185–200.

(1991) *Ancient Egypt: Anatomy of a Civilization.* London: KPI.

(1996) "Meritaten's Bathroom," in *The Ostracon* (newsletter of the Egyptian Studies Society, Denver), Vol. 7, No. 3, 1–5.

Kitchen, Kenneth (1982) *Pharaoh Triumphant: The Life and Times of Ramesses II.* Warminster: Aris and Phillips Ltd.

(1996) *The Third Intermediate Period in Egypt.* Warminster: Aris and Philips.

(1999, in press) "The Wealth of Amun of Thebes under Ramesses II," in *Gold of Praise, Studies on Ancient Egypt in Honor of Edward F. Wente* (E. Teeter and J. A. Larson, eds.). Chicago: The Oriental Institute.

Kramer, Carol (1982) *Village Ethnoarchaeology*. New York: Academic Press.

Lacovara, Peter (1997) *The New Kingdom Royal City*. London/New York: Kegan Paul.

Lauer, Jean P. (1977) *The Pyramids of Sakkarah*. Cairo: IFAO.

Lehner and Zahi Hawass (1997) "Builders of the Pyramids," *Archaeology Magazine* January/February, 30–38.

Leprohon, Ronald (1995) "Royal Ideology and State Administration in Pharaonic Egypt," in *Civilizations of the Ancient Near East*, Vol. I (J. M. Sasson, ed.), pp. 273–287. New York: Scribner's.

Lesko, Leonard (1977) *King Tut's Wine Cellar*. Berkeley, Ca.: B.C. Scribe.

Lichtheim, Miriam (1973) *Ancient Egyptian Literature: A Book of Readings, Vol. I: The Old and Middle Kingdoms*. Berkeley, Ca.: University of California.

(1976) *Ancient Egyptian Literature: A Book of Readings, Vol. II: The New Kingdom*. Berkeley, Ca.: University of California.

(1980) *Ancient Egyptian Literature: A Book of Readings, Vol. III: The Late Period*. Berkeley, Ca.:University of California.

Lloyd, Christopher (1973) *The Nile Campaign*. New York: Newton Abbott.

Logan, Thomas J. (in press, 1999) "Royal Iconography of the Early Archaic Period: Dynasty 0," in *Gold of Praise, Studies on Ancient Egypt in Honor of Edward F. Wente* (E. Teeter and J.A. Larson, eds.), Chicago: The Oriental Institute.

Loprieno, Antonio (1995) *Ancient Egyptian: A Linguistic Introduction*. Cambridge: Cambridge University Press.

Lucas, Alfred (1926) *Ancient Egyptian Materials and Industries*. London: Edward Arnold and Co.

McDowell, Andrea (1990) *Jurisdiction in the Workmen's Community of Deir el-Medîna*. Leiden: Nederlands Instituut voor Het Nabije Oosten.

Maisels, Charles K. (1990) *The Emergence of Civilization: From Hunting and Gathering to Agriculture, Cities and the State in the Near East*. London: Routledge.

Malék, Jaromir (1986) *In the Shadow of the Pyramids: Egypt During the Old Kingdom*. Norman, Okla.: University of Oklahoma Press.

Manniche, Lise (1987) *Sexual Life in Ancient Egypt*. London: KPI.

(1991) *Music and Musicians in Ancient Egypt*. London: The British Museum.

Der Manuelian, Peter (in press, 1999) "Semi-Literacy in Egypt: Some Erasures from the Amarna Period," in *Gold of Praise, Studies on Ancient Egypt in Honor of Edward F. Wente* (E. Teeter and J. A. Larson, eds.), Chicago: The Oriental Institute.

Martin-Pardey, E. (1986) "Wizir," "Wizirat" in *Lexikon der Ägyptologie VI*, cols. 1227–1235. Wiesbaden: Otto Harrassowitz.

Mattha, Girgis (1975) *The Demotic Legal Code of Hermopolis West*. Bibliotèque d'Étude 45. Cairo: IFAO.

Menghin, Oswald (1931) "Die Grabung der Unversitat Kario bei Maadi," *Mitteilungen des Deutschen Archaologischen Instituts Abteilung Kairo* 1, 143–147.

(1932) "Die Grabung der Unversitat Kario bei Maadi,' *Mitteilungen des Deutschen Archaologischen Instituts Abteilung Kairo* 3, 150–153.

(1934) "Die Grabung der Unversitat Kario bei Maadi," *Mitteilungen des Deutschen Archaologischen Instituts Abteilung Kairo* 5, 111–118.

Menghin, Oswald and Moustafa Amer (1932) *Excavations of the Egyptian University in the Neolithic Site of Maadi, First Preliminary Report (Season 1930–1931)*. Cairo: Government Press.

Million, René (1973) *Urbanization at Teotihuacan*. Austin, Tex.: University of Texas Press.

Montserrat, Dominic (1996) *Sex and Society in Graeco-Roman Egypt*. London:KPI.

Moorehead, Alan (1961) *The Blue Nile*. New York: Harper and Row.

Morenz, Sigfried (1973) *Egyptian Religion*. Ithaca, N.Y.: Cornell University Press.

Mumford, Louis (1960) "Concluding Address," in *City Invincible: A Symposium on Urbanization and Cultural Development in the Ancient Near East* (C. H. Kraeling and R. McC. Adams, eds.), pp. 224–248. Chicago: University of Chicago.

Murnane, William J. (1983) *The Penguin Guide to Ancient Egypt*. Harmondsworth: Penguin.

(1995a) "The Kingship of the Nineteenth Dynasty: A Study in the Resilience of an Institution," in *Ancient Egyptian Kingship*, Probleme der Ägyptologie 9 (David Silverman and David O' Connor, eds.), pp. 185–217. Leiden: E. J. Brill.

(1995b) *Texts from the Amarna Period in Egypt*. Atlanta, Geo.: SBL Scholar's Press.

*Nekhen News* (1997) (Newsletter of the Friends of Nekhen), vol. 9. Milwaukee: Milwaukee Public Museum.

Nunn, John, F. (1996) *Ancient Egyptian Medicine*. Norman, Okla.: University of Oklahoma Press.

O'Connor, David (1972a) "A Regional Population in Egypt to circa 600 BC," in *Population Growth: Anthropological Implications* (B. Spooner, ed.), pp. 78–100. Cambridge, Mass.: MIT Press.

(1972b) "The Geography of Settlement in Ancient Egypt," in *Man, Settlement and Urbanism*: *Proceedings of a Meeting at the Research Seminar in Archaeology and Related Subjects at the Institute of Archaeology, London University* (P. Ucko, R. Tringham, and G. W. Dimbleby, eds.), pp. 681–698. London: Duckworth Press.

(1990) *Ancient Egyptian Society*. Pittsburgh, Pa.: Carnegie Museum.

(1991) "Mirror of the Cosmos: The Palace of Merenptah," in *Fragments of a Shattered Visage: The Proceedings of the International Symposium on Ramesses the Great* (Edward Bleiberg and Rita Freed, eds.), pp. 167–198. Memphis, Tenn.: Institute of Egyptian Art and Archaeology.

(1995a) "Beloved of Maat; the Horizon of Re: The Royal Palace in New Kingdom Egypt," in *Ancient Egyptian Kingship*, Probleme der Ägyptologie 9 (David Silverman and David O'Connor, eds.), pp. 263–300. Leiden: E. J. Brill.

(1995b) "The Earliest Royal Boat Graves," *Egyptian Archaeology* 6, 3–7.

O'Connor, David and David Silverman (1979) "The University Museum in Egypt," *Expedition* vol. 21, no. 2, 33–43.

(1995) *Ancient Egyptian Kingship*, Probleme der Agyptologie IX. Leiden: E. J. Brill.

Parker, Richard (1950) *The Calendars of Ancient Egypt*, Studies in Ancient Oriental Civilizations 26. Chicago: University of Chicago Press.

(1971) "The Calendars and Chronology," in *The Legacy of Egypt* (J. R. Harris, ed.), pp. 13–26. Oxford: Oxford University Press.

Parkinson, Richard and Stephen Quirke (1995) *Papyrus*. Austin, Tex.: University of Texas Press.

Peck, William (1996) "Craftsmen and Artist" and "Methods of Representation," in *The Macmillan Dictionary of Art*, Vol. IX, pp. 789–791, 798–799. London: Macmillan.

Peet, T. Eric (1914) *The Cemeteries of Abydos, Part II*, Excavation Memoir 34. London: Egypt Exploration Society.

(1930) *The Great Tomb Robberies of the Twentieth Egyptian Dynasty*. Oxford: Oxford University Press.

Pendlebury, John D. S. (1951) *City of Akhenaten, Part III: The Central City and Official Quarters*, Excavation Memoir 44. London: Egypt Exploration Society.

Petrie, W. Flinders (1900) *The Royal Tombs of the First Dynasty* Vol. I. London: The Egypt Exploration Fund.

(1932) *Seventy Years in Archaeology*. New York: Henry Holt & Co.

Petrie, W. Flinders and A. C. Mace (1901) *Diospolis Parva: The Cemeteries of Abadiyeh and Hu, 1898–9*, Excavation Memoir 20. London: The Egypt Exploration Fund.

Petrie, W. Flinders and J. E. Quibell (1896) *Naqada and Ballas*, BSAE 1. London: Bernard Quaritch.

Piccione, Peter (1990) "Mehen, Mysteries, and Resurrection from the Coiled Serpent," *Journal of the American Research Center in Egypt* 27, 43–52.

Plutarch, *Plutarch Moralia* (trans. Frank C. Babbitt) (1969). New York: Putnum's.

Pritchard, James (1969) *Ancient Near Eastern Texts Relating to the Old Testament,* 3rd edn. Princeton: Princeton University Press.

Quibell, James Edward and Frederick William Green (1902) *Hierakonpolis II*, Egyptian Research Account V. London: Bernard Quaritch.

Quirke, Stephen (1992) *Ancient Egyptian Religion*. London: The British Museum.

Quirke, Stephen and Carol Andrews (1988) *The Rosetta Stone*. New York: Harry Abrams.

Quirke, Stephen and Jeffrey Spencer (1992) *Ancient Egypt*. London: The British Museum.

Ray, John D. (1986) "The Emergence of Writing in Egypt," *World Archaeology* 17, 307–316.

    (1995) "The Mesopotamian Influence on Ancient Egyptian Writing," in *Egypt in Africa* (T. Celenko, ed.). pp. 38–39. Indianapolis: Indianapolis Museum of Art.

Redfield, Robert and Milton Singer (1954) "The Cultural Role of Cities," *Economic Development and Cultural Change* 3, 53–73.

Redford, Donald B. (1984) *Akhenaten, the Heretic King*. Princeton: Princeton University Press.

    (1986) *Pharaonic King-lists, Annals and Day-books*. Mississauga, Ontario: Benben Books.

    (1989) "Prolegomena to Archaeological Investigations at Mendes," MS on file with authors.

    (1992) *Egypt, Canaan and Israel in Ancient Times*. Princeton: Princeton University Press.

    (1995) "The Concept of Kingship During the Eighteenth Dynasty," in *Ancient Egyptian Kingship*, Probleme der Ägyptologie IX (David Silverman and David O'Connor, eds.), pp. 157–184. Leiden: E. J. Brill.

Reisner, George A. (1910) *The Archaeological Survey of Nubia, Report for 1907–08*, Vol. I. Cairo: National Printing Department.

    (1936) *The Development of the Egyptian Tomb down to the Accession of Cheops,* Cambridge, Mass.: Harvard University Press.

    (1942) *A History of the Giza Necropolis*. Vol. I. Cambridge/London: Harvard University Press/Oxford University Press.

Reymond, Eva Anne (1969) *The Mythical Origin of the Egyptian Temple*. New York: Barnes and Noble.

Rice, Prudence (1987) *Pottery Analysis: A Source Book*. Chicago: University of Chicago Press.

Robins, Gay (1986) *Egyptian Painting and Relief*. Aylesbury: Shire.

    (1993) *Women in Ancient Egypt*. London: The British Museum.

    (1994a) *Proportion and Style in Ancient Egyptian Art*. Austin, Tex.: University of Texas Press.

    (1994b) "Some Principles of Compositional Dominance and Gender Hierarchy in Egyptian Art," *Journal of the American Research Center in Egypt* 31, 33–40.

    (1997) *The Art of Ancient Egypt*. Cambridge, Mass.: Harvard University Press.

Roth, Ann M. (1993) "Social Change in the Fourth Dynasty: The Spatial Organization of Pyramids, Tombs and Cemeteries," *Journal of the American Research Center in Egypt* 30, 33–56.

Roux, Georges (1980) *Ancient Iraq*. Harmondsworth: Penguin.

Said, Rushdi (1962) *The Geology of Egypt*. Amsterdam: Elsevier.

    (1975) "The Geological Evolution of the River Nile," in *Problems in Prehistory: North Africa and the Levant* (F. Wendorf and A. Marks, eds.), pp. 7–44. Dallas, Tex.: Southern Methodist University Press.

Sasson, Jack (ed.) (1995) *Civilizations of the Ancient Near East*. 4 vols. New York: Scribner's.

Sauneron, Serge (1960) *The Priests of Ancient Egypt*. New York: Grove.

Schafer, Byron (ed.) (1997) *Temples of Ancient Egypt*. Ithaca, N.Y.: Cornell University Press.

Schäfer, Heinrich (1974) *Principles of Egyptian Art* (trans. J. Baines). Oxford: Oxford University Press.

Schulman, Alan R. (1964) *Military Rank, Title and Organization in the Egyptian New Kingdom*. Münchner Ägyptologische Studien 6. Berlin: Bruno Hessling Verlag.

    (1995) "Military Organization in Pharaonic Egypt," in *Civilizations of the Ancient Near East*, Vol. I (J. Sasson, ed.), pp. 289–301. New York: Scribner's.

Seaton-Williams, Veronica and Peter Stocks (1983) *Blue Guide: Egypt*. New York: W. W. Norton.

Service, Elman R. (1975) *Origins of the State and Civilization*. New York: W. W. Norton.

Shanks, Michael and Christopher Tilley (1987) *Social Theory and Archaeology*. Cambridge: Polity, in association with Blackwell.

Simpson, William K. (ed.) (1972) *The Literature of Ancient Egypt*. New Haven: Yale University Press.

Smith, Grafton Elliot and Warren Royal Dawson (1924) *Egyptian Mummies*. London/New York: Kegan Paul International (original edition reissued 1991).

Smith, Henry S. and Rosalind Hall (eds.) (1983) *Ancient Centres of Egyptian Civilization*. Shooter's Lodge, Windsor Forest, Berkshire: Kensel Press.

Smith, William Stevenson (1949) *A History of Egyptian Sculpture and Painting in the Old Kingdom*. London: Oxford University Press for the Museum of Fine Arts, Boston.

(1958) *The Art and Architecture of Ancient Egypt*. Harmondsworth: Penguin Books.

Spencer, A. Jeffrey (1979) *Brick Architecture in Ancient Egypt*. Warminster: Aris and Phillips.

(1993) *Early Egypt*: *The Rise of Civilization in the Nile Valley*. Norman, Okla.: University of Oklahoma Press.

Stadelmann, Reiner (1979) "Totentempel und Millionjahrhaus in Theben," *Mitteilungen des Deutschen Archaologischen Instituts Abteilung Kairo* 79, 303–331.

(1996) "Temple Palace and Residential Palace," in *Haus und Palast im alten Ägypten* (M. Bietak, ed.), pp. 225–230. Vienna: Verlag der Österreichischen Akademie der Wissenschaften.

Strouhal, Eugene (1992) *Life of the Ancient Egyptians*. Norman, Okla.: University of Oklahoma Press.

Strudwick, Nigel (1985a) *The Administration of Egypt in the Old Kingdom*. London: KPI.

(1985b) Review of Kanawati, *Governmental Reforms of the Old Kingdom*, *Journal of Egyption Archeology* 71 (supplement), 29–30.

(1995) "The Population of Thebes in the New Kingdom: Some Preliminary Thoughts," in *Thebanische beamtennekropen* (J. Assmann, E. Dziobeck, *et al.*, eds.) pp. 97–105. Studien zur Archäologie und Geschichte Altgyptens 12, Heidelberg.

Teeter, Emily (1990) "Hatshepsut," *KMT: A Modern Journal of Ancient Egypt* Spring, 4–13, 56–57.

(1993a) "Female Musicians in Pharaonic Egypt," in *Rediscovering the Muses: Women's Musical Traditions* (K. Marshall, ed.), pp. 68–91. Boston: Northeastern University.

(1993b) "Popular Religion in Ancient Egypt," *KMT: A Modern Journal of Ancient Egypt*, Vol. 4, No. 2, 28–37.

(1997a) "The Life of Ritual," in *Ancient Egypt* (David Silverman, ed.), pp. 148–165. New York: Oxford University Press.

(1997b) *The Presentation of Maat: Legitimacy and Ritual in Ancient Egypt*, Studies in Ancient Oriental Civilizations 57. Chicago: Oriental Institute Press.

(in press) "The Body in Ancient Egyptian Texts and Representations," in *The Body in the Ancient Near East* (C. Jones and T. Wilfong, eds.). Leiden: Styx.

Thompson, Angela P. (1986) *Egyptian Gods and Myths*. Aylesbury: Shire.

Thompson, Jason (1992) *Sir Gardner Wilkinson and his Circle*. Austin, Tex.: University of Texas Press.

Trigger, Bruce G. (1972) "Determinants of Urban Growth in Pre-industrial Societies," in *Man, Settlement and Urbanism*: *Proceedings of a Meeting at the Research Seminar in Archaeology and Related Subjects at the Institute of Archaeology, London University* (P. Ucko, R. Tringham, and G. W. Dimbleby, eds.), pp. 575–599. London: Duckworth Press.

(1985) "The Evolution of Pre-industrial Cities: A Multilinear Perspective," in *Mélanges offerts à Jean Vercoutter* (F. Geus and F. Thill, eds.), pp. 434–453. Paris: Éditions Rescherche sur les Civilisations.

(1993) *Early Civilizations*. Cairo: American University in Cairo Press.

Trigger, Bruce G., Barry J. Kemp, David O'Connor, and Alan B. Lloyd (1983) *Ancient Egypt: A Social History*. Cambridge: Cambridge University Press.

Uphill, Eric P. (1988) *Egyptian Towns and Cities*. Aylesbury: Shire.

te Velde, Herman (1995) "The End of Religious Tradition: the Case of Egypt," in *Abstracts of Papers of the Seventh International Congress of Egyptologists, Cambridge, 3–9 September 1995*, pp. 192–193.

Vercoutter, Jean (1992) *The Search for Ancient Egypt*. New York: Harry Abrams.

Vermeersch, Pierre (1970) "L'Elkabien: Une nouvelle industrie épipaléolithique Elkab en Haute Égypte: sa Stratigraphie, sa Typologie," *Chronique d'Égypte* XLV 89, 45–64.

van den Boorn, Guido P. F. (1988) *The Duties of the Vizier: Civil Admistration in Early New Kingdom Egypt*. London: KPI.

van den Brink, Edwin C. (ed.) (1988), *The Archaeology of the Nile Delta: Problems and Priorities*. Amsterdam: Netherlands Foundation for Archeological Research.

Vogelsang-Eastwood, Gillian (1993) *Egyptian Pharaonic Clothing*. Leiden: E.J. Brill.

Von der Way, Thomas (1987) "Tell el-Fara'in-Buto, Bericht mit einem Beitrag von Klaus Schmidt zu den lithischen Kleinfunden," *Mitteilungen des Deutschen Archaologischen Instituts Abteilung Kairo* 43, 241–250.

  (1988) "Investigations Concerning the Early Periods in the Northern Delta of Egypt," in *The Archaeology of the Nile Delta: Problems and Priorities* (E. C. M. van den Brink, ed.), pp 245–249. Amsterdam: Nederlandse Stichting voor Archeologisch Orderzock in Egypte.

Walker, Christopher B. F. (1987) *Cuneiform*. London: The British Museum.

Watson, Phillip (1987) *Costumes of Ancient Egypt*. New York: Chelsea House.

Watterson, Barbara (1991) *Women in Ancient Egypt*. Stroud: Alan Sutton.

Welsby, Derek (1996) *The Kingdom of Kush*. London: The British Museum.

Wendorf, Fred (1968) *Prehistory of Nubia*. Dallas, Tex.: Southern Methodist University Press.

Wenke, Robert J. (1986) "Old Kingdom Community Organization in the Western Desert," *Norwegian Archaeological Review* 19, 15–33.

  (1990) *Patterns in Prehistory*. Oxford: Oxford University Press.

Wenke, Robert J. and Douglas J. Brewer (1996) "The Archaic-Old Kingdom Delta: The Evidence from Mendes and Kom el-Hisn," in *Haus und Palast im alten Ägypten* (M. Bietak, ed.), pp. 265–285, Vienna: Verlag der Österreichischen Akademie der Wissenschaften.

Wenke, Robert J., Richard Redding, Paul Buck, Michal Kobusiewicz, and Karla Kroeper (1988) "Kom el Hisn: Excavations of an Old Kingdom West Delta Community," *Journal of the American Research Center in Egypt* 25, 5–34.

Wildung, Dietrich (1977a) *Egyptian Saints: Deification in Ancient Egypt*. New York: New York University Press.

  (1977b) *Imhotep und Amenhotep,* Münchner Ägyptologischer Studien 36. München/Berlin: Deutscher Kunstverlag.

Wilfong, Terry (in press, 1999) "Menstruation and the Place of Women in Ancient Egypt," in *Gold of Praise: Studies on Ancient Egypt in Honor of Edward F. Wente* (Emily Teeter and John A. Larson, eds.). Chicago: The Oriental Institute.

Wilkinson, John Gardner (1878) *The Manners and Customs of the Ancient Egyptians*. London: John Murray.

Williams, R. J. (1972) "Scribal Training in Ancient Egypt," *Journal of the American Oriental Society* 92, 214–221.

Wilson, John (1947) "The Artist in the Egyptian Old Kingdom," *Journal of Near Eastern Studies* 6, 231–249.

  (1960) "Egypt through the New Kingdom: Civilization without Cities," in *City Invincible: A Symposium on Urbanization and Cultural Development in the Ancient Near East* (C. H. Kraeling and R. McC. Adams, eds.), pp. 124–164. Chicago: University of Chicago Press.

Wise, Terrance and Angus McBride (1981) *Ancient Armies of the Middle East*. London: Osprey.

Wunderlich, Jürgen (1986) "Investigations of the Development of the Western Nile Delta in Holocene Times," in *The Archaeology of the Nile Delta, Egypt: Problems and Priorities* (E. C. M. van den Brink, ed.), pp. 251–257. Amsterdam: Nederlandse Stichting voor Archeologisch Orderzock in Egypte.

Yoffee, Norman and George L. Cowgill (eds.) (1988) *The Collapse of States and Civilizations.* Tucson, Ariz.: University of Arizona Press.

Zahran, M. A. and A. J. Willis (1992) *The Vegetation of Egypt.* Cambridge: Chapman and Hill.

Zauzich, Karl-Theodor (1992) *Hieroglyphs without Mystery* (trans. A. Roth). Austin, Tex.: University of Texas Press.

# GLOSSARY

**Acheulean**: Tool assemblage characterized by a reduction of stone to make a large multi-purpose instrument such as a hand-ax (*ca.* 50,000–100,000 BC).

**AD**: **anno Domini** (in the year of our Lord).

**Akh**: One of the divisions of the human soul; undergoes transfiguration into blessed status upon rebirth.

**Amarna**: (Tell el Amarna) Modern name for Akhetaten, "Horizon of the Aten," the capital city founded by King Akhenaten in Dynasty 18.

**Amarna Letters**: Cuneiform tablets found at Tell el Amarna detailing the trade and political relationships of Egypt with Western Asia during the reigns of Amunhotep III to Tutankhamun (Dynasty 18).

**Amratian**: Synonym for the Naqada I Predynastic period.

**Amulet**: Good luck/protective charm, often in the form of a hieroglyph.

**Ankh**: Hieroglyph in the form of a looped top cross meaning "to live" and "life."

**Apis bull**: Bull sacred to the god Ptah and later to the god Osiris-Serapis. Buried from the New Kingdom onward in a catacomb at Sakkara.

**Archaeologist**: A scholar who investigates historic or prehistoric cultures through the study of materials such as objects, inscriptions, or architecture; such information is usually retrieved through systematic excavations.

**Assyrians**: Kingdom that gained prominence with the decline of the Mittanians around 1300 BC; center of kingdom at Ashur in northern Iraq; invaded Egypt several times in seventh century BC.

**Aten**: God represented by the disk or globe of the sun; elevated by Akhenaten (Dynasty 18) above all other deities.

**Atum**: Primeval cosmic creator god; appeared spontaneously from Nun; progenitor of elements of the universe.

**Aurochs**: (pl. aurochsen) Wild bovid (*Bos primigenius*) that extended across Euro-Asian continent and much of North Africa; thought to be the progenitor of domestic cattle.

**Ba**: Element of the soul of the deceased that was able to leave the tomb and maintain contact with the realm of the living; shown in the form of a human-headed bird (see fig. 10.1).

**Barque**: A boat; often a sacred boat used to transport a statue of a god or the king (see fig. 6.2).

**Bas relief**: Technique of carving on stone wherein the background is cut away, leaving the design standing above the background.

**BC**: Before Christ (BCE: before the common era); upper case represents a calibrated or calendrical date. Lower case (bc) represents an uncalibrated radio metric or other date.

**Bitumen**: A naturally occurring mineral pitch composed of hydrocarbons resembling tar.

**"Book of the Dead"**: Modern name for series of New Kingdom religious texts intended to protect the soul of the deceased as it traveled through the underworld toward rebirth (see fig. 10.4).

**BP**: Before present, upper case represents calibrated date, lower case (bp) represents an uncalibrated radiometric date.

**C-14**: Radiocarbon dating method based on organic (carbon-based) materials such as wood, plant materials, mollusk shells, and bone.

**Canopic jar**: Vessel of stone or pottery into which mummified organs were stored in the tomb. There were four canopic jars, one each for the stomach, liver, lungs, and intestines. The organs could also be stored in canopic coffins which in turn might be stored in a canopic chest. "Canopic" refers to the Late Period god Canopis who was represented in a form that resembled a jar (see fig. 10.3).

**Cartonnage**: Papier-mâchè-like material made of layers of papyrus, gum, fabric, and plaster, used to make anthropoid coffins and other fittings for mummies.

**Cartouche**: Oval-shaped loop encircling a royal name.

**Cataract**: Outcropping of rock in the Nile that created innavigable rapids. The six cataracts from near Khartoum to Aswan protected Egypt from invasion from the south.

**Cavetto cornice**: Architectural feature; recurved stone surface at top of wall or above doors that represents the frayed reeds at edge of mats once used for walls (see fig. 9.1).

**Cenotaph**: Symbolic tomb.

**Colossi of Memnon**: Name given to a pair of statues in front of the ruined mortuary temple of Amenhotep III in western Thebes.

**Coptic**: Sect of Christianity prevalent in Egypt; from the Greek *aiguptios* and Arabic *gubti* for "Egypt"; also the last stage of the ancient Egyptian language, written in Greek letters.

**Corvée**: Involuntary labor or service to the state theoretically required of all Egyptians.

**Cubit**: Ancient Egyptian measurement based on the width of six palms; approximately 45 centimeters.

**Deben**: Unit of weight; by the time of the New Kingdom, metals were expressed in deben as a monetary referent to establish the worth of a commodity.

**Delta**: Large flat plain lying north of Cairo (ancient Memphis) and drained by the Nile river. Area also known as Lower Egypt.

**Demotic**: Cursive script used to write the Egyptian language from about 600 BC onward.

**La Description (de l'Egypte)**: Twenty-four-volume compilation of Egypt's natural history and culture produced by the savants accompanying Napoleon's invasion of Egypt.

**Determinative**: Unvocalized symbol in the Egyptian writing system that prescribes meaning to a word.

**Diodorus**: Greek historian (*ca.* 80–20 BC) who wrote forty books on world history.

**Dynasty**: A series of rulers, often from the same line of descent; generally traced from father to son.

**Early Dynastic**: Synonym for Archaic period, Dynasties I and II.

**Eastern Desert**: Desert that lies between the Nile and the Red Sea.

**Faience**: Quartz paste-based pottery used to make statuettes, amulets and ritual vessels. Often bright blue or blue green, but it could be glazed in a variety of colors.

**False door**: Architectural feature of tombs and temples; representation of a door. In temples, functioned as the focus of cult activities; in a tomb it was the means by which the soul could travel between the subterranean burial chamber and the tomb chambers (see fig. 10.6).

**Gerzean**: Synonym for the Naqada II Predynastic period.

**Geziras**: Deposits of sand, silt, and clay that appear as islands above the flat plain of the Nile Delta.

**Heb-sed**: Ritual in which the king demonstrated his vitality and ability to rule by running a prescribed course. The ritual was initially celebrated in the thirtieth year of the king's rule and at more frequent intervals thereafter. Also called the "jubilee" (see fig. 6.4).

**Henotheism**: The elevation of one god over others, without eliminating others as in monotheism; characteristic of the religion of Akhenaten.

**Herodotus**: Greek historian (*ca.* 484–430 BC) who traveled widely throughout the Mediterranean world chronicling the cultures of the region. Author of *The Histories*.

**Hieratic**: Cursive form of hieroglyphs used alongside the more complex hieroglyphs (see fig. 8.4).

**Hittites**: Indo-European cultural group occupying central and southern Turkey, *ca.* 1700–1200 BC.

**Hyksos**: People from Western Asia who settled in the delta and ruled parts of Egypt during the Second Intermediate Period.

**Hypostyle**: Architectural term (Greek: many columned), referring to the columned hall in an Egyptian temple.

**Ideogram**: Symbol in Egyptian writing system that represents a word or concept.

**Intaglio**: Technique of carving on stone wherein the design is cut into the background; also called sunk relief.

**Jubilee**: see *heb-sed*.

**Ka**: Part of the soul represented in human form; element of the being that needed food and provisions after death.

**Karnak Temple**: Complex of temples at modern Luxor; dominated by Temple of Amun – the largest structure ever dedicated to any god (see fig. 9.15).

**Khedive**: Title for the Turkish ruler of Egypt (1805–1914).

**Khekeru frieze**: Form of architectural ornamentation; carved or painted representation of bundles of bound reeds; most often at top of wall or above lintels (see fig. 9.1).

**Kingdoms**: Socio-political units of Egyptian history devised by modern scholars as a means to group dynasties into similar socio-cultural units.

**Kom**: An elevated mound representing an ancient archaeological site (synonym for tell).

**Late Predynastic**: Synonym for Naqada II (Gerzean) period.

**Levee**: Natural elevated features created by the annual flooding of the river, usually running parallel to the river's course.

**Logogram**: Symbol in written Egyptian that represents a word.

**Lost wax**: Technique of casting a bronze figure by initially fashioning it in wax and encasing it in clay. The clay jacket was heated to harden the clay and melt the wax, the resulting void was then filled with molten bronze. When the metal had hardened, the clay jacket was broken away from the bronze figure.

**Lower Egypt**: The delta.

**Maat**: Truth, justice, righteousness; also the goddess (Maat) who is the embodiment of truth.

**Mastaba**: (Arabic: bench) Mud-brick or stone rectangular tomb superstructure characteristic of Archaic royal tombs and private tombs of the Old and Middle Kingdoms (see fig. 10.5).

**Medjay**: Desert police force, usually made up of Nubians.

**Menat**: Beaded necklace carried by some priestesses and deities; the sound of the necklace when shaken was thought to be pleasing to the gods.

**Middle Egypt**: Administrative area referring to the area between Cairo and Asyut.

**Mittanians**: Cultural group occupying northern Mesopotamia between Tigris and Euphrates river (*ca.* 1500–1300 BC).

**Mousterian**: Stone tools characterized by a type of flaking technique whereby the stone is reduced by flaking to a dome-shaped core. In this lithic industry it is the flakes that are further shaped into tools, not the core itself (*ca.* 50,000 BC).

**Mulqaf**: An architectural feature for cooling a house, composed of a hooded opening on the roof that catches the prevailing wind, carrying it into the house's interior.

**Naos**: Stone cubicle or shrine, usually in the sanctuary of the temple and in which the cult statue of the god resided.

**Narmer Palette**: A votive palette depicting King Narmer (*ca.* 3100 BC), thought to represent the king defeating delta enemies and commemorating the initial unification of Egypt (see fig. 3.2).

**Natron**: Sodium carbonate and bicarbonate used in the preparation of mummies.

**Neolithic**: Period when evidence of domestication (plants or animals) can be determined. In Egypt the Neolithic precedes the Predynastic.

**Neolithic revolution**: Term applied to the apparent rapid spread of a Neolithic lifestyle throughout the ancient world.

**Nilometer**: Staircase, a simple stone or other surface marked with calibrations to record the height of the Nile flood.

**Nomarch**: Governor of an Egyptian province (nome).

**Nome**: Greek name for administrative districts of Egypt.

**Nubia**: Area between the first and sixth Nile cataracts (today's southern Egypt and northern Sudan).

**Opet**: Annual festival held in Thebes (Luxor) from Dynasty 18 onward in which statues of the gods and the king were carried between Karnak and Luxor Temples. The Opet festival was thought to ritually rejuvenate the spirit of the king.

**Osiris**: Major deity of the afterlife; from the Old Kingdom onward the deceased was associated with Osiris (see fig. 6.3a).

**Ostracon:** (pl. ostraca) Flake of limestone or pottery used for written records or to practice sketching or writing.

**Paleolithic**: Old stone age, a general reference to that period prior to the domestication of plants and animals.

**Palette**: Flat piece of stone used for grinding cosmetic pigments. Votive examples were carved with commemorative or ritual scenes.

**Papyrus**: Paper-like substance made of overlapped strips of the papyrus stalk.

**Pharaoh**: Title for the King of Egypt attested from the New Kingdom onward; from Egyptian *per-aa*: meaning "great house."

**Phonogram**: A sign that represents a phonetic value.

**Pleistocene**: Geological epoch (*ca.* 1.5 million years ago to 10,000 BP).

**Pliocene**: Geological epoch (*ca.* 5–15 million years ago).

**Pluvial**: A period of increased effective precipitation.

**Portico**: Architectural term; row of columns around the perimeter of a court.

**Punt**: Area south of Egypt famed for incense, perhaps Eritrea.

**Pylon**: Monumental gateway of an Egyptian temple; represents the horizon.

**Pyramid Texts**: Religious texts intended to protect the spirit of the king in the afterlife incised on the walls of pyramid burial chambers from Dynasty 5 to 12. Pyramid Texts were usurped by commoners and evolved into Coffin Texts in private tombs of the Middle Kingdom.

**Savants**: Scholars accompanying Napoleon's expedition to Egypt.

**Scarab**: A beetle (*Scarabaeus sacer*); the hieroglyph for "to come into being" or "to exist"; hence its use as an amulet for rejuvenation.

**Sed**: see *heb-sed*.

**Sequence dating**: A relative date established through the study of artifact style and its change through time (see fig. 1.1).

**Serdab**: Statue chamber in an Old Kingdom tomb.

**Shabti** (also spelled *ushebti*): Mummiform statuette deposited in tombs from Dynasty 13 onward to act as a servant for the deceased.

**Sherden**: Peoples thought to have originated near Mt Sardonia in northern Ionia, later migrating to Sardinia.

**Sistrum**: (pl: sistra) Ritual rattle.

**Social complexity** (stratification): Term used to describe a culture with multiple social classes, often used as a synonym for civilization; a socially complex and economically diverse culture.

**Sprue**: An opening in a casting mold.

**Stela** (pl. steles/stelae) Surface of stone or wood carved or painted with scenes or texts; often a monument to the dead or the record of a historical event.

**Stratigraphy**: Layered arrangement of sediments, a series of defined sedimentary layers arranged such that if undisturbed older levels underlay younger levels.

**Sumer**: Complex society located in southern Mesopotamia (Iraq), *ca.* 3000–2000 BC.

**Superposition (Law of)**: In any sequence of sedimentary strata, not later disturbed, deposition was from bottom to top.

**Tell**: Mound consisting of the accumulated remains of one or more ancient settlements, often used in Egypt as a place name (synonym for kom).

**Thinite**: Synonym for Archaic Period (Dynasties 1–2), based on the legend that the earliest kings of Egypt ruled from an area called This.

**Torus molding**: Architectural feature consisting of rounded corner where two exterior walls meet; represents the bound junction of reed mats translated into stone (see fig. 9.1).

**Upper Egypt**: Southern Egypt, traditionally that area south of Cairo. When used with Middle Egypt, it refers to that area south of Asyut.

**Urbanization**: Large population centers where evidence indicates a large proportion of the inhabitants were involved in a number of activities other than agriculture.

**Valley**: Used in reference to the entire Egyptian Nile valley, but can refer specifically to Upper Egypt, that area south of Cairo.

**Valley of the Kings**: (Arabic: Biban or Wadi el Molouk) Valley on west bank of Luxor containing tombs of New Kingdom kings and a few notables.

**Vizier** (*Tjaty*): A position in the Egyptian bureaucracy similar to that of a modern prime minister or Ottoman vizier, who sat as chief advisor, head of administration and supreme court justice.

**Wadi**: An open-ended channel that periodically carries water. A wadi looks much like a dry river bed. In North America it would be referred to as an arroyo.

**Western Desert**: Desert lying west of the Nile also known as the East Sahara or Libyan desert.

**Wilbour Papyrus**: Fiscal text dating to the reign of Ramesses V (*ca.* 1145–1141 BC).

# INDEX

Abadiyeh, 11
Abdel Latif, 5
Abu Haggag, 188
Abu Roash, 155
Abu Simbel, 8, 114
Abu Sir, 155
Abydos, 11, 27, 28, 29, 31, 32, 33, 36, 52, 60, 65,
     88, 110, 126, 155, 156
  architecture, 126
  burial of Osiris at, 88
  destruction in the First Intermediate Period,
    36
  Dynasty 0 at, 31
  early settlement plan, 52
  early state at, 32
  early writing at, 110
  king list, 27
  predynastic cemeteries, 11, 28, 31, 110
  recent work at, 31
  royal tombs at, 155
  urbanism, 65
Acheulean, 22, 202
Adam, Robert, 189
administration, 34, 38–39, 42, 50, 66, 67, 69,
    70–71, 73, 75, 76
  central, 67, 70–71, 80
  of Dynasty 25, 50
  late Middle Kingdom, 38
  priestly, 76
  provincial and regional, 58, 66, 72–74
  state and temple connections, 75–76
  structure of, 34
  temples and divine holdings, 41
administrators, 71
Adoratress, 42
  see also God's Wife
adultery, 96
agriculture, 16, 24, 30, 34–35, 53, 64, 67, 72, 80,
    189
Aha, 29
Ahhotep, 40

Ahmose, 39, 40, 98
  stela of, 40
Ahmose Nofertari, 42
Ahmose son of Ibana, 39
Aida, 9
Åkerbald, Johan, 111–113
akh, 148
Akhenaten, 45–47, 54, 91, 133, 184
  foreign policy of 47
  religion of, 45–46
  see also Amunhotep IV
Akhetaten, see Amarna
Akhtoy, 36
al-Dahr, Mohammed Sa'im, 5
Alexander the Great, 2, 7, 27, 50, 51, 111, 113
Alexandria, 2, 3, 6, 7, 53
Amarna, 43, 46, 47, 54–57, 63–64, 67, 91, 128,
    133, 134, 137, 202
  city plan, 54–55
  Great Temple, 56, 57
  houses at, 54, 133, 134
  North Suburb, 54
  Northern Palace, 54, 137–138, 139
  population during, 54
  religion of, 46, 91
  relocation of capital to, 46
Amarna Letters, 43, 45, 57, 202
Amarna Period, 46, 91, 180
Amasis, 105
Amduat, 42, 164
Amratian Period, 29, 202
amulet, 150, 202
Amun, 2, 41–42, 45, 46, 48, 49, 50, 74, 76, 77, 84,
    85, 90, 91, 119, 142, 143, 164
  domains of, 42, 50, 76
  prophet of, 76, 77
  cult of, 48, 49
  wealth of, 41
  of Karnak, 44, 142, 143, 144
  temples of, 2, 44, 143
    see also Karnak, temple at; Siwa Oasis

Amun-Re, 84, 164
Amunemhet I, 27, 37, 73, 98, 142
    Instructions of, 37
Amunemhet III, 3, 38, 142
Amunet, 85
Amunhotep (family name), 70
Amunhotep I, 45
Amunhotep II, 70
    tomb of, 165
Amunhotep III, 21, 43, 45, 46, 47, 70, 91, 92, 137,
        167, 180
Amunhotep IV, 45, 46, 184
    *see also* Akhenaten
Amunhotep, son of Hapu, 92
Ankhsheshenqy (Instructions of), 108
Ankhtyfy of Moalla, 36
Anukis, 24
Apis, temple of, 3
apprenticeship, 49
Arab, 4–5, 14, 125, 189
    administration of Egypt, 4–5
    architecture, 125
    conquest of Egypt, 4–5
    destruction of pharaonic monuments, 5
    explorers, 4
    language, 110, 122
    travelers, 4
Arabic, 110, 122
Archaic Period, 32–34, 110, 149
architecture, 14, 40, 50, 125–127
    archaizing, 50
    domestic, 127–136
    influence from West Asia,
        mortuary, 152–168
    palaces, 137–141
    recording of, 7
    temples, 141–145
army, 35, 61, 74–75, 188
artisans, 121, 169
Assyria, 43, 44, 48, 50, 188, 202
Aswan, 12, 19, 20, 22, 23, 24, 33
Asyut, 20
Aten, 45, 46, 91, 138, 202
Atum, 85, 202
Avaris, *see* Tell el Daba
Aye, 47

*ba* (soul), 147, 148, 202
Babylon, 43

Badarian Period, 29, 30
Bahr Yusef canal, 20, 21
Bahriya oasis, 20
Ballas, 11
Barthélemy, Jean Jacques, 111
basins, 24
Bay (ruler), 49
beer, 104–105, 107–108, 133, 147, 152
Bekenkhonsu (high priest), 99
Belzoni, Giovanni, 8, 9
Bent Pyramid, 161
    *see also* Dashur; Snefru
Bes, 91
Bible, 4, 50
bitumen, 5, 203
Blue Nile, 22
boats, 3, 25, 30, 31, 86, 88
Book of Exodus, 4
"Book of Gates," 42, 164
"Book of the Dead," 86, 150, 151, 155, 203
"Book of the Heavenly Cow," 42, 164
British Museum, 8
bronze, 50, 74, 127, 171, 173
Bubastis, 53
Buhen, 61–62
bull, 21
burial chamber, 153, 156, 158, 163
burials, 28, 29, 30, 97, 108, 128, 152–155,
        155–168
Buto, 31, 65, 76
Butzer, Karl, 16, 66
Byzantine emperor, 189, 190
Byzantine period, 189

Caesar (Octavian), 2
Cairo, 4, 5, 17, 19, 20
calendars, 27–28
Canaanites, 75
Canopic branch of Nile, 17
canopic jar, 150, 203
capital (of Egypt), 2, 21, 33, 35, 37, 38, 39, 41, 46,
        47, 48, 49, 50
    First Intermediate Period, 35–37
    Hyksos, 38–40
    Late Period, 50
    Middle Kingdom, 37, 38
    New Kingdom, 41, 54
    of Kush, 45
    Old Kingdom, 33, 34, 35, 53

provincial, 53, 54, 57, 65, 66
 Third Intermediate Period, 49
caravan routes, 20
cartonnage, 148, 203
cartouche, 45, 70, 111, 113, 203
cataract, 19, 37, 38, 45, 60, 62, 203
causeway, 161, 162
cavalry, 74
 *see also* military
cavetto cornice, 125, 126, 160, 203
Caviglia, T. B., 1
cedar, 35, 173
Cemetery U (Abydos), 32
ceramics, 11, 12, 13, 30, 31
Champollion, Jean Francois, 10, 11, 113–114
Chapelle Rouge, 41
chariot, 40, 57, 74
child bearing, 97–99
Childe, V. Gordon, 16
children, 86, 91, 97–99, 108
 inheritance of parents' position, 41, 98–99, 108
 duty to parents, 91, 95
Christianity, 4, 190
Christians, 4, 188
circumcision, 98
circumpolar star, 162
city, 33, 52–57, 63–64, 64–67, 71, 133–135
 description, 53, 63–64
 city plans, 32, 132
 life in, 63–64
 patterns, 63–64, 64–67
city-state, 33, 43, 47
class, 100–102
Cleopatra VII, 2, 114
clothing, 85, 99–102, 152
coffin, 30, 58, 88, 148, 155, 158
Colossi of Memnon, 3, 167, 203
conscription, 74, 81
Constantine, 190
copper, 127, 170, 173
copper carbonate, 170
Coptic Church, 110, 118
Coptic language, 10, 110, 111, 113, 114, 117, 118, 123
Coptos, 36, 39, 65
coronation, 70
corvée, 66, 81, 203
craftsmen, 79, 169
creation myth, 85

creator god, 85, 169
Crete, 40
Crusaders, 5
cylinder seals, 33

Dakhla oasis, 20
dancing, 106
Dashur, 37, 155, 126, 161
de Morgan, Jacques, 28–29
de Sacy, Sylvestre, 111
death, 42, 80, 84, 88, 121, 142, 147–148, 148–152, 153, 168
 attitude toward, 80, 88, 147–148
 conception of, 84, 88, 142, 147–148, 148–152, 153, 164, 168
 preparation for, 42, 148–152
Deir el Bahari, 45, 167
Deir el Medina, 42, 49, 58, 79, 128, 133–135
Delta, 17–18, 22, 23, 25, 30, 31, 37, 39, 48, 49, 58, 60, 65, 66, 72, 105, 117, 168, 203
demotic, 7, 111, 112, 113, 114, 115–118, 123, 204
Dendera, 9
*Denkmäler aus Ägypten und Äthiopien*, 11
Denon, Dominique Vivant, 7
*Description de l'Égypte*, 7, 10, 204
determinatives, 117, 119, 204
dialects, ancient, 117
Diodorus, 2, 98, 204
Diospolis Parva, 60
diplomacy, 43
divine birth, 2
divorce, 96, 108
Djoser, 1, 24, 72, 123, 126, 142, 156, 159
 funerary complex, 142, 143, 156–160
Drovetti, Bernardino, 8
drunkenness, 105–106
Dynasty 0, 31
Dynasty 25 (Kushite Period), 50, 75, 77, 155, 168
dynasty (defined), 204

Eastern Delta, 18, 39, 48
Eastern Desert, 17, 170, 204
ebony, 173
ecology, 16
economy, 30, 34, 80–81
Edfu, 9
Edict of Horemheb, 73
education, 79, 99, 121

Egypt Exploration Fund, 11
Egyptian Antiquities Service, 9, 10
Egyptian Museum, 9
El Amrah, 128
el-Mamoun, 6
Elephantine, *see* Aswan
encaustic, 170
entertainment, 3, 103–108
Eonile, 21–22
Esharhaddon, 50
Etheria, 4
Euphrates, 16
evisceration, 149–150
Exodus, 48

faience, 171, 204
false door, 137, 152, 154, 168, 204
Famine Stela, 24
farmers, 34, 40, 54, 58, 65, 73, 80, 81
Fayum, 20, 21, 22, 29, 30, 37
fertility, 97
first cataract, 20, 65
fishing, 30, 80
fixed dates, 27
flood, 19, 23, 24, 25, 35, 51, 58, 60, 86
flood plain, 19, 20, 23, 58, 60, 65
Flying Squad, 57
folk religion, 188
food, 12, 24, 41, 58, 66, 75, 80, 85, 98, 104–105,
        121, 147, 150, 152, 163, 164, 168
    shortage, 24
foreign occupation, 38–39, 50–51
foreign policy, 42, 43–45, 48, 50
foreigners, 38–39, 75, 82
forts, 60–63, 156
Freemasons, 189

games, 103–104, 108, 129
Gaza, 50
Gebel Silsila, 24
Gell, Sir William, 10
Gerzean, 29, 204
gezira, 17–18, 23, 58, 204
Giza 1, 8, 10, 53, 155, 160–163
Giza necropolis, 53, 152, 164
Giza plateau, 5, 10
Giza pyramids, 3, 160-163
goat, 30
god's father, 76

God's Wife, 42, 50, 77
    *see also* Adoratress
gold, 35, 173, 174
gold mines, 35
Graeco-Roman period, 107, 121
Graeco-Roman tradition, 174
Graeco-Roman world, 84
granite, 126
Great Pyramid, 1, 160–163
Greaves, John, 5
Greece, 2
Greek, 1, 14, 114, 115, 116, 121, 123, 188, 189
    intellectuals, 1
    language, 114, 115, 116, 121, 123
    people, 14, 188
    sculpture, 189

Hadrian, 3
hair, 102
Harun Al-Rashid, 4
Hatnub, 36
Hatshepsut, 41, 45, 70, 90, 167
Hawara, 37–38
*heb sed*, defined, 204
    *see also* jubilee
Hebrew people, 48
Hekataios of Miletos, 1
Heliopolis, 77
Hememieh, 52, 60, 128, 129
henotheism, 46, 91, 204
Herakleopolis, 35–37
Herihor, 49
Herodotus, 1–2, 16, 17, 53, 76, 98–99, 149, 163,
        204
Hezekiah, 50
Hierakonpolis, 28, 31, 32–33, 142
hieratic, 115, 117, 204,
hieroglyphs, 10, 78, 110–114, 119
    alphabetic signs, 117, 118, 119
    decipherment of, 10, 110–114
    determinatives, 110, 117, 119
    honorific transposition, 119
    ideograms, 117
    latest written text, 110
    phonetic complements, 119
    phonetic signs, 117
    principles of writing, 117–119
    proto-hieroglyphs, 32
    rebus principle, 33, 119

sign direction, 115
symbolic associations, 111
transposition of, 119
vocalization of, 122–123
High Dam, 12
high priest, 49, 71, 76, 77, 85–86, 99
life of, 76–77
power of, 49
responsibilities of, 76, 85–86
Theban, 49
Hittites, 40, 43, 47, 48, 204
honorific transposition, 119
Horapollo, 111
Horemheb, 47, 69, 73
Edict of, 73
horses, 40
Horus, 33, 45, 69, 86–87, 89, 93, 163
Horus Aha, 33
house design, 127–136
Hu, 11
Hyksos, 38, 39, 40, 42, 48, 188, 204

ideograms, 117, 204
Imhotep, 123
infanticide, 97
infantry, 74
*see also* military
Institut d' Egypte, 6, 7
intermarriage, 49
inundation, 24, 25, 188
Inyotef VII, 39
Inyotef family, 36
irrigation, 25
Isis, 88, 188
Israel, 48, 50
Israel Stele, 48
Israelites, 4, 48
Itchtowy, 21, 37, 38, 41
Iwenmutef priest, 76, 77

jubilee (*heb sed*), 33, 45, 89–90, 91, 159–160,
205
Judah, 50
Justinian, 4

*ka*, 91, 147, 148, 150, 152, 155, 162, 205
Kadesh, 47, 74
Kahun (Lahun), 37, 38, 128, 132
Kaiser Wilhelm IV, 10

Kamose, 39
Karnak, 3, 9, 41–42, 45, 47, 49, 63, 92, 142, 143,
144, 145
city at, 63
excavation of, 9, 63
temple at, 3, 8, 41–42, 45, 47, 92, 142, 143,
144, 145, 205
Kassites, 43
kenbet, 73
Khaemwese, 1
Khafra, 6, 8, 9, 162, 163
Kharga, 20
Khedive Sa'id, 9
khereru frieze, 125, 126, 205
Khnum, 24, 85
Khonsu, 41, 85, 90, 91
Khufu, 6, 34, 160–161, 162, 163
king, 34, 37, 39, 41, 51, 69–70, 86–88, 89, 168,
190
divinity of, 69–70, 86–88
duties of, 69–70, 71, 86
Middle Kingdom, 37
succession, 70
titulary of, 70
king lists, 27, 32, 33, 36, 38, 39, 47
Turin king list, 28, 38
Ramesside, 36, 47
king's son of Kush, 45, 73
Kircher, Anthanasius, 5, 111
Kom Ombo, 20
Kush, 43–45, 50
*see also* Nubia
Kushite Period (Dynasty 25), 50, 75, 77, 155,
168

labyrinth, 3
Lahun, *see* Kahun
Lake Buruillus, 17
Lake Edku, 17
Lake Manzala, 17
Lake Tanganyika, 22
land reclamation projects, 21
language, 110, 114–5, 122–124
dialects, ancient, 117
*see also* Arabic; Coptic language; Greek
language; hieroglyphs
Late Egyptian, 114–115, 123
Late Pliocene, 22
Lebanon, 35, 173

Legal Code of Hermopolis West, 63, 73, 81
legal protection, 6
legal rights, 81, 96, 108
legal system, 73–74, 81
legal texts, 73, 96, 97
Leontopolis, 50
Lepsius, Richard, 9, 10, 11
"Letter to the Dead," 121
levees, 58, 205
Libya, 43, 51, 75
Libyan descent, 49
Libyan Period, 39
life expectancy, 97–98
limestone, 126, 171
linen, 81, 100, 149
Lisht, 37
Litany of Re, 164
literacy, 76, 77, 99, 121
literature, 4, 34, 40, 122
lost wax process, 173, 205
Lower Pliocene, 21
"Loyalist Instructions," 37
Luxor, 3, 7, 8, 9, 20, 38, 188
    *see also* Thebes
Luxor Temple, 3, 9, 41, 47, 188

Maadi, 29, 30, 31, 60, 128
Maat, 205
    goddess, 41, 80, 93, 151
    ethical concept, 70, 80, 86–88, 93, 151–152
mace heads, 33
Mahasna, 128
Makrizi, 4
malachite, 170
Malkata, 137, fig. 9.10
Mamluks, 6
Manetho, 27, 36, 38, 39
Mariette, Auguste, 9, 10, 11
marital property, 108
marriage, 49, 95–97, 108
    contracts, 96
    diplomatic, 43, 47
    monogamous, 95, 108
    terms for, 96
mastaba, 9, 10, 53, 126, 152, 155, 157, 168, 205,
    figs. 10.5, 10.6
medicine, 3, 6, 84
Medinet Habu, 48, 166, 167, 188, fig. 10.16
Mediterranean Sea, 16, 17, 20, 21, 22, 33, 49

Medjay, 37, 75, 205
Megiddo, 43, 74
Meidum, 9, 126, 155
Memnon (statue in Ramesseum), 8
Memphis, 2, 3, 4, 33, 50, 53–54, 65, 66, 68, 71,
    138, 155, 159
    capital at, 33, 41, 53, 65, 72, 155
    city, 53, 65, 66, 68
    conquest of, 50
    foundation of, 53
    palace at, *see* Merneptah
    population, 65
    temples in, 51, 72
Mendes, 53, 65
Menes, 32, 33, 53
Menkaure, 6, 105
Mentuhotep family, 36
Mentuhotep II, 36
Mentuhotep III, 39
mercenaries, 75
Merikare, Instructions of, 36
Merimde, 29, 30, 60, 128
Merneptah, 48
    palace of, 138–141, figs. 9.12, 9.13
Mesheti, 74
Mesopotamia, 33, 40, 42, 43, 48, 50, 52, 64–65,
    73, 75, 96, 110, 188
Middle Egyptian, 114, 115
Middle Kingdom, 37–38, 54, 60–61, 70, 72
    adminstration of, 37, 72–3
    architecture of, 60–61
    capital of, 37, 21
    tombs, 37–38
Middle Kingdom models, 37
Middle Pleistocene, 21, 22, table 2.1
military, 7, 14, 32, 35, 50, 74–75, 82, 106, 188
    award, 40
    barracks, 57
    campaigns, 14, 35, 36, 37, 42–43, 45, 50
    commander, 47, 75
    garrisons, 20, 47
    innovations, 40
    operations, 37, 39, 40, 42, 43, 47, 74
    service, 74
Minshat Abu Omar, 31
Miocene Epoch, 21
Mitanni, 43, 205
Mohammed Ali, 88
monotheism, 46, 91

Montuemhet, 155
mortuary complex, 156–157, 161–164
mortuary cult, 42, 147-148, 152–153, 168
mortuary temple, 42, 155–158, 161–163, 164, 168, fig. 10.13
Mose, 73
mud-brick, 60, 125, 133, 138–139, 142, 145, 155, 157, fig. 9.2
multiplicity of forms of deity, 84
mummification process, 2, 147–150, 152, 163, 168
mummiya, 5
mummy, 5, 8, 39, 93, 148
music, 104, 106, 108
musical instruments, 106–107
musical notation, 107
musicians, 77, 106, fig. 7.7
Mut, 41, 90, 91
myths, 25, 41, 69, 86, 99, 143, 145
mythological descent, 69, 86–88

Naqada (site), 11, 28–33
Naqada I, 29, 30, 60, 128, table 3.1
Naqada II, 29, 30, 31, 60, 128, table 3.1
Naqada II/III, 29, 30, 31, table 3.1
Naqada III, 31, 128
Naqada IIIa, 31
Napoleon Bonaparte, 6–7, 10
Narmer, 32, 33, fig. 3.2
Narmer Palette, 32–33, 206, fig. 3.2
natron, 150, 206
Nauri decree, 81
navy, 74–75
Nebwenenef, 76–77
Necho, 50
Nefertiti, 45, 46, 91, figs. 11.14a, 11.14b
Neolithic Period, 23, 29, 58, 206
Neonile, 22–23, table 2.1
Neoplatonists, 189
niched architecture, 33, 126–127, 137, 155, 158–159, fig. 93
Nile River, 16–25, 51, 53, 65, 188
    sources, 22, 23
Nile Valley, 16, 23, 58
nilometers, 24, 206
Nitocris, 70
nomarch, 34–37, 72, 206
nome, 34, 72–73, 206
nomen, 70
Northern Palace (Amarna), 137–139, fig. 9.11

North Saqqara, 93
Nubia, 35, 37, 39, 43, 74, 75, 168, 173, 206
    administration of, 45, 50, 73
    alliance with Hyksos, 39
    border, 37
    economic resources, 35, 173
    Egyptian policy toward, 5, 35, 37, 40, 43
    Egyptian temples in, 42, 48
    forts, 60–63, figs. 4.4, 4.5
    king, 39, 43, 50, 168
    monuments, 42, 48, 168
    royal tombs, 168
    trade, 35, 173
Nubian campaigns, 42, 50
Nubian Dynasty, *see* Dynasty 25 (Kushite Period)
Nubian commander, 49
Nubians, 35, 37, 75

oases, 20–21, 105, 107
obelisk, 3, 42, 113, 189
Old Egyptian, 114, 115, 123
Omari, 29, 60, 128
Opet festival, 41, 90, 93, 188, 206
oracle statues, 92
oracles, 92–93
Osiris, 69, 86–88, 93, 152, 155, 164, 206, fig. 6.4
ostraca, 73, 208

Pabasa, 155
Paheri, 105–106
Palace, 56–57, 137–141, 145, 164–166, figs. 9.10, 9.11, 9.12, 9.13
    *see also* Northern Palace (Amarna); Malkata; Merneptah (palace of)
Paleolithic, 23, 128, 206
Paleonile, 22, table 2.1
Palermo Stone, 27, 28
Palestine, 43, 48, 50
papyrus, 78, 206
Papyrus Anastasi I, 117
Papyrus Anastasi V, 78, 80
Papyrus Harris, 43, 49
Papyrus Leiden, 48
Papyrus, Wilbour, 48, 208
Patriarch Cyril, 4
Pelusiac branch of Nile, 17
People of the Sea, 48
Pepi I, 53, 173
Pepi II, 163

Persia, 1–2, 5
    rule, 1–2, 50–51, 188–90
Petrie, W. Flinders, 10–12, 14, 29
Philae, 4, 113, 188
phonetic complements, 119
phonetic signs, 110, 111, 113, 117–119, 122,
    123
Pi-Ramesses, 48, 49, 53
Piazzi Smyth, Charles, 11
Piccadilly (Egyptian exhibition at), 8
Pietro delle Valle, 5
pigment, 170–171, 181
Piranesi, 189
Pithom, 4
Piye, 50, 75
Plato, 1
Pleistocene era, 22, 206
Plutarch, 88
pluvial, 22, 23, 206
police, 3, 37, 57, 75
    chief of, 75
    quarters, 57
population, 40, 54, 64, 65
potency, 121
precipitation, 23, 25
Predynastic,
    architecture, 30, 60, 125, 128–129
    burials, 30, 128, 149, 152, fig. 10.2
    cemeteries, 30, 32
    ceremony, 89
    development, 28–32, 72
    language, 110
    sequence, 28–29
    settlements, 30, 52, 60
    sherds, 106
    shrines, 142, 160
    sites, 60, 128
    temple, 160
    towns, 128–129
pregnancy, 97
Prenile, 22, table 2.1
prenomen, 70
priestesses, 42, 50, 76–77
priests, 49, 50, 75–77, 85, 93, 110–111, 166
    Iwenmutef priest, 76, 77
    lector priest, 76
    sem, 76, 77
    wab, 76, 77
primary settlement distribution, 66

prophecy of Neferti, 37
Prophet of Amun, 49–50, 76–77
prostitution, 108
proto-hieroglyphs, 32, 110
Protonile, 22, table 2.1
Prussian survey, 10
Psammethicus, 50
Ptah, 17, 72, 74, 84, 169, fig. 6.1
Ptah-Sokar, 84
Ptahhotep (Instructions of), 73
Ptolemaic Period, 2, 178, 180, 189
Ptolemy I, 2
Ptolemy II, 2
Ptolemy V, 111
Punt, 45, 206
purity, 76, 86
pyramid, 126, 145, 158, 160–163, figs. 10.12,
    10.13
    construction of, 34, 126, 160–161, 163
    Khufu, 6, 34, 160-161, 163
    pyramid complex, 126, 157, 161–164, fig. 10.13
    pyramid texts, 163, 206
    "queen's," 161, fig. 10.12
    satellite, 161
    Stepped, 157–160, 162–163, figs. 10.8, 10.9,
        10.10a, 10.10b
    symbolism, 3, 161–162
    workers, 34, 163
Pythagoras, 1

Qena Bend, 20
quarry technique, 126–127
quartz, 127, 171
queen's pyramids, 161

Ramesses I, 47, 69
Ramesses II, 1, 27, 47, 48, 74, 167
Ramesses III, 48, 49, 75, 166, 167
Ramesses IV, 48
Ramesses V, 48
Ramesseum, 48, 99, 164, 167
rank, 70, 80, 96, 102, 104, 181
Re, 45, 69, 164, 168
Re-Harakhty, 45, 84
rebus principle, 33, 119
Red Sea, 65, 204
rejuvenation, 86–91, 163
Rekhmire, 71, 73, 81, 125, 173, figs. 9.2, 11.1,
    11.4

reproduction, 97
revivification, 163
Roberts, David, 7
Roman,
    administration, 2, 189–190
    civilization, 111, 189–190
    conquest of Egypt, 14, 188
    emperor, 189, 190
    imperial expansion, 189
    monuments, 3, 189
    taxation, 2, 189
    tourists, 3
    travelers, 1
Rome, 2–3
Rosetta (el-Rashid), 7
Rosetta branch of Nile, 17, 31, 47
Rosetta Stone, 7, 111, 117, fig. 8.1
ruling class, 66, 69–71

sacrifices (human), 151
Said Pasha, 9
Sais, 50, 53, 168
Saite Period (Dynasty 26), 1, 50, 168
Salt, Henry, 8
Sand Dwellers, 74
sandstone, 71, 126, 171
Saqqara, 9, 10, 27, 53, 155, 162, 163
    plateau, 10
Satis, 24
scarab, 150, 204
school, 78, 99, 121
school texts, 121
schooling, 78, 99, 121
scribe, 75, 77–79, 99, 115, 170
    class (social), 77
    clothing of, 101
    reputation of, 77, 99
    schools and training, 77, 78, 107, 115, 121
Sea People, 48
Sebennytic branch of Nile, 17
Second Intermediate Period, 38–40, 71
*sed* festival, 33, 45, 89, 93, 158–160, fig. 6.4
    *see also* jubilee
sed court (Djoser), 142, 159–160, figs. 9.14, 10.11
Sehêl Island, 24
Sekhenenre Tao II, 39
Semna, 37, 62, fig. 4.5
Senenmut, 42
senet (game), 103, fig. 7.4

Sennacherib, 50
Senwosert I, 142
Senwosert II, 129, 174
Senwosert III, 37, 60, 72
Septimius Severus, 3
sequence dating, 11–12, 29, 207, figs. 1.1, 1.2
Serapeum, 4, 9
serdab, 152–153, 207, figs. 10.5, 10.6
serfs, 82
Seth, 33, 76, 86–88
Seti (High Priest), 76
Seti I, 8, 166, fig. 10.15
Setna (Tale of), 96, 97, 150
settlement patterns, 52–63, 66, 129–131
settlement types, 52, 57–58, 67–68
shabti, 81, 151, 207
Sharuhen, 39
sheep, 30
Sheik Said, 36
Sherdan, 48, 75, 207
Shoshenq I (Shishak), 50, 74
Shu, 46, 91
Sinai Peninsula, 18, 42, 174
singers, 77, 85, 106–107
    *see also* music
Sirius, 27
Siwa Oasis, 2, 4, 20
slavery, 81–82
Snefru, 126, 161–162
Sobekneferu, 70
social classes, 54, 98–99, 169
    elite, 68, 69–70, 75–79, 98, 104, 107, 129
    lower class, 54, 68, 80, 98, 104, 107
    peasants, 54, 80
soldiers, 74–75
    *see also* military
Sothis, 27
soul, 147, 150–153, 162–163, 169, fig. 10.1
    *see also* ba; ka; akh,
soul house, 128–129, figs. 9.5a, 9.5b, 9.5c
South Tomb (Djoser), 158–159, fig. 10.10
Sphinx, 1, 4
    damage to nose, 4
sports, 103–104
Step Pyramid, 1, 126, 142, 156–160, 161, figs. 10.8, 10.9, 10.10a, 10.10b
Strabo, 3
succession, 47, 49, 69–70, 88
Sudan, xviii, 12

Suez Canal, 9
Sumer, 64, 103, 110, 207
Sumerian language, 33, 110
Syria, 43

Tanis, 49, 53, 167
Tanite kings, 49, 167–168
taverns, 107–108
taxation, 40, 41, 66–68, 72, 73, 80–82, 189
    exemption, 35
Tefnut, 46, 91
Tell el Amarna, 43, 46, 54–57, 64, 91, 129,
        131–133, 137–138, figs. 4.1, 4.2
    *see also* Amarna
Tell el Daba (Avaris), 39–40, 48, 128
Tell El-Maskuta, 4
temples, 41–42, 50, 141–145, 162–164
    administration, 35, 41, 48–49, 71, 75–77, 145,
        167
    of Amun, 41, 45, 48, 49, 50, 76, 142, 143, 145,
        fig. 9.15
    of Isis, 4
    of Luxor, 145
    of Mut, 99, 145
    of Ptah, 53, 72
    of Ramesses II (Ramesseum), 48, 99, 164, 167
    of Ramesses III (Medinet Habu), 48, 166, 167,
        183, fig. 10.16
    of Thutmose III, 142
tent of purification, 163
Thales, 1
Thebes, 41, 48, 50, 52–54, 66, 68, 155
    mayor of, 71
Theodosius, 4, 190
Third Intermediate Period, 39, 49–50, 178
Thoth, 93, 110
Thutmose I, 16, 42, 43, 45, 58, 163
Thutmose III, 43, 45, 70, 74, 142, 173
Thutmose IV, 1, 43, 180
Tivoli (Italy), 3
Tod, 142
Tombos inscription, 16
tombs, 53–54, 72, 150, 168, 170
    mastaba, 9, 10, 53, 126, 152, 155, 157, 168, figs.
        10.5, 10.6
    rock cut, 153, 155, 163–167
    royal, 34, 35, 37–38, 42, 58, 126, 155–168, figs.
        10.14, 10.15, 10.17
tool industry, 22
tools, 22, 126, 170–171

topography, 23-24
torus molding, 125, 142, 160, 207, fig. 9.1
town, 52–60, 128–136
transportation, 24, 25, 58
treasury, 72
    overseer of, 71
    superintendent of, 76
Turin Museum, 8
Tutankhamun, 40, 43, 47, 76, 85, 119, 164
    Restoration Stele of, 46–47, 76, 85
Tutankhaten, 47
    *see also* Tutankhamun

unification of Egypt, 31, 32–33
Unis, 35
    pyramid of, 163
urbanism, 66–67
Uronarti, 37, 62
Uruk, 31
ushebti, *see* shabti

Valley of the Kings, 8, 42, 49, 58, 133, 163, figs.
        10.14, 10.15
Valley of the Queens, 164
Valley Temple, 9, 161, 163, fig. 10.13
Villa Adriana, 3
village, 24, 52–53, 58–60, 63, 68, 131
vizier, 34, 38, 41, 70–71, 73, 81, 82, 123, 207
    duties, 70–71, 73, 75
    title, 70

Wadi Allaqi, 35
Wadi Hammamet, 48
Wadi Natrun, 21
wadis, 65, 208
Walls of the Ruler, 37, 60
waret, 37, 72–73
Weni, autobiography of, 35, 74
Western Asia, 33, 40, 43
Western Desert, 17, 20–21, 22, 23, 25, 107, 208
White Nile, 22
White Walls, 53
wigs, 102
Wilkinson, Sir John Gardner, 9, 10–11
wind, prevailing, 24–25
wine, 31, 86, 105

xenophobia, 43

Young, Thomas, 10, 11, 113